modern publicity

1978

modern publicity

volume 47 1978

Editor Felix Gluck

Studio Vista

The new typeface designs shown on pages 81, 82, 83, 84 and 85 are copyright of the type foundries, designers or photosetting companies. They must not be used without the permission of the copyright holders or their lincensees.

Published in 1977. A Studio Vista book published by Cassell & Collier Macmillan Publishers Ltd, 35 Red Lion Square, London WC1R 4SG and at Sydney, Auckland, Toronto, Johannesburg, an affiliate of Macmillan Publishing Co. Inc., New York.

ISBN 0 289 70785 4

Printed by Sackville Press Billericay Ltd.

Abbreviations
Abkürzungen

AD Advertiser
Client
Auftraggeber

AG Agency/Studio
Agence/Atelier
Reklameberater

DIR Art director
Directeur artistique
Künstlerischer Leiter

DES Designer/Artist
Maquettiste/Artiste
Grafiker/Künstler

ILL Illustrator/Photographer

Contents

Sommaire

Inhalt

Introduction

In this year's edition of *Modern Publicity* we have introduced a new design for the lay-out of the book and hope that this will add to the clarity of the presentation.

The cover design is based on a calendar designed for *BASF Ludwigshafen.* Although one is in general wary of designers using pin-up girls or bathing beauties unless the advertising is trying to sell bathing suits etc., these calendar photos are in effect a sophisticated way of selling printing inks. The black apple is a surrealistic eye-catcher. In their introduction to this calendar the designers explain the psychological effect of using various colours and body language in their illustrations, but I think the photographer would have succeeded superbly even without a strict psychological brief.

In the poster section the openers come from the new *Air India* campaign. This company has maintained a consistently high standard of wit and style in its campaigns and it is always a pleasure to open the parcel of the latest *Air India* material. Other posters of special interest were *Abram Games's* zoo poster with the ingenious use of the London Transport symbol in his design, *Shigeo Okamoto's* elegant fashion posters for a Japanese department store and the posters of the Iranian designers *Morteza Momayez, Ghobad Shiva* and *Farshid Meshgali* with their original designs.

In the advertising section *Mariet Numan* shows the applications of a variety of textile materials and prints through an alphabet. The illustrations are friendly and colourful and the whole design gives the impression of a patchwork quilt.

Other outstanding advertisements were the *Johnny Walker* 'Love thyself' and the *Lloyds Bank* labyrinth advertisements. Press advertisements, like the posters, show a predominance of illustrations and typographical solutions over photographic approaches.

In the postage stamp section the *Swedish Royal Post Office* shows a consistently high standard of design and printing. It is interesting to note that the actual engraving of the designs is mostly done by Czech graveurs, who have a long tradition in this craft and continue it both in Czechoslovakia and abroad. We have made a selection of postage stamps on wild life preservation, which offered designers a variety of approaches. Here the graphic solutions of *Ari Fagundez, Louis Jaeger* and *Wokana Emori* were the most original.

We have not shown a selection of Silver Jubilee stamps from Great Britain and the Commonwealth as they were just too monotonous and not one was outstanding enough to show as an example of good design.

In our chapter on trade marks, however, we found as compensation the official Silver Jubilee symbol designed by *Nicholas Jenkins* and *Richard Guyatt* an excellent example of symbol design.

In the packaging section *St Michael* (Marks and Spencer) is using the appeal of nostalgia in their food packs. The designers of wine and spirit labels still come up with new solutions although often these are nothing more than elegantly scripted labels.

Orda Industries in Israel present a new series of children's toys in a simple, fresh series of packages which sell each other by each showing the whole series of toys on it.

In the TV section *Hans Donner* and *Rudi Böhm* have created a most distinctive graphic style for their titles for *TV Globo. Richard Bailey's* titles for the BBC's *I Claudius* series have captured the spirit of the play. Where commercial TV advertising is concerned we hope to introduce a synopsis of the texts in our next edition and I would like to remind our contributors now to include text when they send in their illustration material for TV commercials.

Our direct mail section is the usual mixture of beautiful prestige publications, company reports and calendars. This section is always difficult to assess as most of the material is expensively produced and does not reach the general public as widely as posters or advertisements do. On the other hand it also gives the designers the most opportunities to experiment with techniques and approaches, and most of the new developments and trends in graphic design probably appear first in direct mail.

I would like to thank our contributors, agencies, clients and art directors, who have submitted their work for this issue, and hope that they will send their new work again as usual and that they will not have been discouraged if none of their work has been published in this present issue of Modern Publicity.

Felix Gluck

Introduction

Dans l'édition de *Modern Publicity* de cette année nous inaugurons une nouvelle disposition typographique qui, nous espérons, aidera à la clarté de la présentation des documents.
Le projet de la couverture est basé sur un calendrier créé pour BASF. Quoique en général nous ne faisons pas trés confiance aux dessinateurs qui emploient des pin-up ou de superbes baigneuses pour une publicité qui n'essaye pas de vendre des costumes de bain, les photos de ce calendrier vendent des encres d'imprimerie de façon trés sophistiquée. La pomme noire trés surréaliste frappe le regard. Dans l'introduction de ce calendrier, les dessinateurs se donnent énormément de mal pour expliquer la psychologie de l'utilisation des différentes couleurs et du langage du corps; mais je trouve que le photographe aurait réussi pleinement même sans un exposé psychologique rigoureux.
Nous ouvrons le chapitre des affiches avec la nouvelle campagne publicitaire de Air India. L'esprit et le style des campagnes de cette compagnie ont toujours été d'un niveau trés élevé et c'est toujours avec un plaisir anticipé que j'ouvre le paquet qui contient les derniers matériaux de Air India. Je trouve d'un intêrèt spécial, les affiches du Zoo d'Abram Games qui utilise astucieusement le symbole du London Transport, les élégantes affiches de mode de Shigeo Okamoto pour un grand magasin japonais, et les dessinateurs iraniens Morteza Momayez, Ghobad Shiva et Farshid Meshgali pour leurs projets pleins d'originalité.
Dans la section publicitaire, l'alphabet textile de Mariet Numan offre une variété de tissus et cotonnades à travers un alphabet montrant leurs emplois. Les illustrations sont sympathiques et pittoresques et l'ensemble donne à l'affiche l'air d'un édredon en patch-work.
Parmi les meilleures publicités, il y a le "Love Thyself" de Johnny Walker et le Labyrinthe de Lloyds Bank: De même que dans le chapitre des affiches, les annonces publicitaires montrent aussi une prédominance de l'illustration et du jeu typographique sur la photographie.
Nous voici au chapitre des timbres poste. La Swedish Royal Post Office a toujours gardé un niveau trés élevé dans le dessin et le tirage de ses timbres. Il est intéressant de noter que la gravure même des dessins est presque toujours accomplie par des graveurs tchèques dont c'est le métier de longue tradition en Tchécoslovaquie et à l'étranger. Nous avons aussi sélectioné une série de timbres sur la nature, qui donne une idée des différentes approches des dessinateurs. Ici Ari Fagundez, Louis Jaeger et Wokana Emoni sont les dessinateurs les plus originaux dans leurs présentations de la préservation de la nature par des réalisations graphiques.
Nous ne donnons pas d'exemple de timbres de Grande Bretagne et du Commonwealth commémorant le Silver Jubilee; d'une monotonie extrême, aucun ne donnerait l'exemple d'un dessin original.
Pour compenser, nous avons trouvé que l'emblême officiel du Silver Jubilee créé par Nicholas Jenkins et Richard Guyatt est un excellent exemple de dessin de symbole.
Dans le chapitre des emballages, St Michael (Marks et Spencer) utilise des emballages plein de nostalgie pour leurs produits d'alimentation. Les dessinateurs des étiquettes des bouteilles de vins et de liqueurs semblent toujours trouver de nouvelles solutions, bien que souvent ce ne soit qu'une autre étiquette élégament calligraphiée.
Les Industries Orda d'Israël présentent de nouveaux jouets en une série d'emballages simples et directs qui, montrant la collection entiére sur chacun d'eux, se vendent les uns les autres.
Dans le chapitre de la télévision, Hans Donner et Rudi Böhm ont créé des titres d'un style très graphique pour TV Globo. Le titrage distinctif de Richard Bailey pour le feuilleton de la BBC "I Claudius" a très bien saisi l'esprit de la pièce.
En ce qui concerne la publicité TV. Nous espérons introduire dans notre prochaîne édition un résumé des textes. J'aimerais rappeler dès maintenant à nos collaborateurs de nous envoyer le texte accompagnant leurs illustrations publicitaires pour la télévision.
Dans notre section des Brochures, nous avons la série habituelle des publications prestigieuses, des rapports de gestion et des calendriers. Ce chapitre est toujours difficile à exclusivement évaluer puisque la plupart des matériaux est produite pour prestige et n'atteint pas le grand public aussi largement que les affiches et la publicité. D'un autre côté, cela donne aux dessinateurs de grades opportunités d'essayer de nouvelles techniques et approches puisqu'il semble que ce soit dans le courier publicitaire qu'apparaîssent la plupart des nouvelles techniques et modes du dessin graphique.
J'aimerais remercier nos collaborateurs, agences, clients et directeurs artistiques, qui ont présenté leurs travaux pour cette édition, et espérons qu'ils continueront à nous les envoyer comme par le passé, sans se decourager si, par manque de place, leur ouvrage n'a pas paru dans cette édition.

Felix Gluck

Einleitung

Für die diesjährige Auflage von *modern publicity* haben wir ein neues lay-out für den Umbruch des Buches entworfen und wir hoffen, dass dies zur Klarheit der Präsentation des Inhaltes beitragen wird.
Unser Umschlag ist auf einen Kalender der *BASF-Gruppe* basiert. Im Allgemeinen ist man skeptisch, wenn Entwerfer Mädchen im Badeanzug zeigen, wenn sie nicht gerade Badeanzüge verkaufen wollen. Die hier verwendete Kalenderillustration verkauft uns aber Druckfarben in raffinierter Weise. Der schwarze Apfel ist ein surrealistischer Blickfang. Die Entwerfer erklären uns in einer Einführung zum Kalender die farbenpsychologischen Gründe zur Auswahl ihrer Motive und Farben.
Im Plakat-Kapitel haben wir die *Air India* Kampagne für die Öffnungsseiten verwendet. Der Humor und Stil dieser Firma hat ein dauernd hohes Niveau und es ist immer ein Vergnügen die Pakete mit den neuesten Plakaten von *Air India* zu öffnen. Andere Plakate die besonders nennenswert waren, sindj *Abram Games'* Zoo Plakat mit genialer Verwendung des London-Transport symbols, *Shigeo Okamoto's* elegante Mode Plakate und die iranischen Grafiker *Meshgali, Momayez* und *Shiva,* die mit ihren Plakaten einen erfrischenden Wind aus dem Osten bringen.
In der Annoncen-sektion zeigt uns *Mariet Numan* eine Menge verschiedener Stoffe und Drucke in einem Textil-Alphabeth. Die Illustrationen sind freundlich und frabenfroh und das ganze Inserat imitiert eine Flickwerk-decke. Andere Inserate die besonders ins Auge fielen sind das *Johnny Walker* Inserat *"Love Thyself"* fur Whisky und das Labyrint für *Lloyds Bank.*
Es ist interessant zu bemerken, dass wiederum wie auch im Plakatenteil Illustrationen und typographische Lösungen in der Mehrheit sind.
Im Briefmarkenkapitel zeigt die *Schwedische Postdirektion* einen konsequent hohen Norm im Entwurf und auch im Druck ihrer Marken. Es ist interessant zu sehen, dass die Mehrzahl von Marken von tschechischen Künstlern graviert wurden, die eine lange Tradition in dieser Technik haben, die sie zuhause und auch im Ausland weiter forsetzen. Marken die in ihrer Mehrzahl zusammen einen Entwurf bilden sind in den vergangenen Jahren mehr und mehr populär geworden. Sie sind aber nicht funktionell und sind fast nur an Sammler gerichtet.
Wir zeigen weiterhin eine Anzahl von Marken zum Thema *Naturschutz. Ari Fagundez, Louis Jaeger* und *Wokana Emori* sind mit ihren graphischen Losungen besonders bemerkenswert.
Obwohl weder die englischen noch die Commonwealth Jubilaeumsmarken interessant waren, fanden wir dass das offizielle Symbol zum *Silver Jubilee* von *Nicholas Jenkins* und *Richard Guyatt* ein ausgezeichnetes Beispiel für guten Symbolentwurf ist.
Im Verpackungsteil verwenden *Marks and Spencer* und auch einige andere Firmen Nostalgie-Verpackungen für Lebensmittel.
Orda Industries entwarfen eine neue Serie von frisch-farbigen Puzzles für *Fernand Nathan.* Die auch gleichzeitig die ganze serie auf den Verpackungen illustrieren.
Im TV Kapitel zeigen wir unter anderem die Arbeiten des Teams *Hans Donner, Rudi Böhm* und *Sylvia Trenka,* die einen varieierten und doch konsequenten graphischen Stil für *TV Globo* in Brasilien eingeführt haben.
Richard Bailey's titel für die BBC Serie von *I Claudius* haben sich im den Geist dieses Schauspiels vollkommen eingefühlt.
Was TV Werbung betrifft, hoffen wir mit dem neuen Umbruch des Buches auch mehr Platz für die Legenden der TV Inserate zu finden. Wir bitten unsere Einsender darum, in Zukunft auch numerierte Dialoge mit den Photos zu senden.
Unser Direct-Mail Kapitel ist wie immer eine Mischung von eleganten Prestige-Broschüren, Jahresberichten und Kalendern. Es ist immer etwas schwierig dieses Kapitel zu beurteilen, weil der grosse Teil dieses Materials Prestigepublizitat ist die ohne grosse Kostenberücksichtigung produziert wird.
Allerdings haben aber die Entwerfer hier die Möglichkeit mit neuen Materialien, Techniken und Ideen zu experimentieren, was beim Massenprodukt weniger möglich ist.
Ich danke wiederum allen Grafikern, Werbeagenturen, Teams Firmen und Postdirektionen, die mit ihren Einsendungen zu der Vielfaltigkeit dieses Buches beigetragen haben. Ich hoffe dass auch jene wiederum teilnehmen werden, deren Arbeiten dieses Jahr nicht erschienen sind.

Felix Gluck

Index

Artists, designers photographers, producers and art directors

Maquettistes et artistes, photographes, production et directeurs artistiques

Entwerfer, Photographen, Produktion und künstlerische Leiter

Ertel, Mengü, 78, 166. San Grafik Saatlaar Atelyesi, Fransiz Gecidi 15-17, Karakiy, Istanbul
Ezquenazi, M., 62. see C. Rolandos & Asoc.

Fabrice, Nicole, 76. see J. Walter Thompson, France
Fagundes, Ari, 96, 100, 102. Av. Epitacio Pessoa 84, Apt. 6Ipanema GB-ZC-37, Rio de Janeiro
Fältman, Gunnar, 22. see Fältman & Malmèn
Farinoli, R., 68. see Adolf Wirz AG
Farrell, Mike, 124. 30 Neal St, London WC2
Feller, Ludvik, 108. 1000 Berlin 61 Mehringdamm 119 BRD
Femesy, Rena, 98. see Crown Agents Stamp Bureau
Fenton, Martin, 58. see Arieli Adv. Ltd
Ferderbar Studios, 74. 2356 S102 Milwaukee Wiskonsin
Ferebee, Bill, 42. c/o Penn State College, Pennsylvania
Fern, Dan, 72. Via Traffic, Amsterdam, Lijnbaansgracht 162, Holland
Fernandez, Enrique, 134. C/Viñeda, 18 Barcelona
Field, K., 162. see Detroit Free Press
Findlay, Dick, 100. c/o Directorate General of Posts, Philatelic Services, Republic of South Africa
Finn, Michael, 48. see ANU Graphic Design
Finn, I. Mickey, 62. 240 Dersing Lam Ave, London E12
Finnerty, Jim, 74. see The Haas Company
Fjeldsted, 72. see Benton & Bowles
Fletcher, Alan, 86, 118. see Pentagram
Flink, Yona, 18, 58, 76. 36 King George St, Tel Aviv
Florschutz, Dick, 110. see Ner Beck Design
Follis, John, 106, 154. see John Follis & Associates
Forbes, Bart, 22. see NBC Advertising Sales Promotion
Ford, Graham, 70. see Collett Dickenson Pearce & Partners
Forster, Anthony D., 104. 7 Stour Rd, New Hall Estate, Tyldesley, Manchester M29 7HH
Forster, Peter, 182. see McCann, Frankfurt
Fowlie, John, 64, 134, 164. Vennemindevej Z100 Khh Ø, Denmark
Fox, Barry, 142. see Leo Burnett Ltd
Franceschi, José, 182. see McCann Erickson, Brazil
Fransson, Greta, 22. see Fältman & Malmén
Frederick, Roger, 170. 216 Friern Rd, London SE23
Freudenreich, Marek, 38. ul Wolowska 88m 17, Warsaw, Poland
Freund, S.E., 102. Director General of Posts & Telegraphs, 1011 Vienna, Austria
Friedeberger, K., 156. 16 Coleraine Rd, London SE3
Friedman, Liz, 148. see BBC Television Centre
Frobisch, Dieter K., 84. Schloss Str. nr. 10, 6238 Hofheim/Taunus, BRD
Frost, Patricia, 128. see Patricia Frost Graphic Design
Fuhrman, Charles, 164. see Charles Fuhrman & Edith Allgood Design
Fürst, Roland, 72, 188. Nerotal 47, D-6200 Wiesbaden

Gaeng, Bruno, 94, 116. Av. du Casino 50, 1820 Montreux, Switzerland
Gagnepain, Gerard, 92. c/o R. Sabater, AGEP, 19 rue Jules Moulet, 13006, Marseille
Gallardi Gervasio 72. c/o Smith Greenland
Games, Abram, 48. 41 The Vale, London NW11
Gandara, Eduardo, 78, 108. Roger de Flor 264, 5º 2ª, Barcelona
Garamond, R.C., 108, 110. see Bureau d'Etude Garamond
Garcia, Antonio, 98. c/o Directorate General of Posts, Philatelic Services, Portugal
Garcia, Axel, 176. see Laboratorio de Diseno y Mercadotecnia
Gardiner, James, 50. see James Gardiner Associates
Garner, Anne, 78. see E/A Records
Gaskin, Malsolm, G.C., 26, 62. 2A Astrop Terrace, London W6
Gassner, Christof, 84, 176. D-6000 Frankfurt/Main, Kaiserstr. 55. BRD
Gauger, David, 66, 74, 106, 158. see Gauger Sparks Silva
Gautier, Ray, 188. c/o Shell Hse, South Bank, London SE1
Geher, Werner, 44. c/o Museum Lausanne
Geiss, Otto, 30. c/o Haindl Papier GmbH, Georg-Haindl-Str. 4, D-8900 Augsburg
Gerlach, Klaus, 62. see Chris Meiklejohn Ltd
Geurts, Arie J., 106, 108, 116, 132, 174, 176. see Laboratorio de Diseno y Mercadotecnia
Ghoshal, N., 62. Sista's Private Ltd, UBI Building, Sir, P.M. Road Bombay 400001, India
Gibbs, John, 162. see Unit 5 Design
Gil, Daniel, 86. Caleruega 20, 13ºF, Madrid 33, Spain
Gink, K., 90. 1118 Budapest, XI, Bezнő Köz
Giovanni, Anthony de, 96. c/o Philatelic Bureau, The General Post Office, Valetta, Malta
Gitzel, Dieter, 160. see Verlag Dieter Gitzel
Gladstone, Gary, 174. 237 East 20th St, NYC, New York
Glemser, Manfred, 160. Silberburgstr. 66, D-7000 Stuttgart 1
Goddard, David, 188. c/o Felix Gluck Press, 72 Northcote Rd, Twickenham, Middx
Goffin, Josse, 180. rue Thomas Decock 12, 5989 Bossut-Gottechain, Belgium
Gogov, Cyril, 126. Tzar Peter Str. 14-16, Sofia 63, Bulgaria
Gorham, John, 174. 30 Neal St, London WC2
Gonzalez, Jose Ros, 106. Dinenador graohico, Avanue Jose Antonio 264, 1º 2ª, Barcelona 4
Gorissen, Götz Gunnar, 84. Osdorfer Str. 21, 1000 Berlin 45
Goslin, Charles, 90, 176, 186. see Barnett/Goslin/Barnett
Gosselin, Gerard, 32. see Union d'Artistes Plasticiens
Graddon, Julian P., 72. 5 Peals Court, 9-10 Colville Terrace, London W11
Granger, Michel, 180. 124 rue de Tolbiac, 75013 Paris
Gratama, 96. Netherlands P & T Service, Korteaerkade 12, Den Haag
Gray, Lyn, 190. Cubitts Yard, James St, London WC2
Green, Stefanie, 160. see Scholastic magazine
Greenberg, Mark, 24. see Raymond Lee & Associates
Grey, Dennis, 154. see Sam Smidt Associates
Grieder, Walter, 88. Bäumleingasse 16, 4000 Basel, Switzerland
Gross, Edith, 38. 44A Morton St, NYC 10014, New York
Grün, Hartmut, 66. see Young & Rubicam, Frankfurt
Grüter, Werner, 70. Leimenstr. 68, CH-4000 Basel, Switzerland
Gruttner, Erhard, 32. 1636 Blankenfelde, Kiefernweg 45, DDR
Guidotti, Paolo, 128. Piazza Risorgimento N7, Milan
Guitart, Francesi, 114, 186. Pasea Manuel Girona, Sotanos 2 Barcelona 17
Guitierez, Pancho, 108. see Laboratorio de Diseno y Mercadotecnia
Guntenaar, Joost, 158. see Will van Sambeek Design Associates
Guyatt, Prof. Richard, 110. see Guyatt/Jenkins
Gyllenhoff, Carl, 134. c/o Folkmar Roll, Brønsholmdalsvej 32, DK-2980 Kokkedal, Denmark

Haars, Peter, 86. Evjegakken 6F, 1346 Gjettum, Norway
Haas, Ernst, 188. c/o Eberhard Bauer, Herausgeber, D-7300, Esslingen-Neckar
Haettenschweiler, Walter, 96. c/o Schweizerische PTT Wertzeichenabteilung Ostermundingenstr. 91, 3000 Berne 29, Switzerland
Hajman, György, 34, 80. 6000 Kecskemét, Hargita u. 9, Hungary
Halas, John, 144. see Halas & Batchelor Animation
Hall, Chad, 62. see Leo Burnett Ltd
Han, Chun Hee, 102. c/o Directorate General of Posts, Philatelic Services, Republic of Korea
Hanna, Wm, 54. see East Ham Graphics
Hansen, Poul Lund, 180. see Poul Lund Hansen/Reklame
Hanson, Paul, 126. see Robert P. Gersin Associates Inc.
Hardacre, Christabel, 180. see HMSO Graphic Design
Harder, Rolf, 170, 178. see Design Collaborative
Hardy, Stewart, 148. see BBC Television Centre
Hargreaves, Brian, 100. see Crown Agents Stamp Bureau
Harold, Peter, 142. c/o KMP, 7 Portland Place, London W1
Harris, David, 130. see David Harris Consultant Designer
Harris, John, 114, 128, 130. see John Harris Design Partnership
Harris, Roger, 120. 25 Anderson Drive, Ashford, Middx TW15 1BG
Hartmann, Erich, 60, 78. 8032 Zürich, Bergstr. 138, Switzerland
Harvey, Len, 160. see Kynoch Graphic Design
Hauch, Walter J., 162. see Graphic Studio Hauch
Hauer, C., 20, 166. see Atelier Noth & Hauer
Häusser, Robert, 44. see Olaf Leu Design
Hayhow, Jeffrey, 28. c/o Victoria & Albert Museum, London
Hayoz, Marcel, 60, 64. Schubertstr. 25, 8037 Zürich, Switzerland
Healey, Gavin, 110, 172. see Gavin Healey Design
Hedberg, Ture, 70. see Marknads Team AB
Heimal, Bob, 106. see Promedeus Arts
Helényi, Tibor, 32. 1075 Budapest VII, Madách Tér 6, Hungary
Henderson, Ed, 70. 1012 Mountain St, Montreal 25, PQ, Canada
Henner-Prefi, 66. see Young & Rubicam, Frankfurt
Henning, Claes, 22. see Fältman & Malmén
Herfurth, Egbert, 42, 88. 701 Leipzig, Flossplatz 36, DDR
Herfurth, Renate, 42. 701 Leipzig, Flossplatz 36, DDR
Hernandez, Sergio, 62. see Carlos Rolando & Asoc.
Herson, Maurice, 190. see Negus & Negus
Hett, Friedemann, 178. 7982 Baienfurt, Weidenstr. 6, BRD
Heuwinkel, Wolfgang, 168, 184. D-507 Bergisch Gladbach, Clemenstr. 7, BRD
Hicks, Roger, 162. see Detroit Free Press
Hidalgo, Francisco, 92. 77 Bd St Michel, 75005 Paris
Hiepler, Gerd, 56, 174. see GGK Basel
Higgins, Peter, 170. see John Nash & Friends
Hill, John T., 112. Amity Rd, Bethany, Connecticut 0652
Hofrichter, Fritz, 44, 72, 176. see Olaf Leu Design
Hollick, Kenneth R., 110. 1/5 Midford Place, London W1P 9HH
Holmes, David, 68. see Dobny Johnson
Holmes, Derrick, 68, 92, 190. see Your Company By Design
Holmquist, R., 96. see Royal Swedish Post Office
Holt, Dave, 70. see Dennis S. Juett & Associates Inc.
Holzing, Heide, 102. c/o Posttechnisches Zentralamt, 61 Darmstadt, BRD
Honeybone, Ian, 22. see Genesis Advertising & Design Consultants
Honeysett, 90. see Weidenfeld & Nicolson
Hoogendoorn, Ton, 64, 192. Weldamstr. 107, Den Haag, Holland
Hornack, Angelo, 180. see HMSO Graphic Design
Hornyik, Istvan, 38. Budapest, Felszabadulás-ter, Hungary
Hristov, H., 102. c/o Postage Stamps Division, Hemus, 6 Ruski Blvd, Sophia, Bulgaria
Hundson, Ross, 42. c/o Penn State College, Pennsylvania
Huet, Michel H.G., 116. see The Buchanan Company
Huguet, Enric, 26, 106. Avenida Gaudi 30 3º 2ª, Barcelona 13
Hunnybun, Gus, 130. see Design for Print
Hunt, Duncan, 176. see Barnett/Goslin/Barnett
Hunt, T. Wayne, 106, 118, 154. see Wayne Hunt Graphic Design
Hunter, Andrew, 160. 13 Buckingham Terrace, Edinburgh
Hutton, 170. see John Nash & Friends
Hynes, Jim, 168. see Burns, Cooper, Donoahue, Fleming & Co Ltd

Ingerlill, 122. see RT
Ireland, John, 122. The Red House, Shelhanger, Norfolk
Isern, Jordi, 190. see ECTA 3
Isern i Castro, Albert, 46, 190. see ECTA 3
Isherwood, Bob, 70. see Collett Dickenson Pearce & Partners
Isles, Terry, 76. c/o McCann Erickson, 151 Bloor St W., Toronto M5S 1S8, Ontario
Itasse, Danièle, 106. see Jean Larcher Studio
Jacki, Gunter, 102. c/o Posttechnisches Zentralamt, 61 Darmstadt, BRD
Jaeger, Louis, 100. Directorate General of Posts, Philatelic Services, Liechtenstein
Jakob, Reinhold, 84. c/o Christof Gassner, D-6000 Frankfurt/Main, Kaiserstr 55, BRD
Jakobson, Jonette, 154, 162. see Peter Bradford & Associates
Jansson, Jan, 28. see Jim Akerstedt AB
Jarrey, Herbert, 34. 3300 Volkmarode, Steinkamp 16, BRD
Jelley, Chris, 148. see BBC Television Centre
Jenkins, Nicholas, 110. see Guyatt/Jenkins
Jenkinson, David, 170. see Gordon Hill Advertising
Jetter, Frances, 90. 57 Montague St, Brooklyn, New York
Jirka, L., 96. c/o Directorate General of Posts, Philatelic Services, Czechoslovakia
Jodlowski, Tadeusz, 30, 34. Al. Swierczewskiego 95/99 prac. 3a, Warsaw, Poland
Johns, Jasper, 38. see Studio Mendell & Oberer
Jones, Barbara, 70. see Dennis S. Juett & Associates Inc.
Jones, Lawrence Fairfax, 184. P.O. Box 70 Blackthorne Rd, Colinbrook, Slough SL3 0AR
Jonkajtys, Marian, 34. ul. Kotowa 20, 03536 Warsaw, Poland
Jørgensen, Jorgen, 134. GL Kongevej 139, Copenhagen
Juett, Dennis S., 70. see Dennis S. Juett & Associates

Kaldelis, Georgos, 62. see K & K Univas Adv. Centre Sarl
Kalderon, A., 96, 122. 8 Kehilat, Budapest St, Tel Aviv
Kambanellis, Pelia, 184. see K & K Univas Advertising Centre Sarl
Kane, Art, 168. 1181 Broadway, NYC 10001, New York
Kantscheff, Stephan, 98, 108. Krasiu Sarafof 17, Sofia 21, Bulgaria
Kapadia, Behram, 90. 38 Chequers Lane, Pitstone, Beds LU7 9AG
Karim, A.F., 98. c/o Directorate General of Posts, Philatelic Services, Bangladesh
Kass, Janos, 102. Budapest 1022, Hankoci u. 15, Hungary
Katzourakis, Agni, 184. see K & K Univas Advertising Centre
Kaveh, Melanie, 176. see Publiciteam
Kawamoto, Roy, 108. see Visual Design Center
Keeble, Chris, 116. Studio D. Floral Hall, Covent Garden, London WC2
Keig, Susan Jackson, 158. 860 Lake Shore Drive, Chicago, Ill 60611
Kellner, Mordechai, 182. Rehov Haas No. 39, Holon, Israel
Kelly, Pete, 60. see Ogilvie Benson & Mather
Kemény, Eva, 38. Budapest 1112, XI, Botfalu — köz 7, Hungary
Kennaway, Adrienne, 100. see Crown Agents Stamp Bureau
Kennerley, Dick, 178. see Smith Kline & French Labs
Keresztes, Lajos, 184. c/o Prof Kurt Weidemann, 7 Stuttgart N, Grünwaldstr. 38, BRD
Khosravi, Ali, 36. c/o Morteza Momayez, 6th St Pakestan Str, Abbass Abad Ave, Tehran, Iran
Kiefte, Kees de, 130. Roelofstr. 44, Nieuwkoop, Holland
Kind, Steffen, 24. see Young & Rubicam, Copenhagen
King, Harold, 92. 13 Clarendon Rd, Ashford, Mddx
King, Pete, 170. see Don Burston & Associates
Klappert, 20, 166. Hauptstr. 32, 1000 Berlin 62, Germany
Klawans, Alan, 178. see Smith Kline & French Labs
Klimowski, Andrzej, 32. Warszawa 03 — 902, ul. Czeska 10m2, Poland
Knezy, C., 66. see Adolf Wirz AG
Kniffin, F. Robert, 174. c/o Johnson & Johnson, New Brunswick, New Jersey 08903
Koblegärd, Per, 60. see Benton & Bowles
Koch, Claus-Joachim, 144, 182. see McCann, Frankfurt
Kopp, Gunther, 84. c/o Christof Gassner, D-6000 Frankfurt/Main, Kaiserstr 55, BRD
Kortemeier, Matthis, 18. see Ariola-Eurodisc GmbH
Kotopoulis, Dino, 144. see Halas & Batchelor Animation
Kraft, Helmut, 28. see Kraftdesign
Kriegel, Harriet, 176. see Barnett/Goslin/Barnett
Kristenson, Stellan, 86. Domherrestigen 6, 150 24 Ronninge, Sweden
Krogh, Ole, 24. see Young & Rubicam, Copenhagen
Krol, Stan, 110. 7 Lowther Rd, London SW13 9NX
Kropivka, José Abel, 22, 70, 76. Rua Bandeira Paulista 147 Apto 43, Sao Paulo SP
Kruse, Wolfgang, 90. John F. Kennedy-Platz, 1000 Berlin 62, BRD
Kujasalo, Kai, 42. Rehbinderintie 5.A.3, 00150 Helsinki 15, Finland
Kurlansky, Mervyn, 86, 94, 174. see Pentagram
Kürti, Esther, 48, 126, 134. see A. Degani & E. Kurti
Kyung, Ahn sung, 100. c/o Directorate General of Posts, Philatelic Services, Republic of Korea

Laeis, Christoph, 90. see Studio Laeis
Laitila, Unto, 22. see G4 Studio
Lam, Ben, 76. 39 Shimon Hatarsi, Tel Aviv
Lane, Tony, 78. see E/A Records
Langer, Bibi, 64. see Young & Rubicam, Stockholm
Langer, Helmut, 52, 68. see Langer Visualisation
Langer-Rosa, Marina, 28, 52, 68. see Langer Visualisation
Larcher, Jean, 26, 106. see Jean Larcher Studio
Larkin, Jack, 88, 90. AD Design, 84 Sycamore St, Caulfield, Melbourne, Australia
Lastrego, Cristina, 88, 94. Corso Casale 2, Turin
Lawson, David, 126, 156. Portland Studios, 30 Bourdon St, London W1
Lazar, Bob, 116. c/o Joe Scorsone, 7823 Spring Ave, Elkins Park, Pennsylvania 19117
Lee, Jared, 88. see Scholastic magazine
Lee, Raymond, 24, 48. see Raymond Lee & Associates
Lee, Sally, 122. see David Tyrell & Associates
Leech, John G., 150. 10 Birch Vale Drive, Romiley, Stockport, Cheshire
Leeds, Martin, 158. see American Express Corporation
Leedy, Jeff, 158. see Gauger Sparks Silva
Lees, Kevin, 172, 182. see E.G. Holt & Associates
Leu, Olaf, 44, 72, 176. see Olaf Leu Design
Levy, Donald, 108. see Visual Design Center
Lewis, M., 172. see E.G. Holt & Associates
Leyge, Roland, 94. Le Vieux Colombier, 95640 Santeuil, France
Liarte, Bartolomé, 190. Roger de Flor, 301 7º 1ª, Barcelona 13
Liesler, 98. c/o Directorate General of Posts, Philatelic Services, Czechoslovakia
Lieve, Meirens, 124. see EDI 2
Lilja, Kirsti, 22. see G4 Studio
Lind, Olle, 54. Kustlaan 7, B-1990 Hoeilaart, Belgium
Lindh, Håkan, 28. see Jim Åkerstedt AB
Linquist, Marita, 146. see The Finnish Broadcasting Company
Liso, Geppi de, 86, 108, 130. see Studio de Liso
Liso, Lilli de, 108, 130. see Studio de Liso
Liuzzi, Sergio, 138. c/o Rudi Böhm, Lopes Quintas 303, Rio de Janeiro
Livingstone, Alan, 190. 37 Ring Dyke Way, Lythan St Annes, Lancashire
Lloyd, Peter, 116. see Forth Studios
Lloyd-Jones, Elphin, 144. see Halas & Batchelor Animation
Lockwood, Arthur, 90. 8 Montague Rd, Richmond, Surrey
Lomeli, Suzy, 174. see Laboratorio de Diseno y Mercadotecnia
Lommel, Wolf, 58. see Young & Rubicam, Frankfurt
Lorente, J., 62. see Carlos Rolando & Asoc.
Löw, Markus, 172. see Ciba-Geigy Corporation, Art Services
Lowe, Dietrich, 144. see Halas & Batchelor Animation
Lum, Marion, 156. see Ad Graphics
Lund, Johnny, 20. see Scherling & Andersen ApS
Lundberg, Birgitta, 96. see Royal Swedish Post Office
Luoto, Laila, 22. see G4 Studio
Luxton, Colin, 48. see Raymond Lee & Associates
Lynch-Robinson, Domonic, 26, 62. see Leo Burnett Ltd

Mac, Joh, 62. see Chris Meiklejohn Ltd
McAllister, Denise, 88. see Transworld Publishers
McBean, George, 38. c/o UNICEF CIS, Box 44145, Nairobi, Kenya
McConnell, 52, 116, 186. see Pentagram
Macdonald, Norman, 176. Herenstr. 14, Voorhout, Holland
McFarland, Mike, 74. see The Haas Company
McGee, Shelagh, 88. 140 Finchley Rd, London NW3
McIness, Ian, 170. see John Nash & Friends
McKenzie, Ian, 172. 77 Victoria Parade, E. Melbourne, Victoria, Australia
McNally, Bruce, 58. see Leo Burnett Ltd
Madsen, Jørgen, 122. see RT
Maessen, Hubert, 104. see ARE Kommunikation
Magin, Wolf, 22. 68 Mannheim 1, Ifflandstr. 8, BRD
Maheux, Denyse, 170. see Gordon Hill Advertising
Majo, William de, 114. see William de Majo Associates
Malecki, St, 98. c/o Directorate General of Posts, Philatelic Services, Poland
Malkemus, Wilhelm, 164. 648 Wächtersbach 1, Bahnhofstr. 31, BRD
Malmén, Kaj, 22. see Faltman & Malmén
Mangiavacca, R., 156. 1 Square Max-Hymans, Paris 15e
Mansky, Marvin, 30. see Ner Beck Design
Mansourpour, Jila, 176. see Publiciteam
Manta, Benito, 22. see CCIA Pubblicita
Man-Yee, So, 54, 106. see Kinggraphic
Marcovecchio, Oscar N., 66. see Oscar N. Marcovecchio, SA de Publicidad
Mariani, Ettore, 28. via Pier Capponi, I Milan
Marquart, Laurent, 40, 112. see Guillon/Designers Inc.
Marquez, Raymundo Leal, 176. see Laboratorio de Diseno y Mercadotecnia
Martin, John, 160. see Forth Studios
Martinez, Sergio, 132. Juan Escutia 45, 5° Piso, Mexico 11, DF
Martins, Carlos, 182. Av. Epitacio Pessoa No. 186 Ap. 7
Maskew, John, 102, 154, 176. see Jeremy Sampson Associates
Mason, Alan, 54. see Kunstschule Alsterdamm
Mason, Les, 130, 132. see Les Mason Graphic Design
Massey, Ray, 18. 158A Camden High St, London NW1
Mastellaro, Alfredo, 126, 128, 132. see Studio Mestellaro & Agenzia Associati
Matsubayashi, Chikako, 176. see The Weller Institute
Matthews, Rick, 24. see Dorland Advertising
Matthies, Holger, 32, 44, 166. 2000 Hamburg 20, Wrangelstr. 13, BRD
Mattingley, Neil, 156. see Trickett & Webb
May, Tony, 18. 1 Portland Mews, London W1
Mayerhofer, Raimund, 126. 1190 Wien, Siebergasse 1, Austria
Medina, Fernando, 106, 164. Santiago Bernabeu 6-7°, Madrid 16
Meer, Ronald van der, 88. 143 Marlborough Rd, Langley, Berkshire
Mehl, Jürgen, 20, 28, 60, 160. see SSM Werbeagentur
Meiklejohn, Chris, 24, 60, 184. 31 King St, Covent Garden, London WC2
Melgarejo, D., 74. see Carlos Rolando & Asoc.
Mendell, Pierre, 38. see Studio Mendell & Oberer
Meola, Eric, New York, 64. see Young & Rubicam, Stockholm
Merisio, Pepi, 182. see Mohn-Gordon Studios
Merwan, B., 140. see Ogilvy Benson & Mather Private Ltd, India
Mesghali, Farshid, 42. 1 77th St, Yosofabad Bala, Tehran, Iran
Metz, Frank, 90. c/o Simon & Schuster Inc., 630 Fifth Ave, NYC 10020, New York
Metz, Frédéric, 40, 106, 112, 164. 306 Place Youville, Suite B-20, Montreal, Quebec H2Y 2B6
Meyer, Ulrich, 90, 160. 61 Av. Simon Bolivar, Paris
Meyers, Bob, 78. see E/A Records
Miettinen, Esko, 22. see G4 Studio
Mietzner, H.G., 184. c/o Prof. Kurt Weidemann, 7 Stuttgart N., Grünwaldstr. 38, BRD
Miho, James, 40, 168. Miho Inc., 217 East 49th St, NYC 10017, New York
Mills, Judie, 90. c/o Franklin Watts Inc., 730 Fifth Ave, NYC, New York
Milne, Jonathon, 172, 182. 11 Maroon Millway, Willowdale M2L 1T9, Ont., Canada
Milon, Reuven, 170. c/o Gordon Gallery, Tel Aviv, Israel
Minor, Wendell, 92. see Wendell Minor Design
Miranda (Miran), Oswaldo, 42, 126, 174. rue Republica da Siria, No 222 Curitiba, Brazil/Parana
Miro, 22, 76. rua Tupi 579, Sao Paulo — Sp
Mitchell, Jim, 28. see Jim Mitchell Adv.
Moei, Dick de, 184. c/o Drukkerij van Wijland bv, Caliskamp 7, Laren nh, Holland
Moisan, Paul Henry, 180. c/o Michel Granger, 124 rue de Tobiac, 75013 Paris
Molen, Ran van der, 124. Heiderweg 45, Soest, Holland
Molho, Yak, 76. Bahat-Molcho, 4 Lambdan Blvd, Ramat Gan, Israel
Momayez, Morteza, 36. 6th Str, Pakestan Str. Abbass Abad Ave, Tehran
Monaghan, Mike, 118. see Monaghan & Beard
Moon, Sarah, 184. 19 Av. de Général le Clerc, Paris 4e
Moore, Brian, 58. see Leo Burnett Ltd
Morgan, Jack, 164. see Robert P Gersin Associates
Morgan, Jonathan de, 192. De Morgan Associates, 13 Moorland Drive, Moortown, Leeds LS17 6JP
Morise, Kazuhiro, 20. Semi Sagiyama Gifu-shi, Japan
Morris, Julie, 122, 128. see Richard C. Runyon Design
Morrison, Derek, 92. Chestergate House, London SW1
Moses, Howard, 150. see BBC Television Centre
Mosinski, Marek, 50. 40 — 133 Katowice, ul. Feliksa Kona 2 m 1, Poland
Motter, Othmar, 54, 106. see Vorarlberger Graphik
Mtodozeniec, Jan, 34. Naruszewicza 3 m 7, 02627 Warsaw, Poland
Muharrqi, Al, 102. see Crown Agents Stamp Bureau
Mullen, Ken, 58. see Leo Burnett Ltd
Müller, Jean Claude, 132. see Ken Parkhurst & Associates Inc.
Munday, John, 88. see Transworld Publishers
Murphy, Rowan Barnes, 88. see Transworld Publishers

Naddeo, Herminio, 182. see McCann Erickson Publicidade
Nagore, Pedro, 134. see Publicidad Mediterranea
Nahmias, John, 178. see Somonte y Associados SA
Naisbitt, Roy, 142. see Richard Williams Animation
Naitou, Fumiko, 20. see photo Suzui Co.
Nakagawa, Kenzo, 108, 158. View Photo 5-4-3, Kita Nagao Cho, Sakai, Osaka, Japan
Nash, Robin, 18. see Young & Rubicam, London
Nathan-Garamond, Jacques, 108, 110, 156. see Garamond
Neate, Elizabeth, 68. see Your Company By Design
Negus, Dick, 190. see Negus & Negus
Negus, Dominic, 190. see Negus & Negus
Nelson, Louis, 126, 164. see Robert P. Gersin Associates Inc.
Netto, J. Natale, 22. rue Miralta 370, Sao Paulo
Neumann, Eckhard, 42. 6 Frankfurt/Main, Seilerstr. 12, BRD
Neuteboom, Boudewijn, 72. NZ Voorburgwaal 266, Amsterdam
Nguyen, Nguyen, 102. c/o Directorate General of Posts, Philatelic Services, Vietnam
Nicholson, J.H., 98. see Crown Agents Stamp Bureau
Nikolov, Nikola Petra, 108, 148. Sofia — C, Post Restante, Bulgaria
Nilson, Kerstin Abram, 96. see Royal Swedish Post Office
Noack, Wolf, 30. Werbestudio Noack, D-8900, Augsburg, D.-Kreuz Str. 16, BRD
Noble, Louise, 92. 2 Park St, Boston, Massachusetts 12107
Nobuyama, Hiro, 108, 158. View Photo 5-4-3, Kita-Nagao Cho, Sakai, Osaka, Japan
Noguera, Javier, 86, 178. Encarnación 140, Barcelona
Noordzig, Gerril, 96. c/o Directorate General of Posts, Philatelic Services, Holland
Norbäck, Lina, 122. see Lintas
Nordbok, 180. Forenings 34, 41127 Gothenburg, Sweden
Noth, Volker, 20, 166. see Atelier Noth & Hauer
Nsd, Masino, 98. c/o Directorate General of Posts & Telecommunications 37 Kebon Sirih, Jakarta, Indonesia
Numan, Mariet, 18, 70. Kouwenoord 601, Amsterdam, Bylmermeer
Nye, John, 54, 176. see Kinggraphic

Oehring, Hans Georg, 154. Braunschweig, Bismarckstr. 14, BRD
Ogilvie, Peter, 74. see Gauger Sparks Silva
Ohashi, Toshiyuki, 40. see Shigeo Okamoto Design Center
Okamoto, Shigeo, 26, 40, 54. see Shigeo Okamoto Design Center
Olbinski, Rafal, 32. Warsaw 03967, Saska 57 u. 8, Poland
Oliver, Rob, 68. see J. Walter Thompson, London
Olmos, Vicente, 74, 160, 178. see Pharma-Consult
Omenamäki, Osmo, 26, 94. Meritullink 9 B 25, 00170 H:kl 17, Finland
Onji, Mostafa, 40. see The Institute for the Intellectual Development of Children & Young Adults
Opperman, Stanli, 24. Pratt Mews, Pratt St, London NW1
Orosz, István, 34, 80. 6000 Kecskemét, Hargita u. 9, Hungary
Oshiga, O.I., 98. c/o Nigerian Philatelic Services, PMB 12647 Tinubu St, GPO Lagos, Nigeria
Otnes, Fred, 180. c/o Exxon Corporation, 1251 Avenue of the Americas, New York 10020
Ott-Heidmann, Eva-Maria, 88. c/o Günther U. Müller, 8 München 81 Cosimastr. 2, BRD

Padova, Ruben, 176. see Laboratorio de Diseno y Mercadotecnia
Page, Tony, 92, 118. see Tony Page Associates
Pallares, Jose, 134. Mineria 28, Barcelona
Pallut, Dominique, 54. 2 rue Pas de la Mule, Paris 75003
Pambouthi, Pavline, 62. K & K Univas Adv. Centre Sarl
Park, Malcolm, 160. see Forth Studios
Parker, Robert J., 178. see Smith Kline & French Labs
Parkhurst, Ken, 132. see Ken Parkhurst & Associates
Parnaby, Jane, 94. see Pentagram
Parry, David, 22, 170. see Burns, Cooper, Donoahue, Fleming & Co Ltd
Pasini, Mario, 92, 94. see Atelier de créations Belin
Pasture, M.A., 90. c/o Le Directeur, General Administration of Postal Services, Centre Monnaie 1000, Brussels
Pateman, Michael, 154. see Peter Bradford & Associates
Patiwael, Donald, 98. c/o Netherlands P & T Services, Korteaerkade 12, Den Haag, Holland

Pavlicek, Emanuel, 38. c/o Artia, Prague, Czechoslovakia
Pawletta, Rolf, 24. see Kunstschule Alsterdamm
Payne, Colleen, 90. see Weidenfeld & Nicolson
Payne, Len, 114. 6 Dorset St, London W1H 3FE
Peake, John, 62. see Chris Meiklejohn Group
Pearce, David, 118. see Pentagram
Pearson-Taylor, John, 22. see Genesis Advertising & Design Consultants
Pedersen, Jonson Hinrichs, 178. 605 Third Ave, NYC, New York
Pergson, J., 100. c/o Philatelic Services, Tel-Aviv-Yafo, Israel
Persson, P.A., 96. see Royal Swedish Post Office
Peters, Christa, 62. see Leo Burnett Ltd
Petit, Gilbert, 76, 94. 55 rue Orfila, Paris 20e
Pettersen, Tor, 106. see Lock/Pettersen Ltd
Petzak, Christina, 88. 117 Berlin, Puchanstr. 37, DDR
Pfister, A., 68. see Adolf Wirz AG
Phil, Göran, 112. St. Nygatan 13, Stockholm
Pichard, Erik, 68. see RT
Pino, Giusseppe, 94. see Publicite Bornand & Gaeng
Pittmann, Stuart, 72. c/o Smith Greenland
Pokora, Milos, 124. c/o Ladislav Rada, Praha 10, Belocerkevská 1303, Czechoslovakia
Pollard, John, 188. see Cato Hibberd Hawksby Design
Popcorn, Faith, 72. c/o Smith Greenland
Poppe, Martha, 102. rua Laranjeiras, 55/1405 Rio de Janeiro
Prechtl, Michael Mathias, 28, 92. 8500 Nürnberg, Josef Simonstr. 16, BRD
Preston, Fred, 24. see Young & Rubicam, Copenhagen
Preston, Jerry, 24. see Leo Burnett Ltd
Pritchard, Susan, 164. see Guillon/Designers Inc.
Profeta, Alfredo, 26. Vico Paradiso all Salute 25, Naples
Proto, Peter, 134, 172. see Peter Proto Associates
Pstrowski, Stefan, 150. see BBC Television Centre
Puech, Andres, 132. see Diseño y Creacion Grafica
Pugh, Anna, 94. 32 Cheapstow Rd, London W2
Puhovski, Nenad, 166. c/o Zeljko Borcic, Jurisićeva 26/111, 41000 Zagreb
Purdum, Dick, 142. see Richard Williams Animation

Queva, Patrick, 180. c/o Josse Goffin, rue Thomas Decock 12, 5-89 Bossut — Gottechain, Brussels
Quick, Jim, 148. see Granada TV

Rabascall, Joan, 28. see Atelier Joan Rabascall
Rada, Ladislav, 124. Praha 10, Belocerkevská 1303, Czechoslovakia
Rajlich, Jan, 30. Uvoz 88, Brno 60200, Czechoslovakia
Randall, Chris, 144. see Wyatt Cattaneo Productions
Randall, K., 170. see John Nash & Friends
Rasqui Lorca, Jaime, 136. c/o Olivo, 10 pral. 1ª, Barcelona 4
Rau, Hans Jürgen, 44, 54. see Studio Rau
Raut, S.T., 16. see Air India
Rauter, Peter, 22. see Genesis Adv. & Design Consultants
Raz, Varda, 170. c/o Gordon Gallery, Tel Aviv, Israel
Ready, Mark, 60. see Ogilvie, Benson & Mather
Réber, Laszlo, 88. Pozsonyi ut. 12, Budapest 1137, Hungary
Reid, A., 162. see Kynoch Graphic Design
Rej, Bent, 68. Bent Rej Studios, 17 Vesterbrogade, DK 1620, Copenhagen V
Rey, N., 18, 58, 62, 68. see Nucleo de Comunicacion & Marketing/Publis
Ri, Nguyen Van, 102. c/o Directorate General of Posts, Philatelic Services Vietnam
Richardson, Ilana, 132. 101 Marlborough Rd, London N19 4PA
Riedemann, Kristin, 42. c/o Eckhard Neumann, Seilerstr. 12, D-6000 Frankfurt 1
Rindlisbacher, Max, 60, 64. see Gisler & Gisler
Risbeck, Philip E., 20. 3521 Canadian Parkway, Fort Collins, Colorado 80521
Robin, Randi, 110. see The Design Partnership
Rodat, Pierre, 26. see Jean Larcher Studio
Rohonyl, Charles, 190. Clos Beau Sejour 18, Waterloo, Belgium
Rolando, C., 24, 62, 74, 92, 114, 164. see Carlos Rolando & Asoc.
Roll, Folkmar, 112, 134. Bronsholmdalsveg 32, DK 2980 Kokkedal, Denmark
Roodnat, Bas, 184. c/o Drukkerij van Wijland BV, Caliskamp 7, Laren nh Holland
Roos, Urs, 60. see Gisler & Gisler
Rostron, 170. see John Nash & Friends
Rourigh, Marta, 92, 114. see Carlos Rolando & Asoc.
Rowold, Ben, 140. see NPO — Nationale Publiciteits Onderneming
Ruffolo, Sergio, 146, 160. see Ruffolo

Saha, Binay, 136. see Bata Studio
Sahib, Mian Mohammad, 98. c/o Directorate General of Posts, Philatelic Services, Pakistan
Saint, Kenny, 116. see Grapplegroup CJA
Salahuddin, Adil, 98, 100. c/o Directorate General of Posts, Philatelic Services, Pakistan
Salaroli, Sergio, 88. Via dei Gracchi 285/1, Rome
Salcedo, R., 18, 58, 62, 68. see Nucleo de Communicacion & Marketing/Publis
Salinas, Luis, 178. see Somonte y Asociados
Sambeek, Will van, 158. see Will van Sambeek Design
Sampson, Barry, 154. see Jeremy Sampson Associates
Sampson, Jeremy, 102, 110. see Jeremy Sampson Associates
Sanhandri, Uri, 18. see Bauer — Vershavsky Adv.
Sands, Colin, 156. see Trickett & Webb
Santis, Alfredo de, 50, 108, 146. see Studio de Santis
Santo, Antonio dal, 128. see Studio Mastellaro
Sarker, Benoy, 96, 98, 100, 102. L 1/1 Hauz Khas, New Delhi 110016, India
Saveta, Masic, 92. Beograd 11000, Vojvode Brane 7, Yugoslavia
Savitzky, Martha, 88. see Scholastic magazine
Scarzafava, Sondra, 130. see Pepsi-Cola Company
Schaap, Jeann, 50, 192. Meester Pankenstr. 12, Bergeijk, Holland
Schaap, Robert, 50, 90, 192. Meester Pankenstr. 12, Bergeijk, Holland
Schejbal, Danuta, 32. Warszawa 03-902, ul. Czeska 10 m 2 Poland
Schillinger, Heinz, 102. c/o Posttechnisches Zentralamt, 61 Darmstadt, BRD
Schillinger, Hella, 102. c/o Posttechnisches Zentralamt, 61 Darmstadt, BRD
Schlageter, Paulus, 186. c/o Wilhelm Kumm Verlag, Tulpenhofstr. 45, 6050 Offenbach/Main, BRD
Schleger, Hans 108. see Hans Schleger & Associates
Schlesinger, Maurice, 174. see Graphic Concept
Schlosser, Cyril John, 164. 4317 York Ave. South, Minneapolis, Minnesota 55410
Schlüter, Harald, 20, 28, 60, 160. Brunhofstrasse 1, 4330, Mühlheim/Ruhr Germany
Schmid, Helmut, 104. 403 Coporas Shimoi, 3-29-26, Tarumi-Cho, Suita-shi, Osak-fu, 564 Japan
Schmidt, Chuck, 106. see John Follis & Associates
Schmidt, Peter, 128, 132. 2000 Hamburg 13, Poseldorferweg 7, BRD
Schneider, Dominic, 60. see Gisler & Gisler
Schulz, Peter, 60, 64, 78. see Gisler & Gisler
Schulze, Wolfgang, 84. 1000 Berlin 20, Neuhausweg 2, Germany
Schuster, Gerd A., 84. c/o Dieter K. Frobisch, Schloss Str. 10, 6238 Hofheim/Taunus, BRD
Schutter, De, 188. see De Schutter SA
Schütz, Wieland, 108, 166. see Studio für Grafik — Wieland Schütz Design
Schwartz, Erick, 132. see Young & Rubicam, Mexico
Schwarz, R., 48. c/o Israel Homes & Real Estate Corp., 71A Ben Yehuda St, POB 3450, Tel Aviv
Scorsone, Joseph, 44, 114, 116. 7823 Spring Ave, Elkins Park, Pennsylvania 19117
Scott, Tom, 160. see Forth Studios
Seeff, Norman, 78. see E/A Records
Segura, Ramiro, 134. Paseo Maragall 73, Barcelona
Seidler, Ger, 64. see HVR Studio
Serény, Eva, 58. see Young & Rubicam, Frankfurt
Setzke, Gerd F., 24, 54. Hamburg 1, Ferdinandstr. 17, BRD
Shanosky, Don, 168. see Cook & Shanosky Associates
Sharma, Billy, 70, 170. see Gordon Hill Advertising
Shek, Michelle, 112. see Design Development
Shimizu, Takashi, 96. c/o Directorate General of Posts, Philatelic Services, Japan
Shiva, Ghobad, 26, 36. see NIRT, Sorush Press Graphic Dept
Showell, Russ, 70, 170. see Gordon Hill Advertising
Silvonen, Noora, 22. see G4 Studio
Silva, J.R., 70. see Bureau Tecnica de Publicidade — BTP
Silva, Larry, 66, 74, 106. see Gauger Sparks Silva
Silva, Suzana Fonseca d'Arinos, 118. Ruaigarapava 59 — 4° Leblon, Rio de Janeiro
Simond, Monique, 170, 178. see John Nash & Friends
Simons, Kurt, 22. Sulitelmavägen 18, 161 33 Bromma, Sweden

Index

Advertising agents, and studios

Agences et studios

Werbeagenturen, und Studios

Index

Advertisers
Clients
Auftraggeber

Posters
Affiches
Plakate

1a-d India
AD Air India
AG Air India Art Studio
DIR J.B. Cowasji
DES (a) S.T. Raut
(b-d) S.N. Surti
save wild life, protegez les bêtes sauvages,
Naturschutz

1a

1b

1c

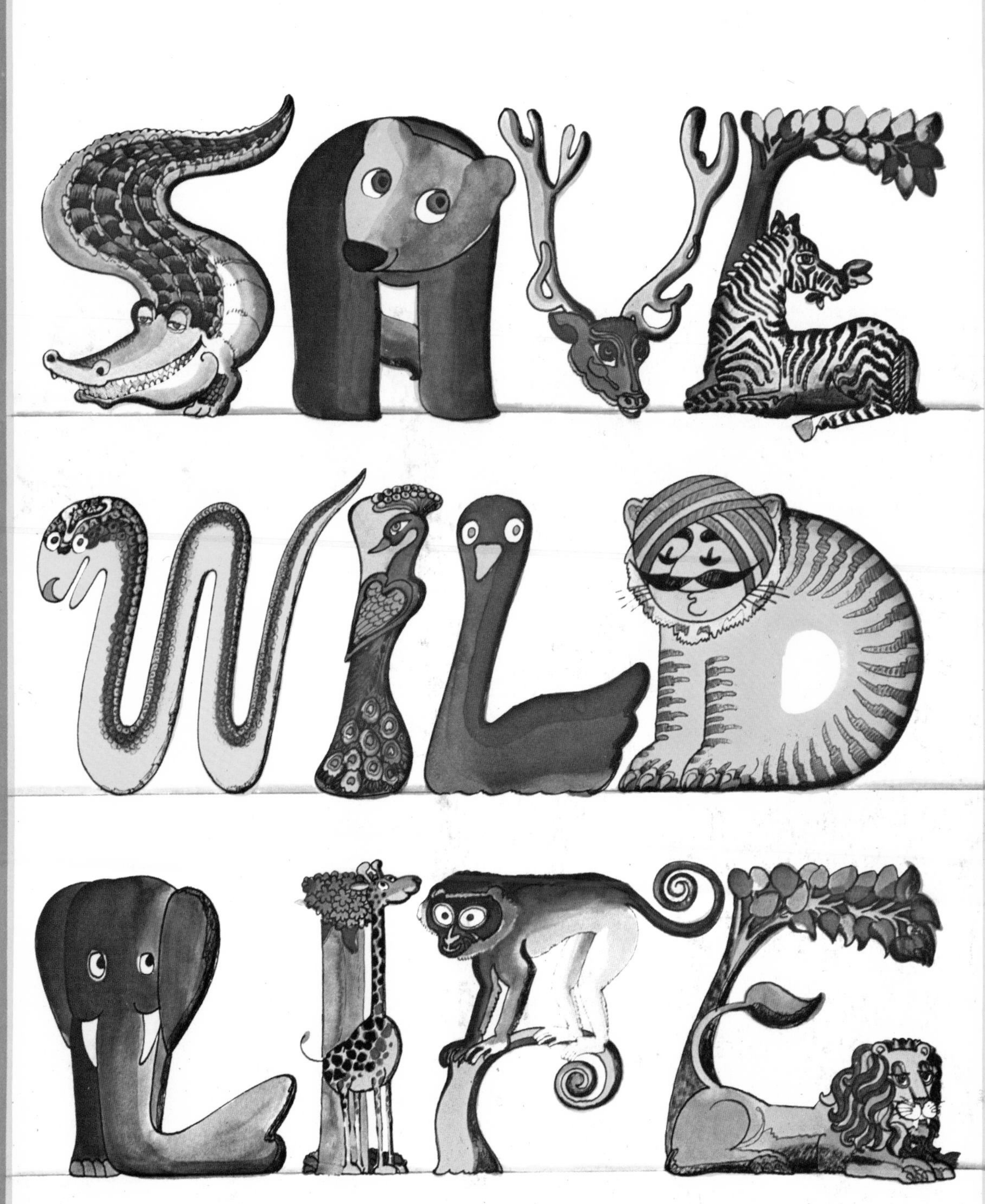

CREATED BY AIR-INDIA FOR WORLD WILDLIFE FUND

Posters
Affiches
Plakate

1a-b Great Britain
AD Heinz
AG Young & Rubicam Ltd
DIR Creative Group
ILL (1a) Tony May
(b) Billy Wrencher
soup, Suppen

2a-c Great Britain
AD (a, b) IDV
AG Young & Rubicam Ltd
DIR (a, b) Robin Nash
ILL (a) Julian Cottrell
(b) Ray Massey
(c) Bob Cramp
Copy Kate Batteau
vodka

3 Holland
AD 'De Ploeg' NV
AG NPO — Nationale Publiciteits Onderneming BV
DIR/DES Huib Ebbinge
ILL Mariet Numan
COPY Joop Cranendonk
textiles

4 Holland
AD Het Nederlands Zuivelbureau
AG Prad BV
DIR/ILL Jan Cremer
milk, lait

5 Great Britain
AD Scottish & Newcastle Breweries Ltd
AG Leo Burnett Ltd
DIR/DES Doug Buntrock
ILL Jack Bankhead
COPY Peter Smith

6 Spain
AD Pulco
AG Nucleo de Comunicacion & Marketing/Publis
DIR/DES Salvatore Aducci
COPY R. Salcedo, N. Rey
lemon juice, jus de citron, Zitronensaft

1a

1b

2a

3

4

7 Germany
AD/AG Ariola-Eurodisc GmbH
DIR/DES Manfred Vormstein
ILL Manfred Vormstein, Matthis Kortemeier
records, disques, Schallplatte

8 Israel
AD Acrilan
AG Bauer-Vershavsky Adv Ltd
DIR/DES Uri Sanhandri
ILL Yona Flink

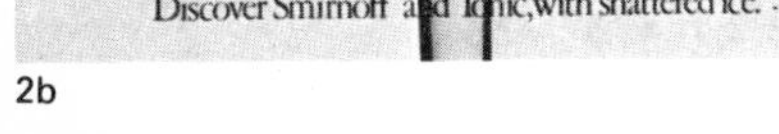

2b

2c

5

6

7

8

Posters
Affiches
Plakate

1 Japan
AD Oriental Nakamura Dept Store
AG Photo Suzui Co
DES Kazuhiro Moriste
ILL Sachio Suzui
COPU Fumiko Naitou
department store, grand magazin, Warenhaus

2 France
AD Absorba
AG Mafia
children's clothes, vêtements enfant, Kleidung für Kinder

3 Denmark
AD The Danish Post and Telegraph Service
AG Scherling & Andersen ApS
DIR/DES Johnny Lund
send Christmas post in good time

4 Hungary
AD Hungexpo
DIR Nándor Szilvásy
exhibition of agricultural machines

5 France
AD Peroche
AG Mafia (Maime Arnodin, Fayolle, International, Associés)
ready-to-wear women's clothes, prêt-à-porter femme, Moden

6 United States
AD Johns-Manville
AG Colorado State University Art Department
DIR/DES Philip E. Risbeck
symphony concert

1

2

3

4

7 Germany
AD Zanders
AG SSM Werbeagentur
DIR/DES H. Schlüter
COPY J. Mehl
fine papers, papier

8 Germany
AD Birkle & Thomer
AG Atelier Noth & Hauer
DES Noth, Hauer, Sodemann
ILL Klappert
Easter poster, affiche pour Pâques

5

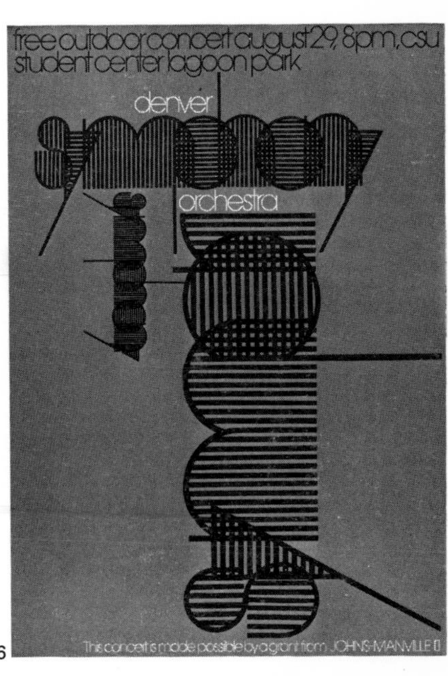

6

7

8

Posters
Affiches
Plakate

1 Sweden
AD Trafiksäkerhetsverket
DIR Kurt Simons
road safety, sécurité de la route, Unfallsverhütung

2 Germany
AD Maimarkt
DIR/DES Wolf Magin
cars, autos

3 Finland
AD Helsinki City Transport
AG Studio G4 HKL
DIR Esko Miettinen
DES Noora Siivonen
ILL Unto Laitila
COPY Laila Luoto, Kirsti Lilja
campaign for public transport

4a-b Canada
AD Dominion Bridge Steel Service
AG Burns, Cooper, Donoahue, Fleming & Co Ltd
DIR Robert Burns
DES Jim Donoahue
ILL Heather Cooper
COPY David Parry
steel company, acier, Stahl

5 Italy
AD Carlo Crespi & C.
AG CCIA Pubblicita
DIR/DES Innocenzo Careccia
ILL Adamo Photographer
office equipment

1

2

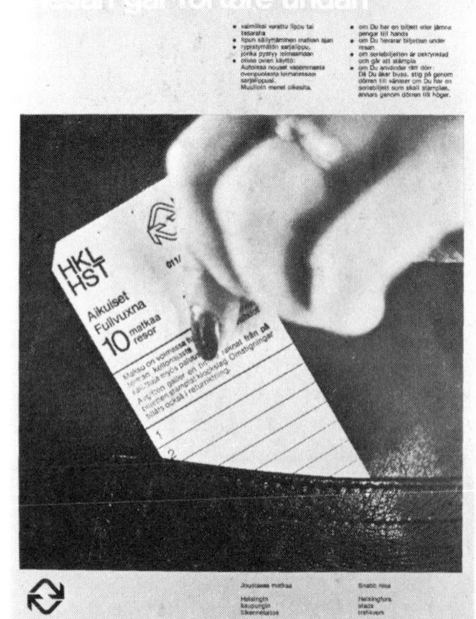

3

4a

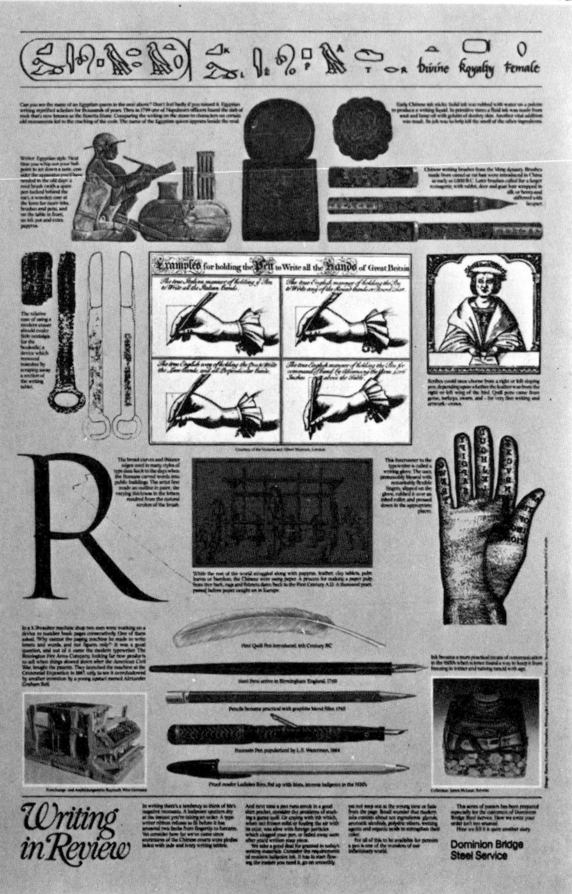

4b

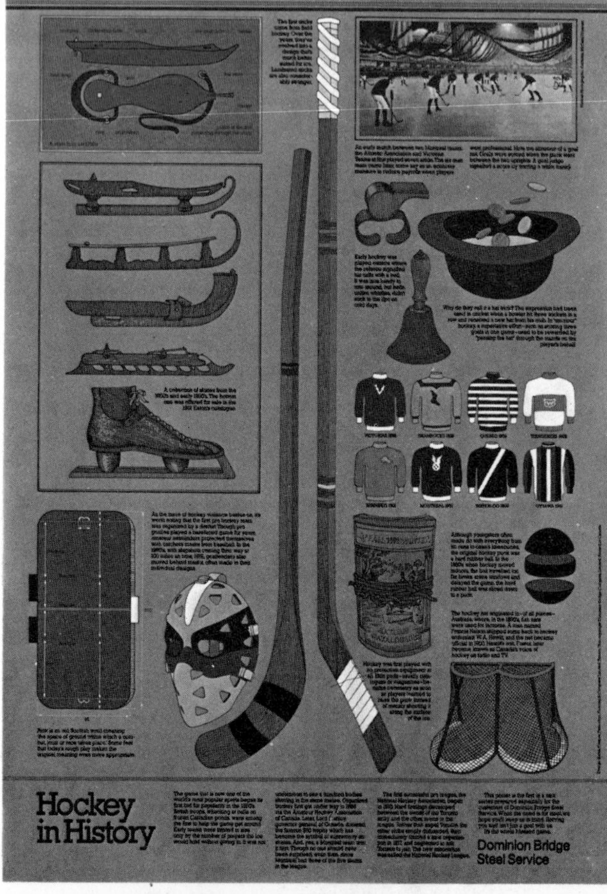

6 Italy
AD Innocenzo Careccia
AG CCIA Pubblicita
DIR/DES Innocenzo Careccia
ILL Benito Manta
promotion

7 United States
AD NBC Sports
AG NBC Advertising Sales and Promotion
DIR/DES Nicholas M. Stano
ILL Bart Forbes
COPY Hal Alterman

8 Great Britain
AD Airfix Products Ltd
AG Genesis Advertising and Design Consultants Ltd
DIR/DES John Pearson-Taylor
ILL Ian Honeybone (model maker), Peter Rauter (photographer)
plastic toys, jouets, Spielzeuge

9 Brazil
AD Golden Cross
AG Bureau Tecnico de Publicidade
DIR Jose Abel Kropivka
ILL Miro
COPY J. Natale Netto
health insurance, assurance maladie

10 Sweden
AD RFSU (Swedish Association for Sex Education)
AG Fältman & Malmén
DIR Gunnar Fältman
DES Claës Henning
ILL Claës Henning, Greta Fransson
COPY Kaj Malmén
condoms

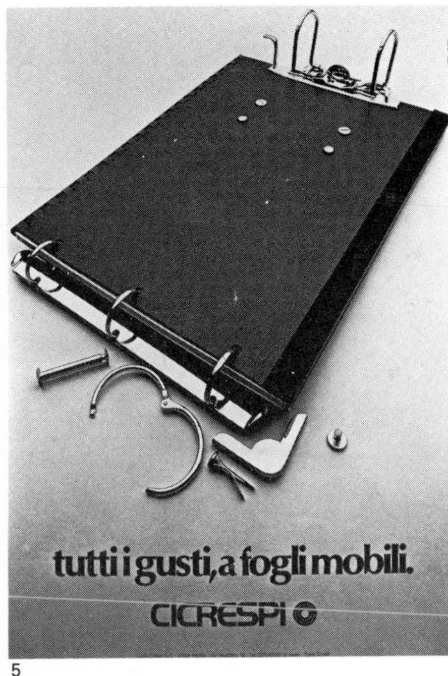

5

6

7

8

9

10

Posters
Affiches
Plakate

1 Great Britain
AD British Transport Hotels
AG Cato Johnson GLH
DIR/DES Richard Tilley
ILL Reg Cartwright
inclusive holidays by train

2 Germany
AD Verband Deutscher Reeder
AG Kunstschule Alsterdamm
DIR Gerd F. Setzke
DES Rolf Pawletta
travel by sea, voyages en mer, Seeschiffahrt

3 Denmark
AD Mols Linien
AD Young & Rubicam
DIR Steffen Kindt
ILL Fred Preston
COPY Ole Krogh

4 France
AD/AG Edition Bernard Grasset
DES Manelle Corner
childrens books

5 Spain
AD I.P. Mark
AG C. Rolando & Asociados
DIR/DES C. Rolando
seminar on creativity

6 Great Britain
AD Cadbury
AG Leo Burnett
DES Group: Chris Meiklejohn
ILL Jerry Preston

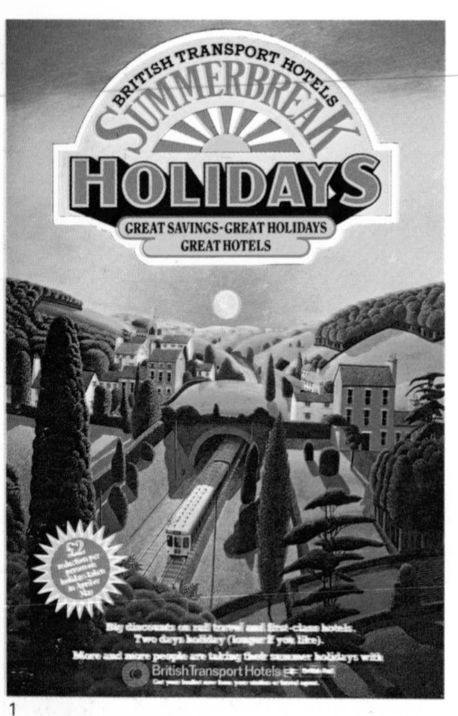

1

2

3

4

5

6

7 Great Britain
AD Tuborg
AG Dorland Advertising
DIR Rick Matthews
DES Group: Chris Meiklejohn
ILL David Bull

8 Canada
AD McGregor Hosiery Mills
AG Raymond Lee & Associates Ltd
DIR/DES Raymond Lee
ILL Greg Zajack
COPY Mark Greenberg
socks, chaussettes, Socke

9 Great Britain
AD Fitzrovia Festival
AG Castle Chappell & Partners Ltd
DIR/DES Robert Steward
ILL Theo Brown (model maker),
Stanli Opperman (photographer)
street festival

10 Great Britain
AD London Borough of Hammersmith
DIR/DES Ken Watson
ILL T. Austin Smith
newspaper, journal, Zeitung

7

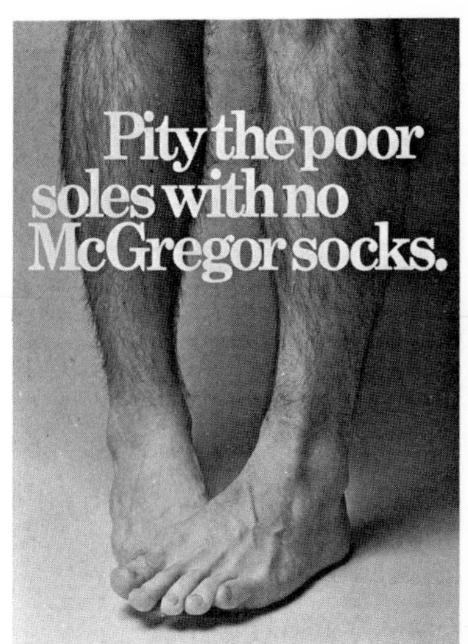

8

9

10

Posters
Affiches
Plakate

1 Great Britain
AD Times Newspapers Ltd
AG Leo Burnett Ltd
DIR/DES Malcolm G. C. Gaskin
COPY Dominick Lynch-Robinson
newspaper, journal, Zeitung

2 Italy
AD Refrain Record Shop
DIR/ILL Alfredo Profeta
records, disques, Schallplatten

3 Finland
AD Svenska Teatern
AG Ateljee Omppu
DIR/DES Osmo Omenamäki
theatre

4 France
AD Izason
AG Jean Larcher Studio
DIR/DES/ILL Jean Larcher
COPY Pierre Rodat
record and audio-visual

5 Spain
AD Salón Nautico
DES Enric Huguet

6a-b Japan
AD Meitetsu Sakae Melsa
AG Shigeo Okamoto Design Center
DIR/DES Shigeo Okamoto
department store

7 Iran
AD NIRT
AG Sorush Press Graphic Dept
DIR/DES Ghobad Shiva
National Iranian Radio & TV chamber
orchestra

THERE'S NOT LONG TO GO AND YOU HAVEN'T EVEN STARTED THINKING ABOUT PRESENTS and who to give what ≈ and the shops are packed solid with hot sweaty bad-tempered people just like you ≈ and anyway the best stuff's gone already ≈ and your legs ache ≈ your wallet's empty ≈ your mind's numb ≈ it's raining and the crowds are murder ≈ and oh could you use some help this Christmas. Slow down and relax. ≈ Get your help through The Times Christmas Gift Guide. ≈ You'll find presents for everyone, for every age, at every price. ≈ And there's a daily competition with Christmas prizes like vintage wines, Habana cigars and French perfume.

THE TIMES CHRISTMAS GIFT GUIDE
Shop in peace this Christmas.

1

2

3

4

5

Melsa sakae

燃えるこころ、ひろげよう。——冬の栄メルサ。

Winter Original Collection 1976/77

6a

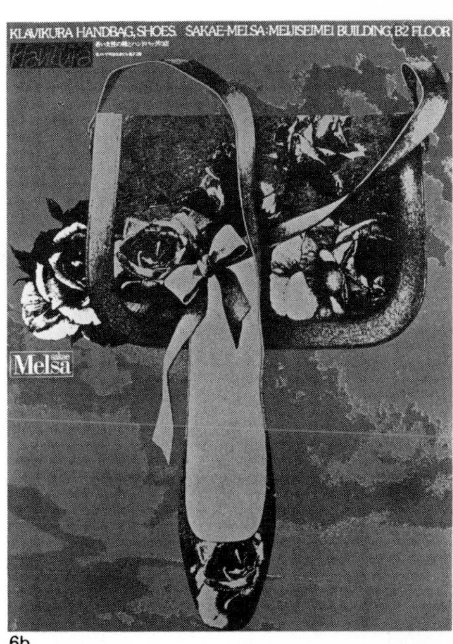

6b

7

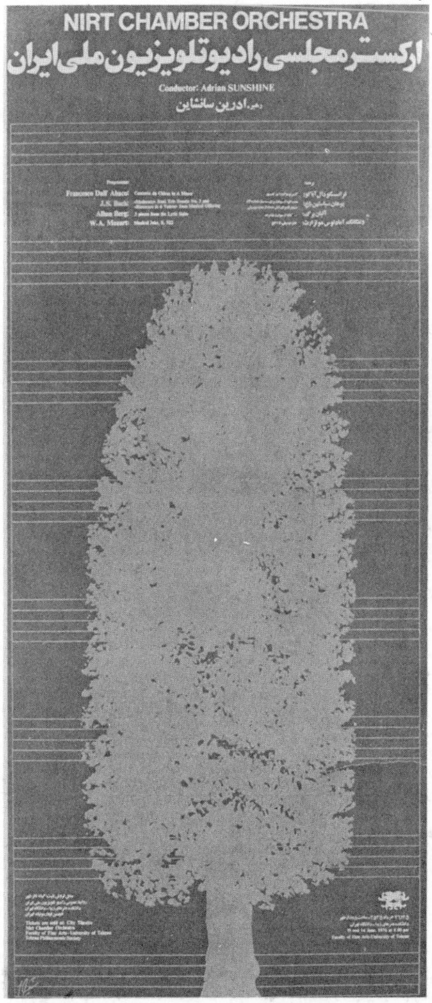

NIRT CHAMBER ORCHESTRA

ارکستر مجلسی رادیو تلویزیون ملی ایران

Conductor: Adrian SUNSHINE

Posters
Affiches
Plakate

1 Belgium
AD TR Sibel
AG Aid
DIR/DES Luk Vangheluwe
carpets and covers, tapis, Teppiche

2 Germany
AD Zanders Feinpapier
DIR Marina Langer-Rosa, Helmut Langer
ILL Marina Langer-Rosa
office paper

3 United States
AD Dartmouth Outdoor Sports
AG Jim Mitchell Advertising
DIR/DES Bob Coonts
COPY Jim Mitchell
boots, chaussures, Stiefel

4 Germany
AD GST Gruppe
AG SSM Werbeagentur
DIR Harald Schlüter, Jürgen Mehl
typefaces

5 France
AD Fête de la Lettre
AG Joan Rabascall
DES Waxmann Junior, Belgium
exhibition

6 Sweden
AD Robert Bosch AB
AG Jim Akerstedt AB
DIR/ILL Jan Jansson
ILL Haken Lindh
eggboiler, boulleur d'oeufs, Eierkocher

1

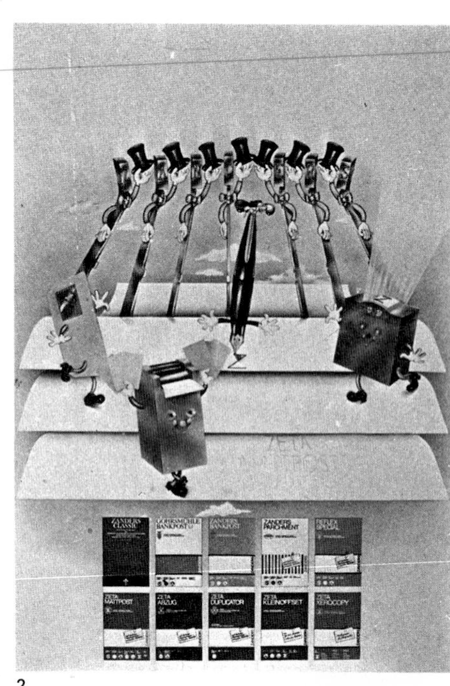
2

3

4

5
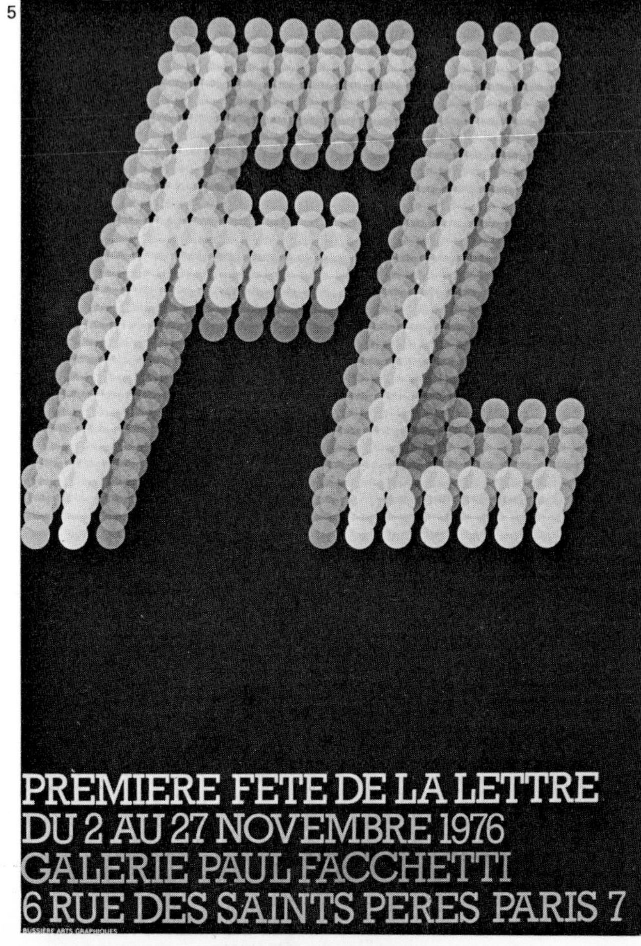

7 Great Britain
AD Victoria & Albert Museum
AG Her Majesty's Stationery Office
DIR/DES Peter Branfield
ILL Jeffrey Hayhow
travelling exhibition

8 Italy
AD Rinasceute
DES Ettore Mariani
DH Adver Photo
textiles

9 Germany
AD Ev. Kirche Frankfurt/Main
AG Kraftdesign
DIR/DES Helmut Kraft
religious promotion

10 Germany
AD Sozialistische Jugend Deutschlands
DES Michael Mathias Prechtl
children's day, jour de l'enfant, Tag des Kindes

6

7

8

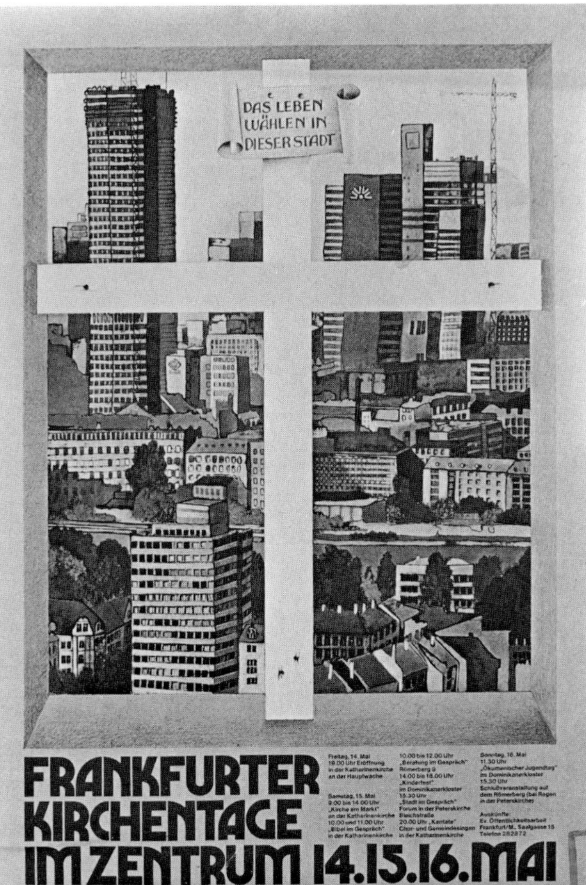

9

10

Posters
Affiches
Plakate

1a-b Great Britain
AD Bush Theatre
DIR/DES Oscar Zarate
ILL (b) Oscar Zarate
theatre

2 United States
AD Ratskeller Restaurant
AG/DES Lanny Sommese
sports

3a-b Haindl Papier GmbH
AG Werbeberatung Peter Seidler
DIR Andreas Asam
DES Werbestudio Noack
ILL Otto Geiss
paper, Papier

4 Poland
AD Panstw. Prezedsiebiorstwo Rozrywkowe
AG KAW
DIR B. Bocianowski
DES T. Jodlowski
circus

5 United States
AD Graphi Care
AG Ner Beck Design
ILL Ner Beck
COPY Maruin Mansky
oral hygiene

6 Czechoslovakia
AD Oblastní galerie vytvarného umený Gottwaldov
AG Propagacní Tvorba
DIR/DES Jan Rajlich
exhibition of toys, jouets, Spielwaren

1a

1b

2

3a

3b

7 Germany (DDR)
AD Progress Filmtrieb
DIR/DES Manfred Bofinger
film

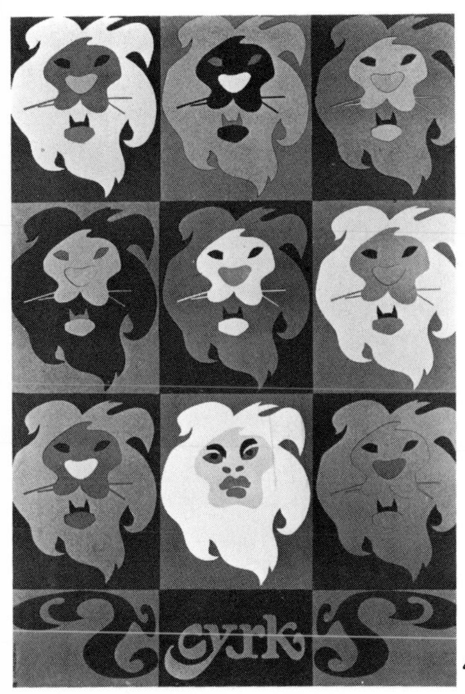

4

5

6

7

Posters
Affiches
Plakate

1 Hungary
AD Kiállitási Intézmények
DES/ILL Tibor Helényi
'Studio' exhibition

2 France
AD/AG Union d'Artistes Plasticiens
DIR Gerard Gosselin
DES Roman Cieslewicz
exhibition

3 Hungary
AD Institute of Cultural Relations
DES Tibor Helényi
exhibition

4 Poland
AD The S. Jaracz Theatre
DES J. Rafal Olbinski
theatre

5, 9 Germany
AD 5) Bühnen der Hansestadt Lübec
9) Thalia Theater, Hamburg
DES Holger Matthies
theatre

6 Hungary
AD Kiáll Int. Mücsarnok
DIR Vizy Otto
DES/ILL Bányai Istvan
exhibition

7 Germany (DDR)
AD VEB Progress-Film-Vertrieb
DES Erhard Grüttner
film

8 Poland
AD Zjednoczenie Rozpowszechniania Filmów
DES/ILL Mieczystaw Wasilewski
film

10 Poland
AD/AG ZRF
DES Andrzej Klimowski, Danuta Schejbal
ILL Andrzej Klimowski

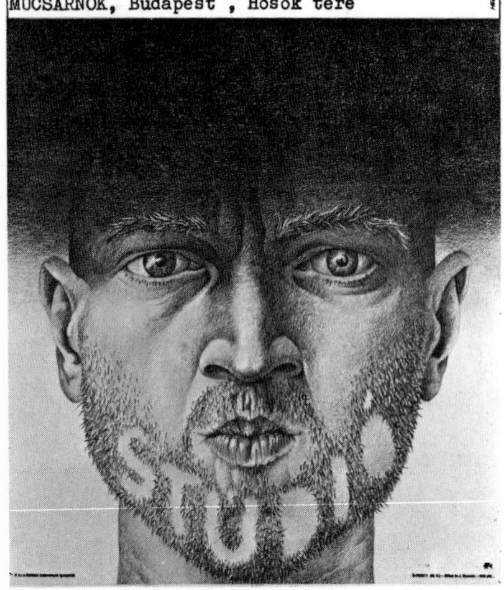

1

2

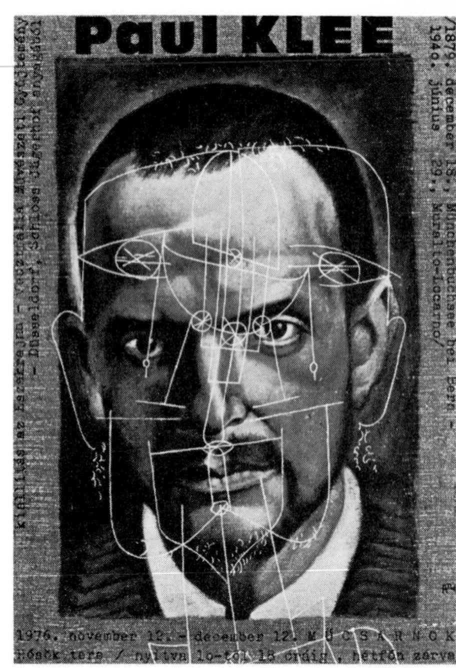

3

4

5

BÁNYAI ISTVÁN
NYITVA Hétfő kivétel 10–18 h
MÁJ 27– JÚN 20
GRAFIKUSMŰVÉSZ KIÁLLITÁSA A HELIKON GALÉRIÁBAN
BUDAPEST – 1976
V. Eötvös Loránd u 8

6

Ein DEFA-Film aus dem Jahr 1951 wieder im Kino
Werner Peters in
Der Untertan
Nach dem gleichnamigen Roman von Heinrich Mann
mit Paul Esser, Eduard von Winterstein
Ren
Fischer, Sabine Thalbach
Ernst Legal, Friedrich Gnass
REGIE: WOLFGANG STAUDTE
DREHBUCH: W. und F. STAUDTE
Kamera: Robert Baberske

7

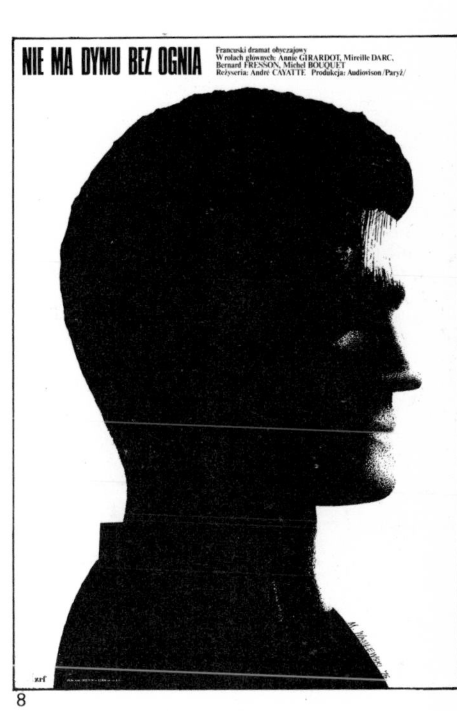
NIE MA DYMU BEZ OGNIA
Francuski dramat obyczajowy
W rolach głównych: Annie GIRARDOT, Mireille DARC,
Bernard FRESSON, Michel BOUQUET
Reżyseria: André CAYATTE Produkcja: Audiovison /Paryż/

8

Leben
Eduards des Zweiten
von England
Hamburger
Thalia
Theater

9

10

nagrodzony Oscarem 75 za najlepszą piosenkę
NASHVILLE
NASHVILLE
reżyseria ROBERT ALTMAN
produkcja: USA
w rolach głównych
KAREN BLACK GERALDINE CHAPLIN BARBARA HARRIS

Posters
Affiches
Plakate

1a-c Hungary
AD Magyar Iparmüvészeti Föiskola
DIR György Hajman
ILL (a, b) Keresztes Dora
(c) István Orosz

2 Poland
AD Teatr TV 'Kwadrat'
DES T. Jodlowski
theatre

3 Poland
AD Teatr na Tarbòwku
DIR Marian Jonkajtys
DES Jan Mtodozeniec
theatre (musical)

4 Germany
AD Landestheater Halle
DES Helmut Brade
theatre

5 Bulgaria
AD Satiric Theatre
DES Ludmil Chehlarov
theatre

6 Germany
AD Landesmuseum
DES Herbert Jarrey
museum

7 Germany
AD Staatstheater Stuttgart
DES Roman Weyl
opera

1a

1b

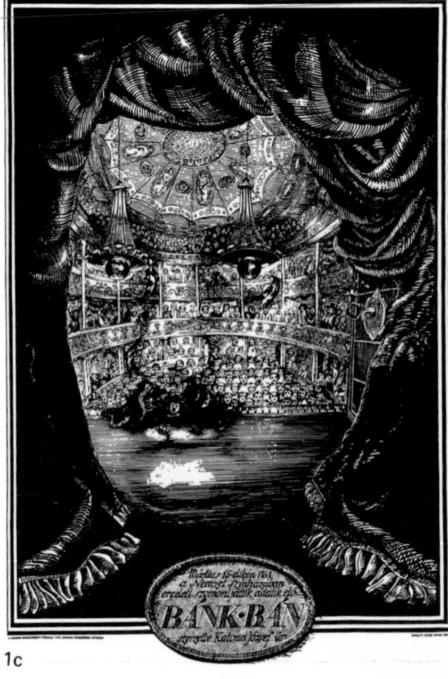

1c

2

3

4

5

6

7

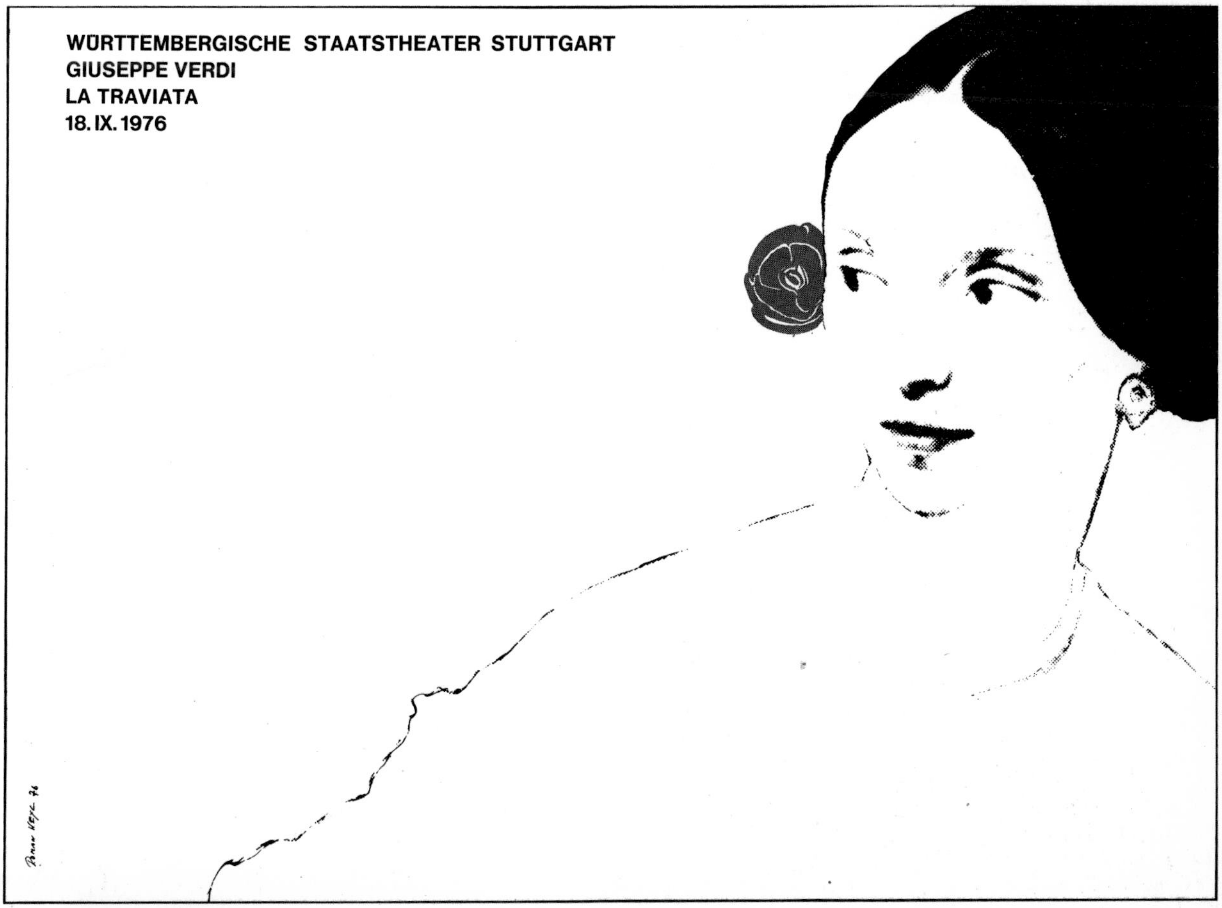

WÜRTTEMBERGISCHE STAATSTHEATER STUTTGART
GIUSEPPE VERDI
LA TRAVIATA
18. IX. 1976

Posters
Affiches
Plakate

1 Hungary
AD Mokép
AG Magyar Hirdetö
DIR Jozsef Adorjan
DES/ILL Jozsef Arendas
film

2 Hungary
AD Mokép
AG Magyar Hirdetö
DIR Ilona Biró
DES/ILL Paul Antal
film

3 Holland
AD Volkshochschule der Stadt Aachen
AG Endrikat
DIR/DES Klaus Endrikat
school, école, Schule

4 Hungary
AD Mokép
AG Magyar Hirdetö
DIR/DES Bakos István
film

5 Germany
AD Landestheater Halle
DES Helmut Brade
theatre

6 Iran
AD Tehran International Film Festival
DIR/DES Morteza Momayez

7 Iran
AD Tehran International Film Festival
DIR/DES Morteza Momayez
ILL Ali Khosravi

8 Iran
AD Independent Artists Group
DIR/DES Morteza Momayez

1

2

3

4

5
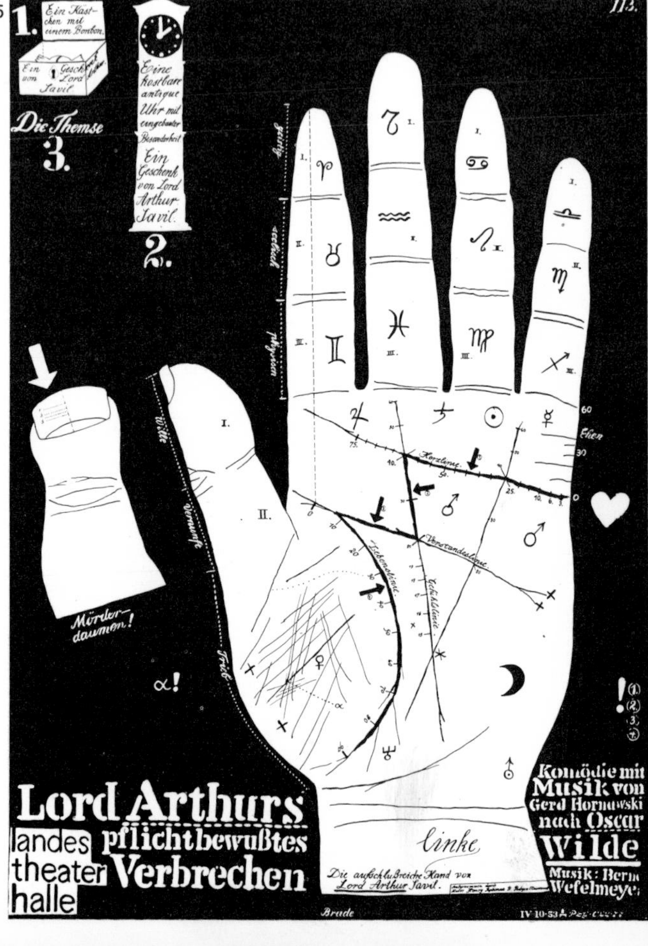

9 Iran
AD NIRT (National Iranian Radio and TV)
AG Sorush Press Graphic Dept
DES Ghobad Shiva
chamber orchestra, Kammerorchester

10 Iran
AD NIRT (National Iranian Radio and TV)
AG Sorush Press Graphic Dept
DIR/DES Ghobad Shiva

6

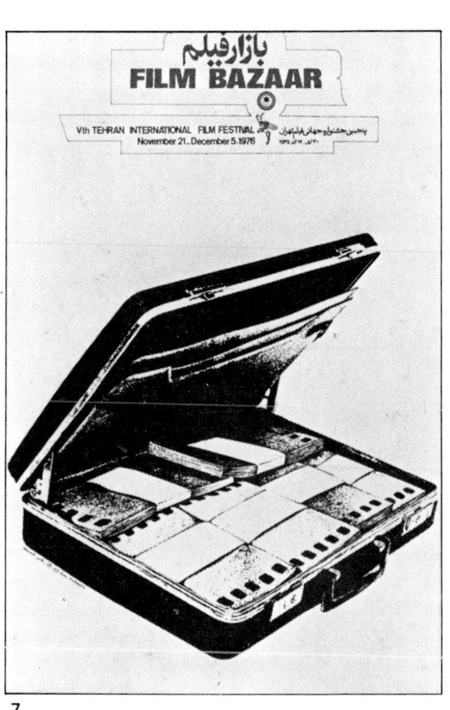

7

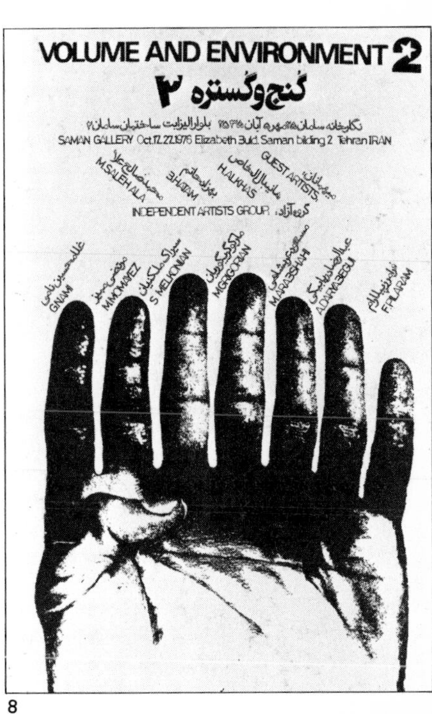

8

9

10

Posters
Affiches
Plakate

1a-c United States
AD Mobil Oil Corporation
AG Chermayeff & Geismar Associates
DIR/DES Ivan Chermayeff
COPY Gordon Bowman

2 Poland
AD PZU (Staatliche Versicherungsanstatt)
DES/ILL Marek Frudenreich
stop accidents poster

3 Germany
AD Nationalgalerie Berlin
AG Studio Mendell-Oberer
DIR/DES Pierre Mendell
ILL Jasper Johns
exhibition

4 Czechoslovakia
AD/AG Jaroslav Súra
DIR Emanuel Pavlicek
DES Jaroslav Súra
exhibition

5 Kenya
AD United Nations Children's Fund
DES George McBean

1a

1b

1c

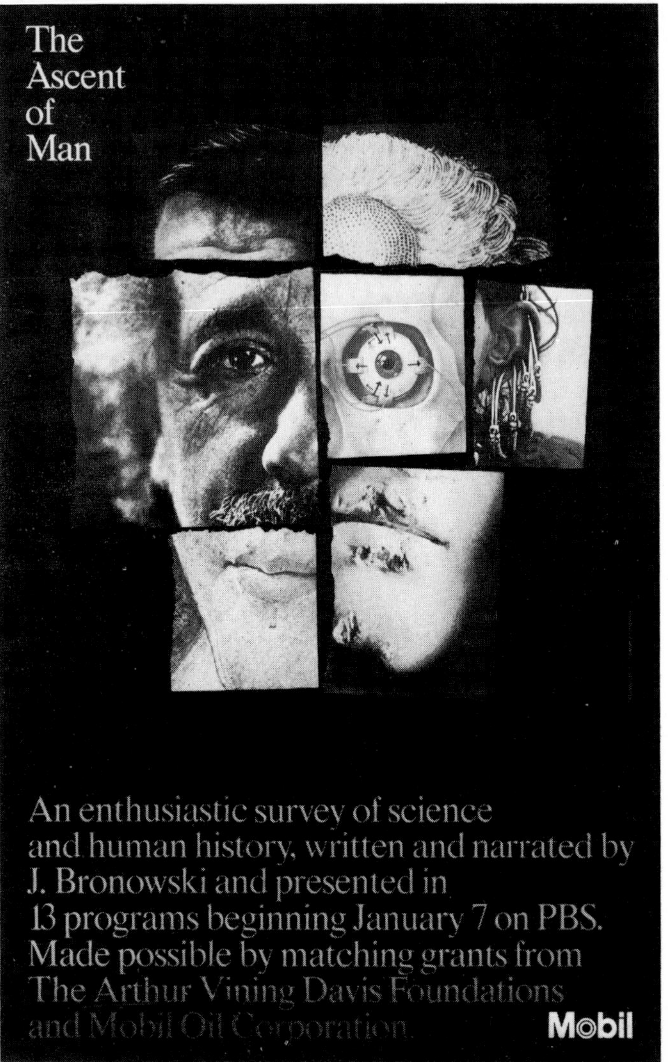

2

6 Hungary
AD/AG Ibusz
DIR István Hornyik
DES Laszló Sós, Eva Kemény
tourism

7 United States
AD/AG Amnesty International
DIR Edith Gross
DES Roman Cieslewicz
help for political prisoners, aide pour les prisonniers politiques

3

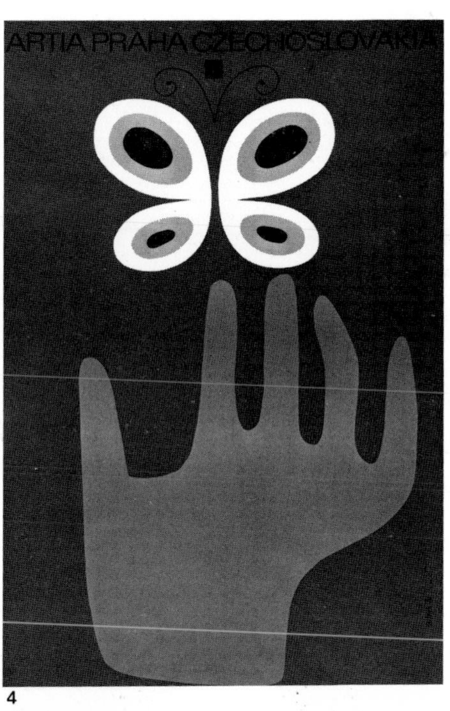

4

5

6

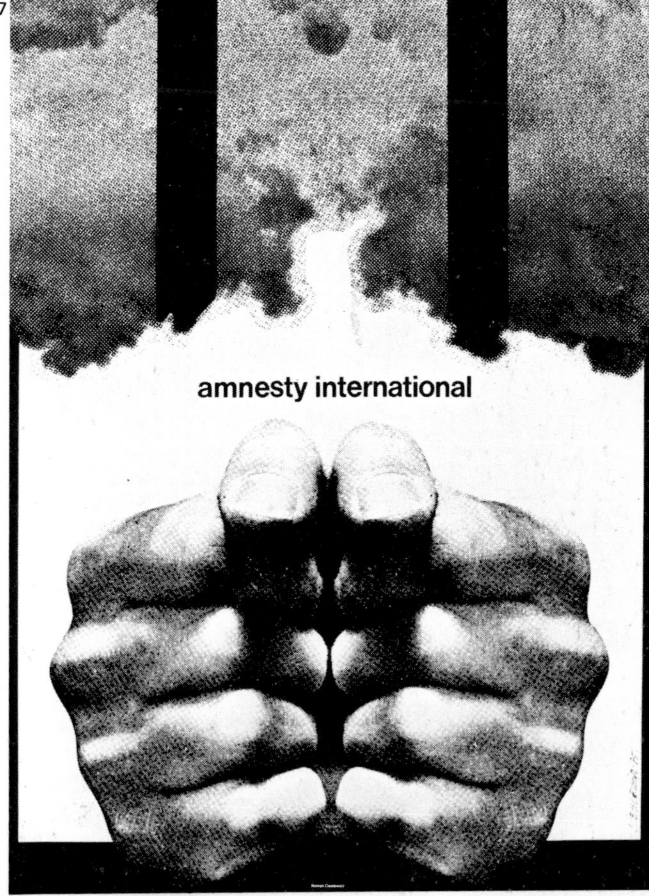

7

Posters
Affiches
Plakate

1 United States
AD Champion Papers
DIR/DES Miho
ILL Alexander Calder
exhibition

2 Japan
AD Sakura Gallery
AG Shigeo Okamoto Design Center
DIR/DES Shigeo Okamoto
ILL Toshiyuki Ohashi
exhibition

3 Spain
AD Federación Catalan de Gimnasia
AG Estudi Ariño
DES Pere Ariño
Catalan gymnasium Federation

4 Iran
AD/AG The Institute for the Intellectual Development of Children and Young Adults
DIR/DES Mostafa Onji
book, film, music, record for children

5 Canada
AD/AG Guillon/Designers Inc
DIR Laurent Marquart
DES Frédéric Metz
ILL Binette & Associes
invitations

6 Germany
AD/DES Prof. Jürgen Spohn
Tourism

1

2

3

4

7a-b Japan
AD (a) Shikishima Baking Company Ltd
(b) Meitetsu Sakae Melsa
AG Shigeo Okamoto Design Center
DIR/DES Shigeo Okamoto
(a) bakery, Boulangerie, Bäckerei
(b) fashion, modes

5

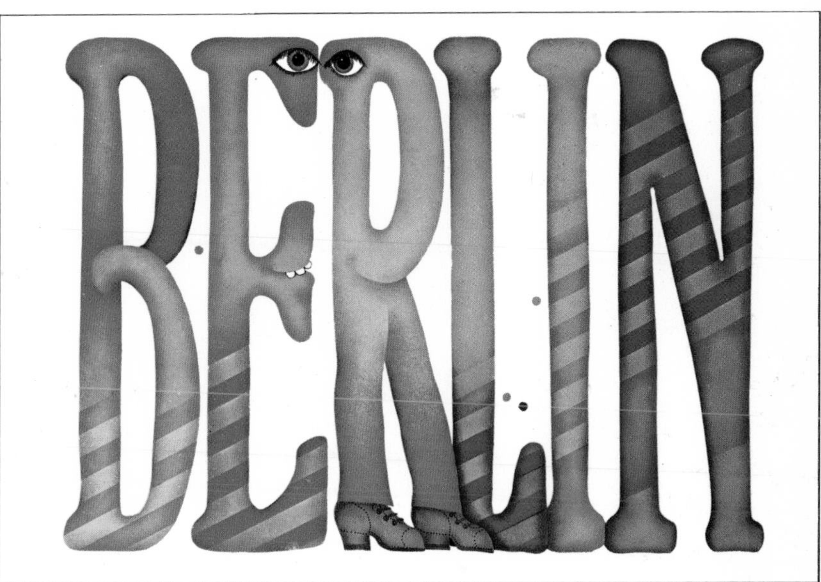

6

7a

7b

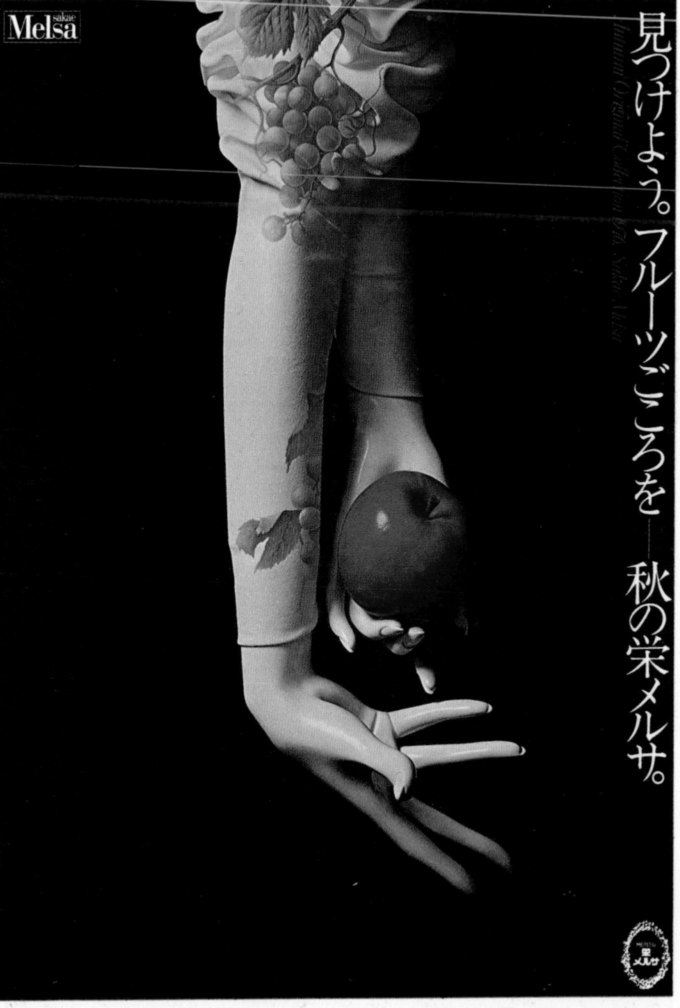

Posters
Affiches
Plakate

1 Germany
AD Internationales Design Zentrum Berlin
DES Eckhard Neumann
COPY Kristin Riedemann
exhibition of kindergarten art

2 Germany (DDR)
AD VEB Druckmaschinenwerk Polygraph Leipzig und Deutscher Turn- und Sportbund der DDR
DES Renate Herfurth
sport

3 Germany (DDR)
AD Museum der Stadt Neustrelitz
DES Egbert Herfurth
graphic exhibition

4 Brazil
AD/AG Associados Propaganda
DIR/DES Oswaldo Miranda (Miran)
music-festival

5 Brazil
AD Colaboracao CR Almeda SA
AG Associados Propaganda
DIR/DES Oswaldo Miranda (Miran)
ornithological congress

6a-b Finland
AD Lilla Teatern
DIR(DES Kai Kujasalo
theatre

7 United States
AD Department of Music, Penn State University
AG Lanny Sommese Freelance Design
DIR/DES Bill Ferebee
ILL Lanny Sommese
orchestra

IDZ Berlin
Kindertagesstätte -
erste Begegnung mit der organisierten Umwelt
Notwendigkeiten und Ansätze für die Gestaltung

1

2

3

4

8 Iran
AD/AG Institute for the Intellectual Development of Children and Young Adults
DES Farshid Mesghali
animated films festival

5

6a

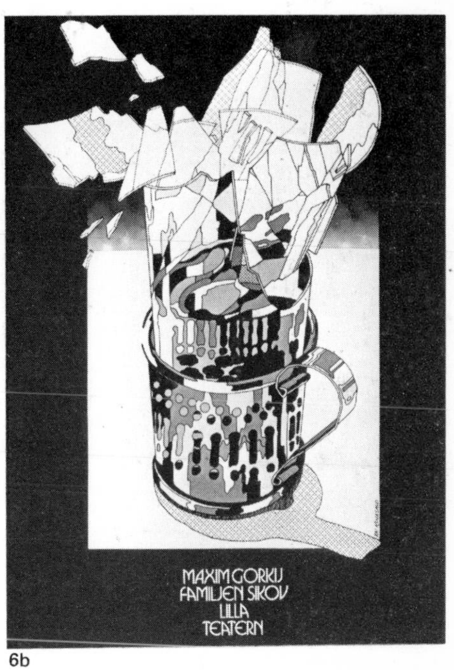

6b

7

8

Posters
Affiches
Plakate

1 Switzerland
AD Museum Lausanne
DES Werner Geher
ILL M. Delessert
carnival-masks

2 Germany
AD Theater in der Kunsthalle
DES Holger Matthies
theatre

3 United States
AD Temple University
DIR/DES Joe Scorsone
COPY Michael Becotte
art school exhibition series

4 Germany
AD Evangelische Kirche
AG/DES Studio Rau
religious promotion

5 Spain
AD Salón de la Infancia y la Juventud
AG Pena SA
DIR/DES Francisco Bas
childrens exhibition

6 Canada
AD Festival of Festivals
AG Burns, Cooper, Donoahue, Fleming & Co Ltd
DES Dawn Cooper Tennant
film festival

7 Germany
AD Bayerischer Rundfunk München
DES Walter Tafelmaier
children's radio, programme pour les enfants

1

2

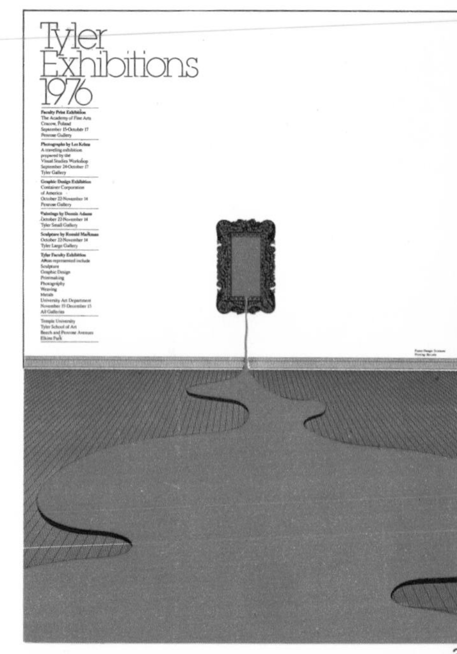

3

4

5

8 Germany
AD Druckfarbenfabrik Gebr. Schmidt
AG Olaf Leu Design
DIR/DES Olaf Leu, Fritz Hofrichter
ILL Robert Häusser
printing inks

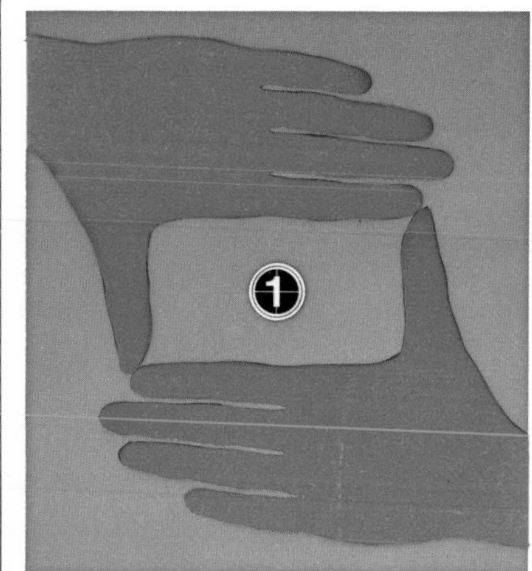

6

7

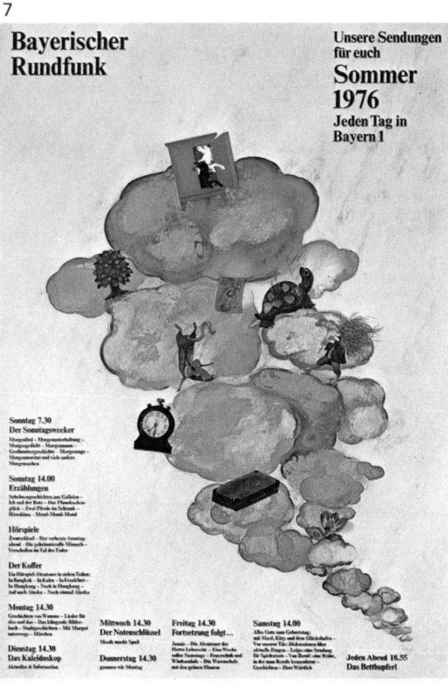

ROBERT HÄUSSER

MIT GEBR. SCHMIDT DRUCKFARBEN

8

Posters
Affiches
Plakate

1 United States
AD Kino International Inc
AG Art Dept Colorado State University
DIR/DES John J. Sorbie
film tour

2 Great Britain
AD The Golden Masque
DES Glenn Tutssel
exhibition of dance posters

3 United States
AD Rocky Mountain Dance Theatre
AG Art Dept Colorado State University
DIR/DES John J. Sorbie
dance, Tanz

4 United States
AD Penn State University Museum
AG Lanny Sommese Free Lance Design
DIR/DES Lanny Sommese
exhibition

5 United States
AD University Arts Services Penn State University
AG Lanny Sommese Free Lance Design
DIR/DES Lanny Sommese
theatre

1

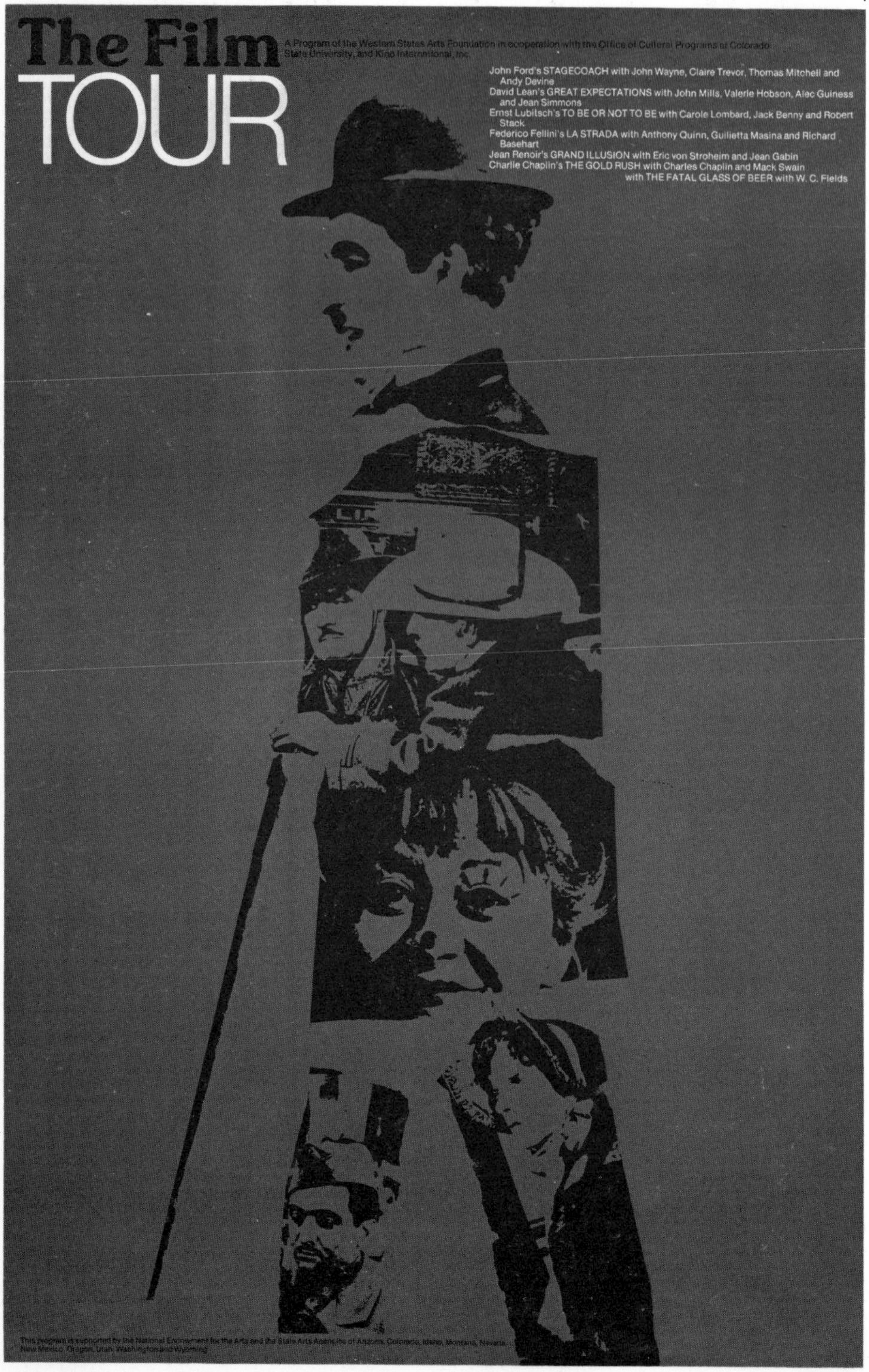

The Film
TOUR
A Program of the Western States Arts Foundation in cooperation with the Office of Cultural Programs at Colorado State University, and Kino International, Inc.
John Ford's STAGECOACH with John Wayne, Claire Trevor, Thomas Mitchell and Andy Devine
David Lean's GREAT EXPECTATIONS with John Mills, Valerie Hobson, Alec Guiness and Jean Simmons
Ernst Lubitsch's TO BE OR NOT TO BE with Carole Lombard, Jack Benny and Robert Stack
Federico Fellini's LA STRADA with Anthony Quinn, Guilietta Masina and Richard Basehart
Jean Renoir's GRAND ILLUSION with Eric von Stroheim and Jean Gabin
Charlie Chaplin's THE GOLD RUSH with Charles Chaplin and Mack Swain
with THE FATAL GLASS OF BEER with W. C. Fields

2

3

6 Spain
AD Tecnogar FAD
AG ECTA 3
DIR/DES Albert Isern i Castro
exhibition of interior decorating

7 Germany
AD Künstlerhaus Bethanien Berlin
DES Christian Chruxin
concert

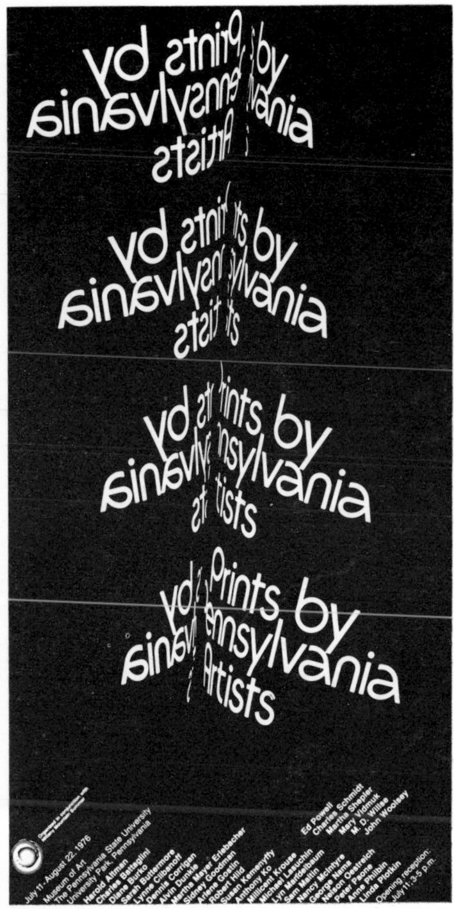

4

5

6

7

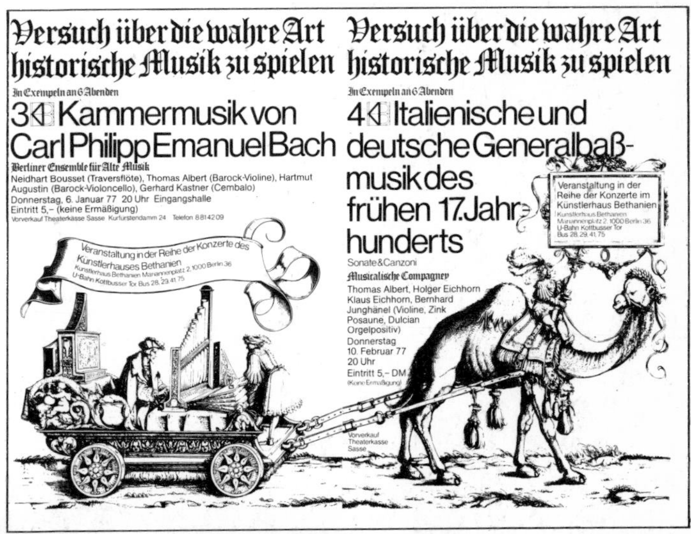

Posters
Affiches
Plakate

1a-b Great Britain
AD London Transport
DIR Publicity Officer, London Transport Executive
DES (a) Abram Games
(b) Tom Eckersley
(a) London Zoo
(b) ceremonial London

2a-b Israel
AD Haifa Municipality
DES R. Schwarz
tourism

3 Israel
AD Israel Homes Real Estate Corp
DES E. Weishoff

4 Holland
AD Lijempf Ijscream & Milkpowder
AG Weda/D&A
DIR/DES Theo de Witte
ILL Studio Kral

5 Australia
AD Australian National University
AG ANU Graphic Design
DIR/DES Adrian Young
ILL Michael Finn
children's holiday

6 Israel
AD Eilat Tourist Association
AG A. Degani & E. Kurti
DES Alona Degani, Esther Kurti
tourism

7 Canada
AD Garlick Films Ltd
AG Raymond Lee & Associates Ltd
DIR/DES Raymond Lee
ILL Rudi Von Tieterman
ILL Colin Luxton
cameras

1a

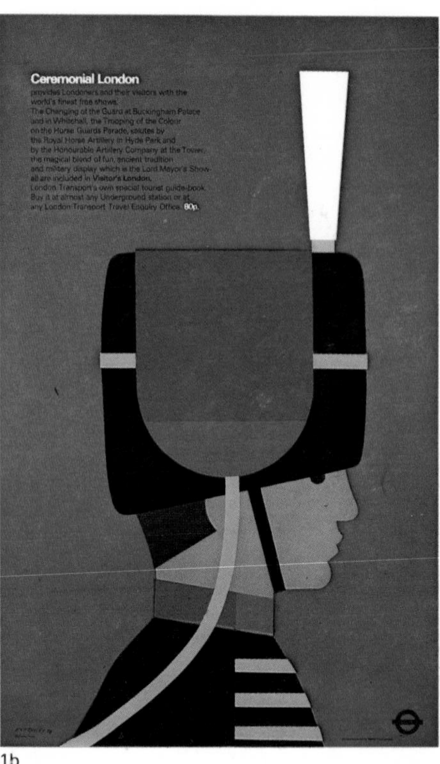

1b

2a

4

5

תערוכת
כ״ה שנים
לחיל הים

2b

WELCOME HOME TO ISRAEL

3

תכניות מיוחדות למבקרים באילת!
special festives for visitors in
Eilat
Eilat tourist association אגודת גורמי תיירות·אילת

6

7953
7 automatic cameras by KONICA.
THIS VEHICLE STOPS AT
ALL RAILWAY CROSSINGS
MAR-77
BU2 342
ONTARIO
ONT 1975
4433
PUBLIC-VEH

7

Posters
Affiches
Plakate

1 Holland
AD Stichting Gemeenschapswerk Bergeyk
AG I.D. Unit
DES Jeanne & Robert Schaap
music group

2 Germany
AD/DES Dirk Streitenfeld
election campaign against CDU and CSU,
Bundestagswahlkampf 76, gegen CDU und CSU

3 Germany (DDR)
AD Kulturbund Leipzig
DES Lutz Dammbeck
COPY R. Zwicker
gallery, Kleine Galerie Jungekunst

4 Germany
AD Sender Freies Berlin
AG/DES Reinhart Braun
concert, Konzert

5 Italy
AD Dumocks studio di registrazione musicale
AG Studio de Santis
DIR Alfredo de Santis
music recording studio

6 Poland
AD B.W.A.
DES Marek Mosinski
exhibition

1

2

3

4

7 Great Britain
AD Scottish Arts Council
AG James Gardiner Associates
DIR James Gardiner
DES/ILL James Gardiner, Ian Woodyer
exhibition

8 Germany
AD/ Sender Freies Berlin
AG/DES Reinhart Braun
folklore show from Tunisia

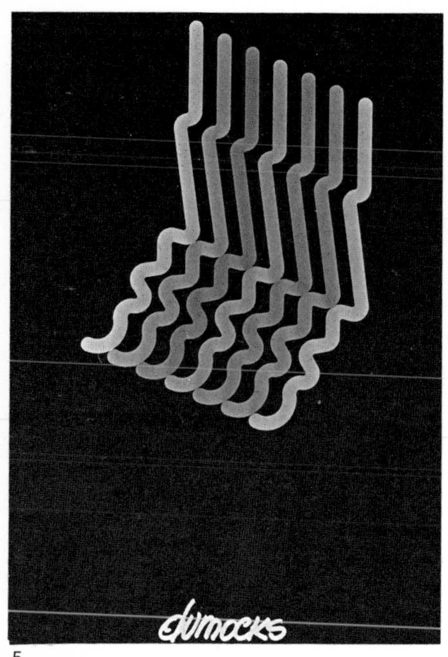

5

6

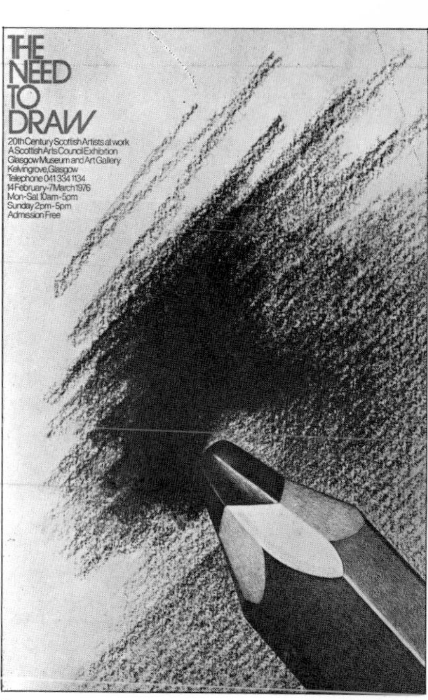

7

8

Gäste aus
Tunesien

Aufzeichnung für das
Deutsche Fernsehen (ARD)

RTT Tunis präsentiert
in Kooperation mit dem
Sender Freies Berlin
zum ersten Mal

Tunesische
Folklore mit:
Hedi Jouini
Zouheira Salem
Safoua
Kacem Kefi
Mohamed el Euch
Beya Nebil
Hajer Rassaa
Zohra Ounis

Das Orchester
der RTT
Leitung:
Ali Chalgham

Ansage:
Rekaya Dekhil

SFB
31.1.

Eintrittskarten
DM 3,-; 5,-; 7,-; 10,-
im SFB-Pavillon,
Theodor-Heuss-
Platz, Montag
bis Freitag
14 – 18 Uhr
und bei den
Theaterkassen

31. Januar 1976
Beginn 20 Uhr
Großer Sendesaal
Haus d. Rundfunks
Masurenallee

Posters
Affiches
Plakate

1 Germany
AD Phantasialand Amusement Park
AG Langer Visualisation
DIR/DES Helmut Langer
ILL Marina Langer-Rosa
amusement park

2 Germany
AD Staatliche Museen, Berlin
DES Prof. Jürgen Spohn
museum

3 Germany
AD Schiller Theater, Berlin
DES Prof. Jürgen Spohn
theatre

4 Hungary
AD Miskolci-Galeria
DES Jozsef Arenddás
exhibition

5 United States
AD The American Institute of Architects
AG Peter Bradford & Associates
DIR/DES Peter Bradford
AIA convention

6 Great Britain
AD The Designers and Art Directors Association
AG Pentagram
DIR/DES John McConnell
ILL Howard Brown
D & AD's graphic workshop

7 United States
AD The Phoenix Art Museum
DES Massimo de Stefani
exhibition

1

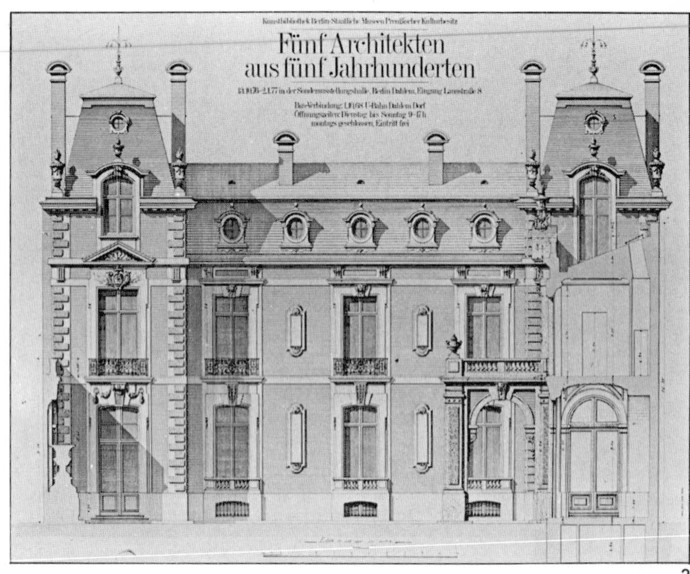

2

3

4

8 Nigeria
AD Arts Council Port Harcourt
AG Haig-Betanova
DIR/DES Haig David-West
exhibition

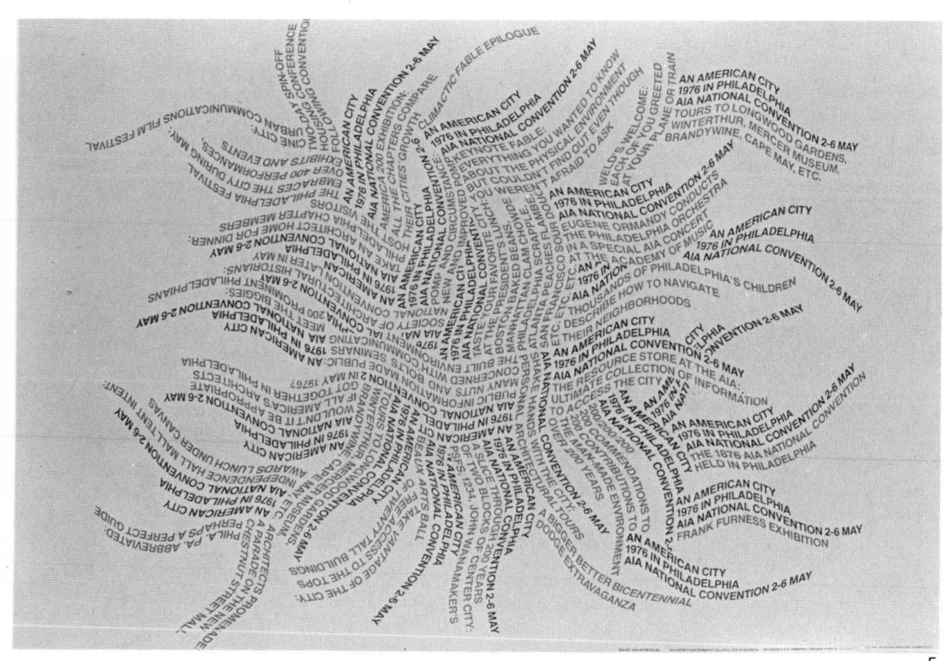

5

The Graphic Workshop (Sponsored by The Designers and Art Directors Association)

The Graphic Workshop once again provides the opportunity, instruction and creative atmosphere for exciting experiment in visual communication; to make the participants more effective as Art Directors, Designers, Illustrators, Typographers, Photographers etc.

In the past the Graphic Workshop has invited many distinguished guests to criticise students' work and to help with their problems. These include David Bailey, Saul Bass, Peter Blake, Mark Boxer, Robert Brownjohn, Germano Facetti, Alan Fletcher, Colin Forbes, Abram Games, Bob Gill, John Glashan, Henrion, David Hockney, Patrick Hughes, Jonathan Miller, Marcello Minale, Norman Parkinson, Hans Schleger, Feliks Topolski, and others.

The Workshop seeks participants who are art school graduates or who have had equivalent experience. Exceptions will be made, however, in unusual cases.

The Workshop is highly selective in its choice of members and the number of participants is necessarily limited so that discussion and criticism may be intense.

Applicants must submit portfolios of their work, together with their name and address. These must be brought to the Des:gn & Art Directors Association office, Third Floor, Nash House, 12 Carlton House Terrace, London SW1Y 5AH, not later than noon on Friday 15 October 1976, and will be reviewed by the Selection Committee in the afternoon of that day. Applicants will be notified by post whether or not they have been accepted for the Workshop.
The D&AD will not be responsible for work not collected by noon on Monday 18 October.

There will be six sessions of the Workshop on the evenings of 25 October, 1, 8, 15, November, 6, 16 December from 6.30 to 9.00 pm. at the D&AD office.

Participating instructors for the six sessions will be Neil Godfrey, John McConnell, Marcello Minale and guests. There will be a £10 fee.

6

7

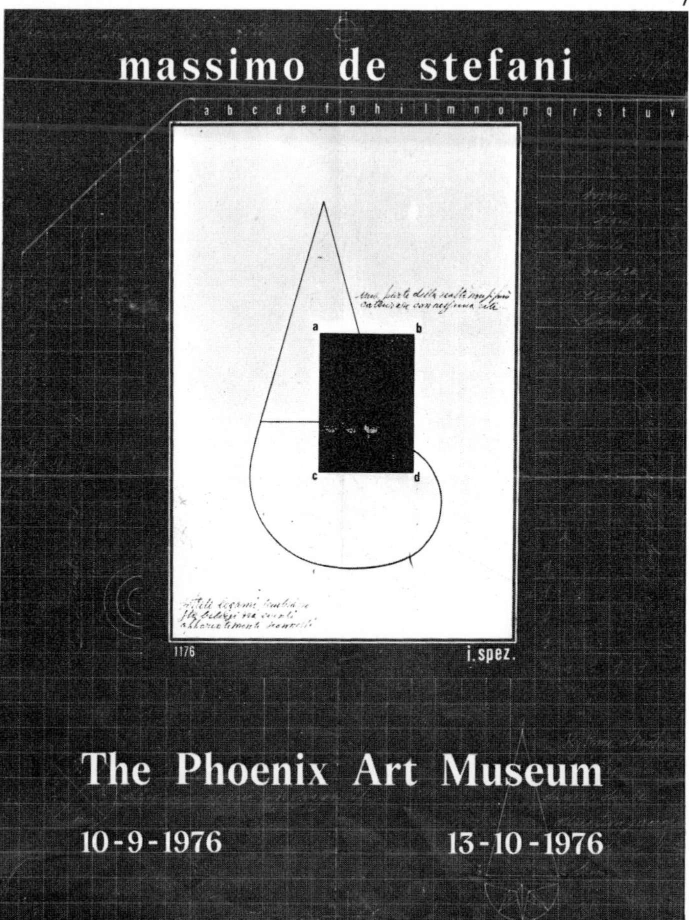

8

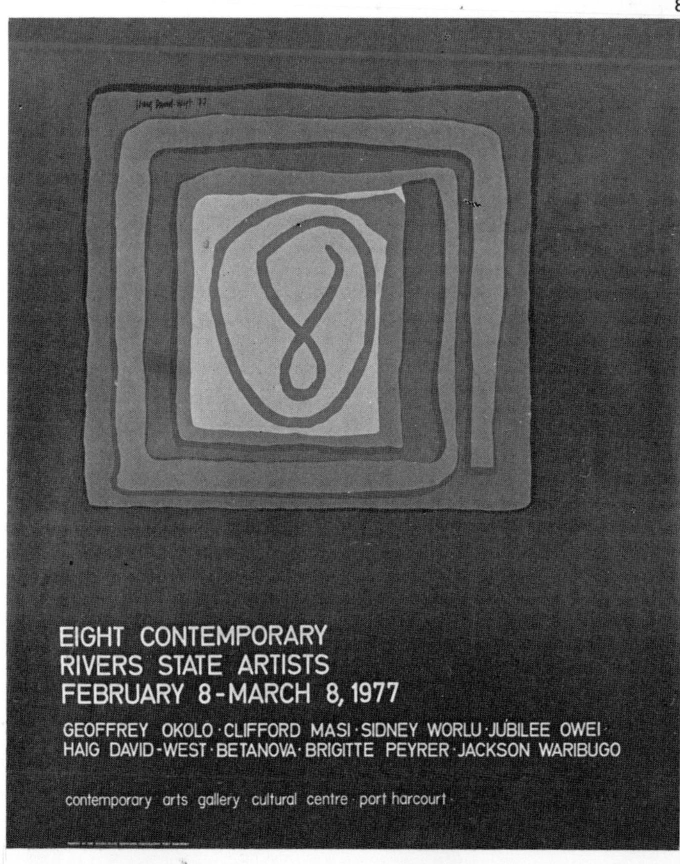

Posters
Affiches
Plakate

1 Germany
AD Germany
AG Kunstschule Alsterdamm
DIR Gerd F. Setzke
DES Alan Mason
sea travel, voyages par mer, Seeschiffahrt

2 Great Britain
AD Bexley Libraries & Museum Service
DES Graeme Campbell
exhibition

3 Japan
AD Sakura Gallery
DIR/DES Shigeo Okamoto
exhibition

4 Germany
AD Evangelische Kirche
AG Studio Rau
DES Studio Rau
religious meetings

5 France
AD/AG Festival d'automne à Paris
DIR Dominique Pallut
DES Roman Cieslewicz
painting exhibition, exposition de la peinture

6 Belgium
AD Honeywell
AG Inhouse Production
DIR/DES Olle Lind
ILL Marcel Deligne
switches, interrupteurs, Schalter

1

2

3

4

5

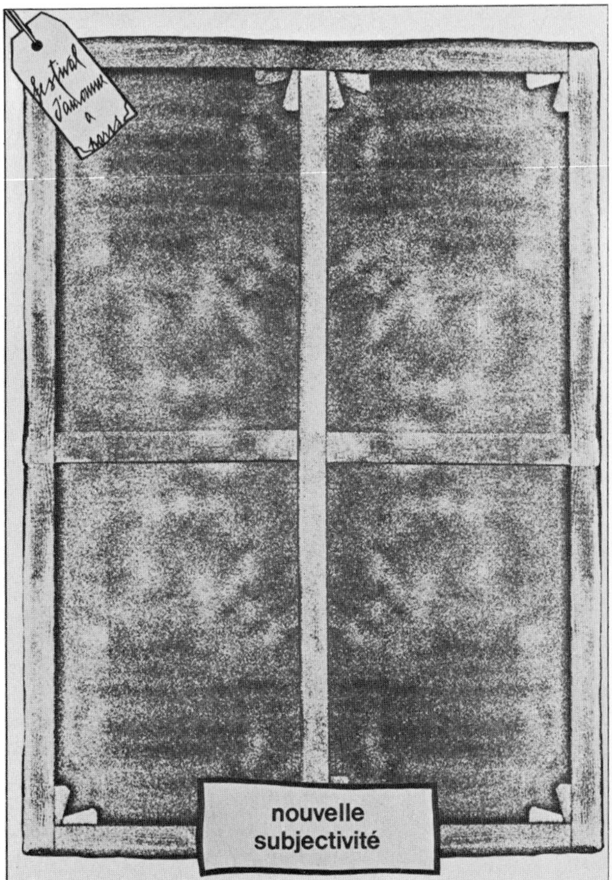

festival d'automne à Paris

nouvelle subjectivité

11 rue Berryer Paris 8e 28 octobre-19 décembre 1976 12h-19h fermé le mardi

7 Great Britain
AD/AG East Ham Graphics
DIR Ethan Ames, Richard Doust, Valerie Allam
DES/ILL Ethan Ames, Richard Doust
ILL Wm Hanna
graphic design course

8 Hong Kong
AD Hongkong & Yaumati Ferry Co Ltd
AG Kinggraphic
DIR Hon Bing-Wah
DES So Man-Yee
ILL John Nye
charity gala in support of textbooks

9 Austria
AD Export u. Mustermesse GmbH
AG Vorarlberger Graphik
DES Othmar Motter
fair, foire, Messe

10 Great Britain
AD David Cropper
AG/DES Richard Dragun
concert, Konzert

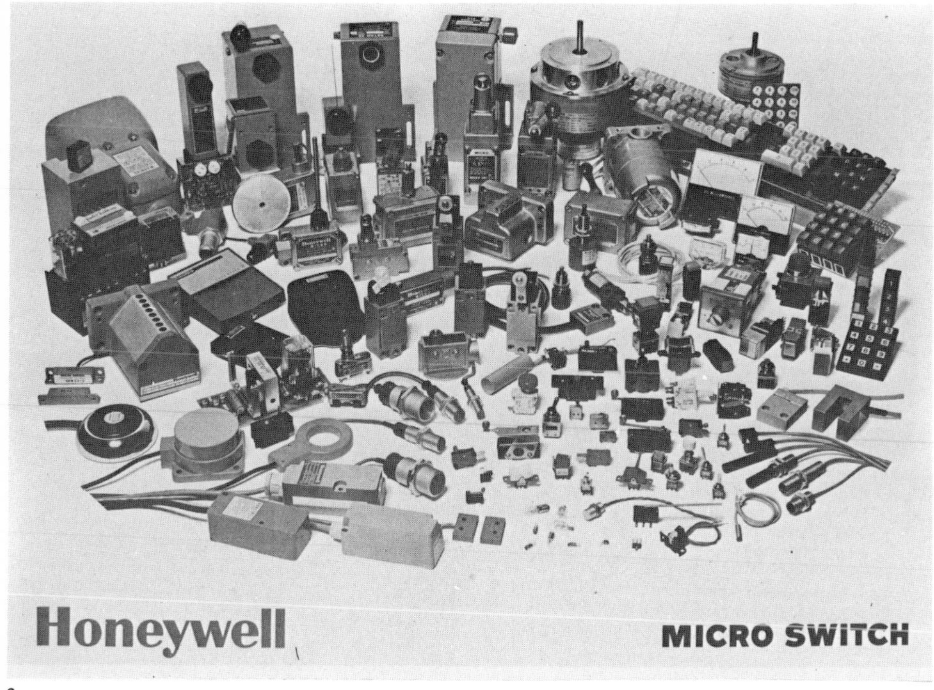

6

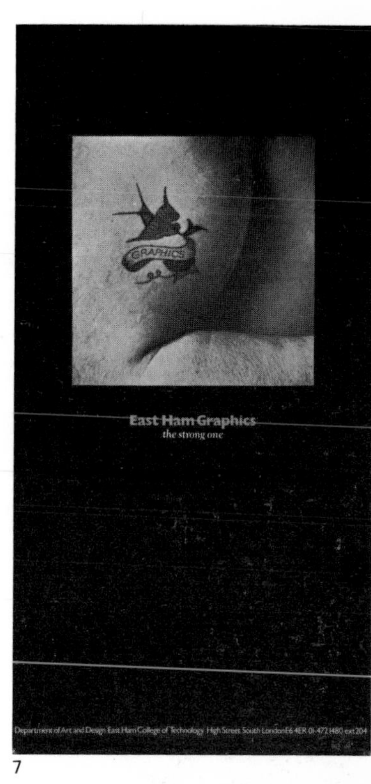

7

8

9

10

Press advertisements
Annonces de presse
Zeitungs-Inserate

1a-b Switzerland
AD Swissair
AG GGK Basel
DIR (a) Guido Stuber
(b) Gerd Hiepler
ILL (a) A. von Steiger
(b) Bollmann Bildkartenverlag
airline promotion

1a

Jeden Tag in einer anderen Stadt. Und jede Nacht im gleichen Bett.

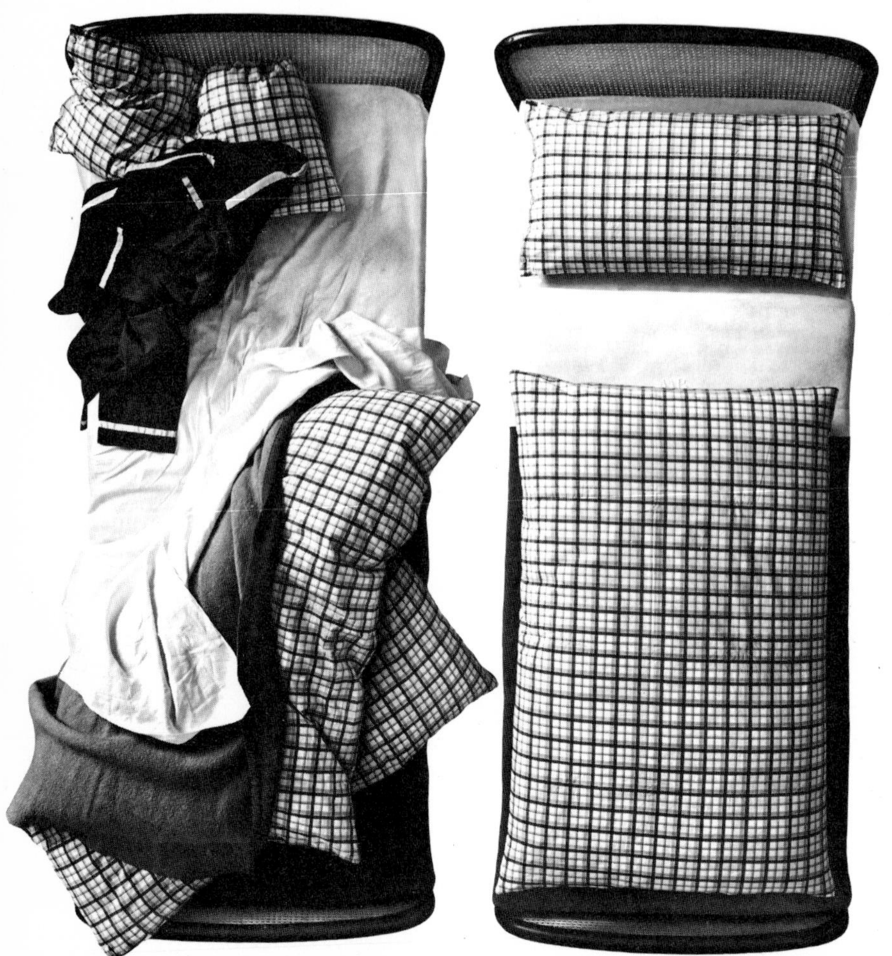

Mit den Eintagsflügen der Swissair können Sie am Morgen aus den Federn springen, ein paar hundert Kilometer zur Sitzung nach Rom, Paris, London, Wien usw. fliegen und nach einem ausgefüllten Arbeitstag abends wieder ins eigene gemachte Bett sinken. Soviel Zeit haben Sie in 14 Städten für Ihre Geschäfte:

Von Zürich aus.

In London	10.45 Stunden	In München	10.00 Stunden*
In Paris	12.00 Stunden	In Stuttgart	11.10 Stunden
In Brüssel	11.05 Stunden	In Kopenhagen	8.15 Stunden*
In Amsterdam	11.40 Stunden	In Wien	11.40 Stunden
In Düsseldorf	11.15 Stunden	In Mailand	7.45 Stunden
In Hamburg	8.40 Stunden*	In Rom	11.30 Stunden
In Frankfurt	12.00 Stunden	In Genf	13.40 Stunden

Von Basel aus.

In London	10.35 Stunden	In München	10.00 Stunden*
In Paris	13.35 Stunden	In Stuttgart	11.10 Stunden
In Brüssel	8.25 Stunden*	In Kopenhagen	7.55 Stunden*
In Amsterdam	7.20 Stunden	In Wien	11.40 Stunden
In Düsseldorf	11.15 Stunden	In Mailand	11.20 Stunden
In Hamburg	8.40 Stunden*	In Rom	11.30 Stunden
In Frankfurt	12.10 Stunden	In Genf	14.40 Stunden

* In Zusammenarbeit mit Sabena, Lufthansa, SAS.

Sie sehen, wie man fliegt, so bettet man sich.

Die Swissair oder die IATA-Reisebüros geben Ihnen gerne weitere Auskünfte.

GGK

1b

This city is

Here, with all the splendid boul
and monuments of a continent cl
Swissair's new DC-9s are consid
fast, dependable, and convenient
tation. Of the 40 stops on its lin
special mention as transfer poi
Geneva.
A trip through our fair city by Sw
no longer than traversing the m
own country.
Do you know your way around the
Alcazaba. **2.** *Genoa:* Porta Sopra

GGK

ous for its public transportation: Swissair. Next stop: Basel-Mulhouse.

Designed by Bollmann-Bildkarten-Verlag KG · 33 Braunschweig · West-Germany

Mallorca: Château Bellver. **4.** *Cologne:* Cathedral. **5.** *Hamburg:* St. Michael's and St. Paul's landing stages. **6.** *Zurich:* Grossmünster, Lindenhof and Bahnhofstrasse. **7.** *Frankfurt:* St. Paul's Church and Römer (Town Hall). **8.** *Manchester:* Town Hall. **9.** *Oslo:* Town Hall. **10.** *Barcelona:* Church of the Holy Family and Columbus Column. **11.** *Salzburg:* Hohensalzburg Fortress. **12.** *Basel:* Minster. **13.** *Budapest:* Chain Bridge. **14.** *Geneva:* Ile Rousseau and Jet d'Eau. **15.** *Istanbul:* Hagia Sophia. **16.** *Prague:* Charles' Bridge. **17.** *Berne:* Minster and Time Bell Tower. **18.** *Warsaw:* Old Town. **19.** *Helsinki:* Cathedral. **20.** *Lisbon:* Praça do Comércio and Torre de Belém. **21.** *Brussels:* Atomium and Grand'Place. **22.** *Stockholm:* Town House and Riddarholm. **23.** *Paris:* Eiffel Tower and Notre Dame. **24.** *Amsterdam:* Westerkerk and Royal Palace. **25.** *Copenhagen:* Stock Exchange and Château Christiansborg. **26.** *Moscow:* Kremlin. **27.** *Düsseldorf:* Thyssen Building and Schauspielhaus. **28.** *Munich:* Frauenkirche and Town Hall. **29.** *London:* Parliament and Tower Bridge. **30.** *Nice:* Promenade des Anglais. **31.** *Vienna:* St. Stephen's Cathedral. **32.** *Belgrade:* Parliament. **33.** *Bucharest:* Athenaeum. **34.** *Stuttgart:* Collegiate Church, Old and New Châteaux. **35.** *Milan:* Cathedral. **36.** *Madrid:* Plaza Mayor. **37.** *Rome:* Colosseum. **38.** *Marseilles:* Notre Dame de la Garde. **39.** *Zagreb:* St. Mark's Cathedral. **40.** *Athens:* Acropolis.

Information is available through your IATA travel agency or Swissair. Including information, of course, on the excellent connexions to all of the other 87 Swissair stops around the world—for instance, the daily flights to Montreal and Toronto (in cooperation with Air Canada).

Press advertisements
Annonces de presse
Zeitungs-Inserate

1a-b Great Britain
AD Scottish & Newcastle Breweries Ltd
AG Leo Burnett Ltd
DIR Doug Buntrock
ILL (a) Brian Moore
(b) Bruce McNally
COPY Doug Buntrock, Peter Smith
beer, bière, Bier

2 Great Britain
AD H.P. Bulmer Ltd
AG Leo Burnett Ltd
DIR/DES Stuart Cooper
ILL Holly Head NTA Studios
COPY David O'Connor Thompson
cider, cidre

3 Great Britain
AD Aquilac Alimentaire/Perrier
AG Leo Burnett Ltd
DIR Stuart Cooper
ILL Philip Castle
Perrier water

4 Israel
AD Gold Star
AG Arieli Adv Ltd
DIR/DES Dali Bahat
ILL Yona Flink Studio Vision
COPY Martin Fenton
natural fruit drinks, jus de fruit

5a-b Great Britain
AD Times Publishing Co
AG Leo Burnett Ltd
DIR Ken Mullen, Bob Byrne
newspaper, journal, Zeitung

6 Spain
AD Bodegas Berberana SA
AG Nucleo de Comunicacion & Marketing/Publis
DIR/DES Salvatore Adduci
COPY R. Salcedo, N. Rey
wine, vin, Wein

1a

1b

What can you drink if you talk with a plum in your mouth?

You may be labouring under the illusion that the speaking of the Queen's English is an asset.

True it's a passport to Ascot, Henley and those sort of do's, but it does have its drawbacks. Apart from making verbal communication damnably awkward, it also gives you this unnaturally dry palate.

Fortunately the chaps down at Bulmers know the odds.

In fact, they discovered the solution years ago when they created this excellent beverage, Bulmers No 7. It's a cider, but so very, very dry it'll do wicked things to your taste buds unless you know what's what.

First chilled in the trout stream, then decanted in a long glass is how No 7 performs at its best.

It enriches the vocal chords. It soothes the ruffled palate. And it tells you that here at last is a drink to separate the plums from the prunes.

BULMER'S NUMBER 7
The extra dry, dry drink.

2

3

They sell a million bottles a day in France.

They sell a million bottles a year in England.

But then it took us a while to catch on to denim.

Ask a Frenchman why he drinks Perrier, and he'll probably ask you why you don't.

To them it comes naturally, perhaps because it comes naturally. A natural, sparkling spring water bottled as it comes out of the ground. They drink it with or without a lemon slice. They drink it straight from the fridge.

And just in case you think the French can never point the way, cast your mind back to who made jeans respectable. It wasn't a cowboy.

With added je ne sais quoi.

4

VISION

7 Spain
AD Marie Brizard
AG Nucleo de Comunicacion & Marketing/Publis
DIR/DES Salvatore Adduci
COPY R. Salcedc, N. Ray
liqueur

8 Germany
AD Peter Eckes 'Eckes Edelkirsch'
AG Young & Rubicam Werbung
DIR Wolf Lommel
ILL Eva Sereny
COPY Renate Velten
liqueur

5a

5b

7

6

Lacón con grelos y Berberana Carta de Plata. ¡Intimos!

Una buena comida en casa, un vino de calidad y un recuerdo inolvidable...

Año tras año. En una fecha. Siempre con la misma alegría, renace para los dos un recuerdo inolvidable: un día, en el que se forjaron tantas y tantas ilusiones, que poco a poco van siendo realidad.

Una comida íntima, en casa, con un plato especial, y un vino de cuerpo redondo, de acidez fija, de calidad reconocida, un buen vino: Berberana Carta de Plata.

BERBERANA
El Fruto de la Tierra de Rioja.

8

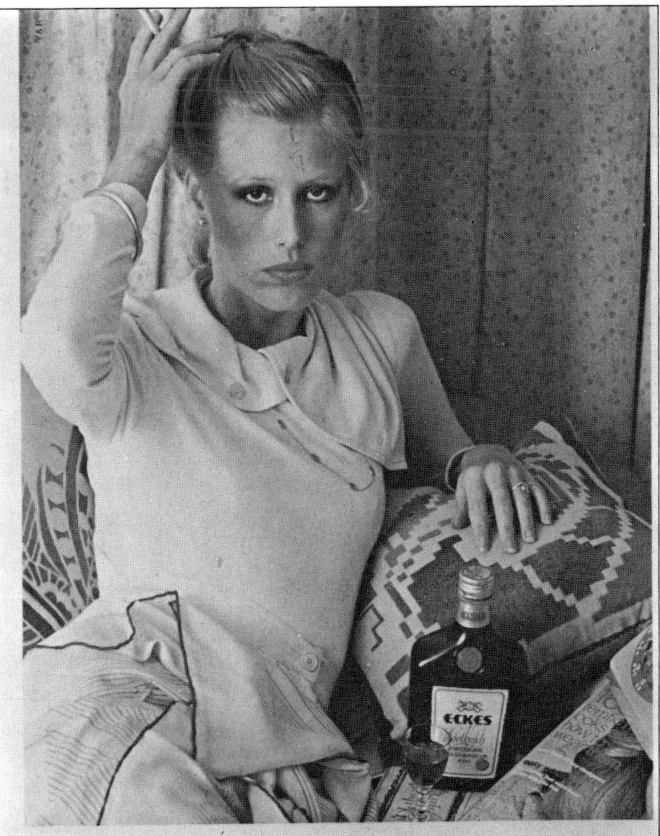

Press advertisements
Annonces de presse
Zeitungs-Inserate

1 Italy
AD Zucchelli Forni
AG Studio Arletti
DIR Ebro Arletti
DES Elis Arletti
electric ovens for bakers, fours électriques de boulangeries, Backöfen

2 Switzerland
AD Thomi & Franck AG
AG Gisler & Gisler
DIR/DES Max Rindlisbacher
ILL Marcel Hayoz
COPY Francis Sulzer
coffee, café, Kaffee

3 Switzerland
AD G. Widmann & Söhne
AG Gisler & Gisler
DIR Erich Hartmann
DES Urs Roos
ILL Dominic Schneider
COPY Peter Schulz
coffee machine, Kaffeautomat

4 Denmark
AD Hafnia-Haand I Haand
AG Benton & Bowles AS
DIR John Andersen
DES Per Koblegård
ILL Claes Ekmann
life insurance, assurance-vie, Lebensversicherung

5 Switzerland
AD Schweiz Käseunion
AG Gisler & Gisler
DIR/DES Fredy Steiner
ILL Dominic Schneider
cheese, fromage, Käse

2

3

4

Hvornår skal De til at nyde livet?

Tænk på det nu hvis De er mellem 35 og 50.

Der kommer en tid, hvor De kan nyde livet i fulde drag. Landligger-livets lyksaligheder er for mange det skønneste på jord, hvis der bare er råd til sommerhus.

Andre vil hellere rejse, spise ude på spændende steder eller dyrke søsportslivet. Der er nok at glæde sig til.

Det er op til Dem selv, hvor meget De vil have ud af livet, når De engang ad åre ikke længere er så aktivt beskæftiget med arbejdet.

Men en ting er sikker. Der skal penge til at opretholde en tilværelse, der er lige så god, som den De lever nu.

Folkepensionen alene gør det ikke.

Men så er der Hafnia-Haand i Haand. Med Indeks-Liv.

Den mest fordelagtige opsparingsform i livsforsikring. De kan vælge. Gennem præmiereguleringer tager vi automatisk højde for, at den sum De eller Deres familie til sin tid råder over, rimer med det prisniveau, vi har til den tid.

Endelig lægger vi en klækkelig bonus oveni summen, så De er sikret en høj forrentning af Deres penge.

Med andre ord. De får både en livsforsikring og en opsparing, der følger inflationen. Kan man forlange mere.

Indeks-Liv kan tegnes i 3 udgaver. Risiko-liv, kapital-liv og rate-liv. I de to første kan De fradrage indtil 3.000 kr. årligt på selvangivelsen. Med rate-liv formen har De fri fradragsret på selvangivelsen.

Tag en samtale med en af Hafnia-Haand i Haand's 500 assurandører.

Tegn Indeks-Liv i Hafnia-Haand i Haand. Lev livet efter de 60.

Kupon
sendes i kuvert til
Hafnia-Haand i Haand, Informationsafdelingen, Holmens Kanal 22, 1097 København K.
Jeg vil gerne vide mere om fordelene ved Hafnia-Haand i Haand Indeks-Liv og ønsker
☐ brochure tilsendt ☐ besøg på min bopæl
Navn ....
Adresse ....
Postnr. .... By ....

HAFNIA - HAAND I HAAND
Helsikring i hverdagen.

5

Donner une saveur nouvelle à la vie...
Gruyère, emmental, sbrinz.
Fromageons en choeur! Union suisse du commerce de fromage SA, Berne

Kleine Wassermusik. Ohne Eintrittskarten.
Emmentaler, Greyerzer, Sbrinz.
Chästeilet macht einig. Schweizerische Käseunion AG, Bern

Donner une saveur nouvelle à la vie...
Gruyère, emmental, sbrinz.

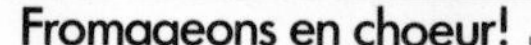

Fromageons en choeur!

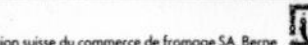

Union suisse du commerce de fromage SA, Berne

6
AD Licher Bier
6 Germany
AD Ihring-Melchior Lich
AG SSM Werbeageutur
DIR/DES Harald Schlüter
Copy: Jürgen Mehl
beer, bière, Bier

7 Italy
AD Josiah Wedgwood & Sons Ltd
AG Comunicazione Visive
COPY Gordon W. Wright
tableware, faience fine, Töpferware

8 Great Britain
AD Shell Oil
AG OBM
DIR Mark Ready
DES Group: Chris Meiklejohn
ILL Pete Kelly

9 Germany
AD Kawasaki
AG Young & Rubicam Werbung
DIR/ILL David Corbett
COPY Thomas Wulfes
motorcycles

6

7

8

Don't risk your investment in farm machinery by using an inferior oil.

Today, your machines have never had to work harder or longer to justify their cost.

That's why Shell have put the full weight of their technical know-how behind new Shell Universal Farm Oil.

Shell Universal Farm Oil exceeds all the latest, toughest manufacturers' specifications. And being truly multi-purpose it does every job: engine, transmission, hydraulics and oil immersed brakes.

Quite simply it's the best farm oil we've ever made.

For further information and your nearest stockist phone your local Shell Office.

You can be sure of Shell

9

NSU Quickly, Vespa, VW, Borgward Isabella, Porsche 911 S... und dann?

Die Geschichte eines Mannes ist oft die Geschichte seiner fahrbaren Untersätze. Die Geschichte des sie verfügt über eine damenfreundliche Sitzbank. Ein Umstand, der seiner unaufhaltsamen Entwicklung zum Manne sehr entgegenkommt. Und so ist es nicht weiter ver-

Die erste Liebe!

Auf der Vespa mit der zweiten ersten Liebe.

Mannes dieser Anzeige beginnt 1952 mit einer NSU Quickly, die nicht viel jünger ist als er selbst. Aber was macht das schon? Es ist das erste Gefühl von Macht über eine Maschine, von Überlegenheit gegenüber den anderen, die ihn bei 32 km/h etwas vom Rausch der Geschwindigkeit ahnen läßt.

Zwei Jahre später ist dieser Rausch verflogen und eine silberne Vespa gekommen. Sie ist stärker, komfortabler, und – wunderlich, daß diese erste Tuchfühlung auf der Vespa-Bank, wieder zwei Jahre später, in einem kaffeebraunen VW mit Liegesitzen ihre Fortführung findet. Der Rest der Geschichte ist schnell erzählt: Die lauen Sommernächte bleiben nicht ohne Folgen – eine Familie wird gegründet, auf den heißgeliebten VW folgt

Das erste eigene Auto! Ein VW, Baujahr 1953, in Kaffeebraun mit Liegesitzen.

Es ist geschafft: Familie gegründet, Borgward Isabella gekauft!

eine Borgward Isabella – ein wunderbarer Familienwagen. In den nächsten Jahren wächst sein Wohlstand weiter, und mit dem Wohlstand wachsen auch seine Autos, bis er sich schließlich 1972 einen – wie er meint – Jugendtraum erfüllen kann: einen Porsche 911 S. Ist er damit am Ziel seiner Wünsche? Nein! Denn irgendwann, als er sich auf der Autobahn der 160 PS seines Porsches bedient, fallen ihm die 1,4 PS seiner ersten Liebe wieder ein und das unvergleichliche Vergnügen, das sie ihm bereitet hatte.

Auf Geschäftsreise im neuen 911 S.

Die Folge: Heute fährt seine Frau den Porsche und er seine Kawasaki Z 1000! Ein Motorrad, das ein Maximum an Kraft, Sicherheit und Fahrkomfort bietet. Eine Maschine, die ihn das Fahren pur erleben läßt. Und den Spaß und das Glück, das einmal auf dem Rücken der alten „Quickly" begonnen hatte.

Kawasaki

Die neue Kawasaki Z 1000 – 1009 ccm, Vierzylinder-Viertakt, obenliegende Nockenwellen, 85 PS, drei Scheibenbremsen, von 0 auf 100 km/h in etwa 3,2 Sekunden, Spitze über 200 km/h, empf. Verkaufspreis 9000 Mark.

Ein Verzeichnis aller autorisierten Kawasaki-Händler finden Sie auf der nächsten Seite.

Press advertisements
Annonces de presse
Zeitungs-Inserate

1 Spain
AD Productos Lea
AG Nucleo de Comunicacion & Marketing/Publis
DIR/DES Salvatore Adduci
COPY R. Salcedo, N. Rey
shaving cream, savon à barbe, Rasierkreme

2 Great Britain
AD Disophrol
AG Deltakos
DIR John Peake
DES Group Chris Meiklejohn
ILL John Mac

3 Spain
AD Camper Shoes
DES Carlos Rolando
ILL C. Rolando, M. Ezquenazi
(photo) Sergio Hernandez
COPY J. Lorente
desert boots

4 Great Britain
AD Philip Morris Ltd
AG Leo Burnett Ltd
DIR/DES Doug Buntrock
ILL Chad Hall, Christa Peters
cigarettes

5 Great Britain
AD Melitta, Germany
AG G.F.P.
DIR Klaus Gerlach, Bernie Dienst
DES Group: Chris Meiklejohn
ILL Ken Thompson

6 India
AD HMT
DES Niranjan Ghoshad
watches, montres, Taschenuhren

1

2

3

4

7 Greece
AD Sportex SA
AG K&K Univas Advertising Centre
DIR Frederick V. Carabott
DES Georgos Kaldelis
COPY Pavlina Pambouthi
sport and leisure shoes, souliers, Schuhen

8 Great Britain
AD National Benzole Co Ltd
AG Leo Burnett Ltd
DIR Malcolm G.C. Gaskin
DES Cliff Butler
ILL Mickey Finn, (photo)
P. John Turner
COPY Dominick Lynch-Robinson

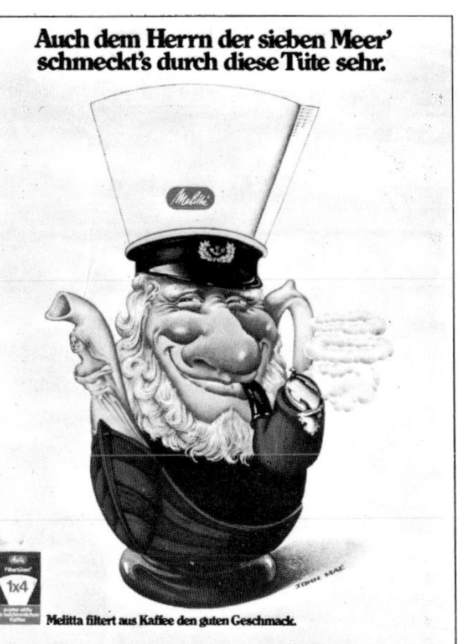

5

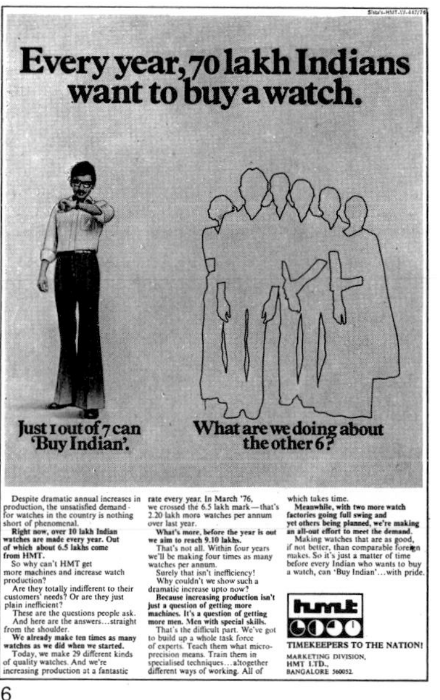

6

7

8

We know it takes more than this to get you going.

We're not averse to a bit of glamour ourselves you know.

It's just that when we're talking to our dealers we'd rather talk business than talk pretty girls.

And we know that's the way you like it as well.

'76 was a year of expansion for National. But it was you, the National dealer, that made it so.

A large number of dealers have already converted to National and many more are in the process of doing so. We've helped to renovate and redecorate more sites, from million-galloners to country service stations, than in any other year. And now we're involved in rebuilding a large number of sites with dealers who have come over to us.

Now the public know we're on the move.

It wasn't just the trade that saw more of us this year. The public did as well. After seeing National giant-sized posters, the 'Join the National Clan' TV commercial and hearing our radio commercials, more people are going to be thinking and buying National than ever before.

And next year we'll be creating even more customer goodwill.

1976 was no one year wonder.

You put in the work. We put in the support. With staff training schemes, loans and financial advice, advertising, free point-of-sale material and successful promotions. We're planning to continue opening more sites all over the country because our first priority is to have a growing network of satisfied National dealers.

So if you haven't joined the National Clan, why not make it your New Year's resolution?

And as for the glamour?

Well, she's not bad looking is she?

National

You'll be seeing a lot more of us.

JAN 1 2 3 4 5 6 7 8 9 10 11 12 13 14 15 16 17 18 19 20 21 22 23 24 25 26 27 28 29 30 31

Press advertisements
Annonces de presse
Zeitungs-Inserate

1a-b Holland
AD Stichting Ideële Reclame (SIRE)
AG Prad NV
DIR Dick v.d. Beemt
DES (concept) Paul Mertz
ILL Marjolein Bastin
COPY Paul Mertz
non-commercial campaign about trees for children's magazines

2 Holland
AD Dutch Flower Growers' Council
AG HVR Studio
DIR Ger Seidler
DES Ton Hoogendoorn
flowers, fleurs, Blumen

3 Sweden
AD General Foods AB
AG Young & Rubicam AB
DIR/DES Bo Zaunders
ILL Eric Meola, New York
COPY Claes Bergquist, Bibi Langer
coffee, café, Kaffee

4 Switzerland
AD Thomy & Franck AG
AG Gisler & Gisler
DIR/DES Max Rindlisbacher
ILL Marcel Hayoz
COPY Francis Sulzer
sandwich spread, paté, Brotaufstrich

5 Denmark
AD Carno Denmark
AG SB Grafisk Design
DIR/DES Søren Balle
ILL John Fowlie
conserves

6 Switzerland
AD Eswa AG
AG Gisler & Gisler
DIR/DES Max Rindlisbacher
ILL Marcel Hayoz
COPY Peter Schulz
detergents, Waschmittel

1a

1b

2

3

BIBI OM GEVALIA

Bibi Langer berättar om hur Sveriges mest älskade kaffe kommer till. Brev 2

Högt uppe på en bergssluttning mitt i Colombia ligger Saras och Antonios lilla kaffefarm.

De är båda 35 år och har en liten son – Hever – på tio. Sara väntar dessutom sitt andra barn när som helst och hon har bestämt sig för att föda det hemma. "Jag vill ha Antonio hos mig och vara omgiven av vanda ting", berättar hon.

Tillsammans med modern Maria, 70, bor de i två rum och kök och försörjer sig förutom kaffeskörden på bananer, majs och höns.

Utanför boningshuset växer deras kaffebuskar fulla med bär, i skydd av bananplantor och carbonerotråd – de vet att sol och regn är bäst i lagom doser. Under de två skördetiderna hjälps hela familjen åt – Hever får ledigt från skolan under plockningen.

Som de flesta colombianska småfarmare kan Sara och Antonio själva klara av allt förarbete med de nyplockade kaffebären. I det lilla uthuset står en gammal handdriven maskin som tar bort skalen från de röda bären, så att bara bönorna blir kvar.

Torkningen försiggår i lådor på hjul, som kan skjutas in under uthuset när det regnar. Är solen framme står Antonio bland bönorna och vänder dem med en raka för att få en jämn torkning.

Ingen i familjen kan tänka sig något bättre än kaffe. De är stolta över att odla en av världens förnämsta kaffesorter. Eller som Maria med strålande ögon säger: – När det är dags att skörda, spränger hjärtat av lycka.

PS. Fick ett brev från Sara just nu: "*La ciguena me visitó el 7 de septiembre a las 2 de la manana y recibí un nino. Nacio muy alentado y yo estoy muy bien*". (Storken kom med en pojke klockan 2 på morgonen den 7 september. Födde lugnt och mår mycket bra". DS.

I Gevalia ingår nästan en tredjedel milt aromrikt Colombiakaffe.

Gevalia, Gävle, 026-11 54 20

THOMY Tartinade bringt ein bisschen Abwechslung auf unser täglich Brot.
Mit Petersilie entdeckte es Tante Emilie.
Mit Pfeffer macht's scharf auf mehr.
Mit Spargeln wird es Spitze.
Mit Schnittlauch schmeckt's auch.
Mit Servelats ist es wie mit Klöpfern.
Mit Poulet nimmt man's gern zur Brust.
Mit Sardinen kommt's einem spanisch vor.
Mit Tomaten stellt es alles in den Schatten.
Mit Thon kann man ein Lied davon singen.
Mit kaltem Braten lässt es keinen kalt.
Mit Konfitüre schmeckt's chinesisch.
Mit Radieschen liebt es das Lieschen.
Tartinade ist der neue Delikatess-Brotaufstrich von THOMY. Die neue THOMY Tartinade lässt sich leicht von der Tube direkt aufs Brot streichen.
Und das schönste daran ist: die THOMY Tartinade schmeckt immer wieder anders. Zum Beispiel mit einem Wurstzipfel zum Znüni. Mit etwas Käse zum Zvieri. Und mit Tomaten, Sardinen, Eiern oder Kümmel als ausgewachsenes Nachtessen. Je nachdem, was Sie noch im Kühlschrank haben. Mit der THOMY Tartinade ist Brotessen ein feines und abwechslungsreiches Zusammensetzspiel geworden.
Mit Kümmel bleibt kein Krümel.
Mit Cornichons macht's keinen sauer.
Mit Kapern wird's am Spass nicht hapern.
THOMY Produkte gibt's in der Tube, weil's appetitlicher und einfacher zu dosieren ist.
THOMY
TARTINADE
Delikatess-Aufstrich
neu
Mit Gurken lieben's auch die kleinen Schurken.
Mit Kresse kommt es in die Tagespresse.
Mit Ei schmeckt es an Ostern.
Denn Gutes kommt von THOMY.

4

Nu sælger CARNO to krydderiserier, det kendte grønne glas og nu det mere eksklusive med korkprop.
Køb hele den spændende nye krydderiserie med 30x6 glas og få 22% nyhedsrabat
CARNO har fremstillet en ny og spændende krydderiserie med særligt udvalgte krydderier som Edelsuss-paprika Cassia Lignea-kanel, Ostindisk-carry, Blå-birkes m.m.
Serien består af 30 forskellige krydderier i smukke glas med den ægte korkprop som gør glasset til andet end bare et krydderiglas, en god gaveidé, der efter brugen kan bruges til alt muligt nips.
peber
carry
kanel
paprika
CARNO's konsulentservice hjælper Dem gerne med opstillingen af den ny krydderiserie.
CARNO har ladet fremstille skillerum til Deres trådhylder, og små fikse skilte der fortæller, hvor de forskellige krydderier skal stå.
Alt sammen uden nogen udgift for Dem.
CARNO
Midtager 28, 2600 Glostrup. Tlf. (02) 96 79 00

5

6

Gabeh-Luri, ca. 119 × 189 cm Fr. 975.–
„Du, Dein Nomade macht sich gut!"
Tatsächlich, dieser urwüchsige Teppich liegt am rechten Platz und verdient ein Kompliment. Um sich in Nomadenteppiche zu verlieben, müssen Sie aber kein altes Bauernhaus bewohnen. Denn die »Nomaden« fühlen sich überall wohl, wo sich Menschen ursprünglich oder bewusst einfach einrichten – also in rustikaler oder moderner Atmosphäre.
Nomadenteppiche haben unabhängig von ihrer Herkunft etwas gemeinsam: ihre Schönheit lebt nicht von der Feinheit der Muster und der Knotenzahl – ihre starke Ausstrahlung kommt vom Ungekünstelten der Motive und von der unregelmässigen Arbeit der wandernden Knüpfer. Aber wie lange fertigen Nomadenstämme in Afghanistan noch Hausrat-Taschen und Türschmuck für ihre Zelte an? Und wann verschwindet das traditionelle Ziegenhaar aus den südpersischen Gabeh-Teppichen? Unsere Einkäufer reisen seit Jahren im ganzen Orient und verfolgen das Sesshaftwerden der Nomaden und die damit einhergehende Qualitätseinbusse ihrer Teppichproduktion genau.
Die bevorstehende Verknappung der noch immer sehr preiswerten Nomaden-Produktion macht deshalb jedes schöne Stück zu einem der wertsteigerndsten Orientteppiche.
Unsere Orientteppich-Abteilungen in der ganzen Schweiz verfügen über eine ansehnliche Auswahl dieser urwüchsigen Gattung. In Ihrer nächsten Möbel-Pfister-Filiale hin und wieder in den Stapeln stöbern lohnt sich jedenfalls – aber bevor die Preise davonspringen.

Jeder abgebildete Teppich ist ein Einzelstück. Wenn er verkauft wird, finden Sie bei uns aber ebenso schöne Stücke der gleichen Herkunft und Preislage.
Afghan, semi-alt, ca. 114 × 179 cm Fr. 775.–
Ait-Ouzguit, ca. 101 × 151 cm Fr. 255.–
Beloutch-Torba, ca. 60 × 105 cm semi-alt, Fr. 275.–
Beloutch, ca. 84 × 117 cm Fr. 375.–
Afghan-Djaler, ca. 27 × 106 cm Fr. 245.–
Khar, ca. 147 × 292 cm Fr. 2150.–
Koliay, ca. 142 × 228 cm Fr. 1200.–
Afghan-Djaler, ca. 42 × 120 cm semi-alt, Fr. 215.–
Boullou, ca. 121 × 241 cm Fr. 855.–
Sumakh, ca. 100 × 128 cm Fr. 495.–
Gabeh-Schuli, ca. 106 × 200 cm Fr. 950.–
Alle Preise sind Mitnahmepreise.
Möbel-Pfister
hat Nomadenteppiche von Sachwert-Niveau
Avry-Centre b. FR Bellinzona Biel Delémont Lausanne Luzern Neuchâtel St. Gallen Suhr Zug
Basel Bern Contone TI Genf Lugano Mels-Sargans Schönbühl b. BE St. Margrethen Winterthur Zürich
h/j OT 10

Press advertisements
Annonces de presse
Zeitungs-Inserate

1 Spain
AD/AG Nucleo de Comunicacion Marketing/Publis
DIR/DES Salvatore Adduci
ILL Fernando de Bustos
motorcars, automobile

2 United States
AD Nycom, Inc
AG Gauger Sparks Silva
DIR/DES/ILL David Gauger
COPY Larry Silva
car rally

3 Germany
AD Bosch
AG Young & Rubicam Werbung
DIR Manfred Dittrich
ILL Henner — Prefi
COPY Hartmut Grün
toolmaking machine, Werkzeugmaschine

4a-b Switzerland
AD Haldengut Brewery Inc
AG Adolf Wirz ag
DIR/DES/ILL C. Knezy
beer, bière, Bier

5 Switzerland
AD Philips AG
AG GGK Basel
DIR Guido Stuber
car radio, Autoradio

6 Argentina
AD Deville SA
AG Oscar N. Marcovecchio SA de Publicidad
DIR Nestor Denis
DES Oscar Marcovecchio
ILL Guillermo Balboa
bra, soutien-gorge, Büstenhalter

1

2

3

Hecken sind wohl das Beliebteste, was in deutschen Gärten wächst. Sie bieten Windschutz und Sichtschutz, gliedern ein Grundstück, sehen schön aus, und sie machen viel Arbeit.

Wie Sie schneller und sicherer – ohne Blasen an den Händen, ohne viel Schweiß zu vergießen und ohne Muskelkater – zu einer schönen Hecke kommen, wollen wir Ihnen im folgenden beschreiben.

Zuerst einmal: Warum Sie sich eine Bosch-Heckenschere kaufen werden.

Die Messer der Bosch-Heckenscheren sind tropfenförmig ausgebildet. Sie umschließen jeden Zweig, halten ihn fest und kappen ihn sauber ab. Auch das kleinste Ästchen kann Ihnen nicht entwischen.

Der kräftige 350-Watt-Motor ist verantwortlich dafür, daß selbst 10 mm starke Äste spielend geschnitten werden. Mit 65 cm Schnittlänge der P 80 SL zum Beispiel sind Sie selbst breiten Hecken mühelos gewachsen.

Die gegenläufigen Messer sorgen für eine größere Schnittleistung und machen die Maschine angenehm vibrationsfrei. Die beidseitig schneidenden Scherblätter machen die Arbeit schneller und einfacher. Der schwenkbare Handgriff läßt immer eine günstige Gewichtsverteilung zu, und Sie können auch hohe und breite Hecken ohne ausgerenkte Arme bearbeiten.

Sie und der Motor stehen unter Schutz.

Sollte mal ein Zaundraht die Messer blockieren, schützt die eingebaute Rutschkupplung den Motor vor dem Durchbrennen. Und selbst wenn mal aus Versehen das eigene Stromkabel zwischen die Messer gerät, kann Ihnen nichts passieren. Denn das vollisolierende Polyamidgehäuse schützt Sie vor elektrischem Strom.

Für Hecken fern von jeder Steckdose.

Und zum Trimmen und Ausputzen ist die Akku-Strauchschere P 801 zu empfehlen. Sie ist besonders leicht und handlich und hat doch eine eindrucksvolle Schnittleistung, für die vier aufladbare Nickel-Kadmium-Zellen von 4,8 Volt sorgen. Eine Akkuladung reicht bis zu 30 Minuten Schnittzeit.

Das Ladegerät wird mitgeliefert und kostet keinen Pfennig extra.

Wichtige Hinweise zur Anlage und Pflege von Hecken.

Vor der Pflanzung einer Hecke muß eine gute Bodenvorbereitung vorgenommen werden. Je laufenden Meter braucht man etwa 4 bis 5 Pflanzen, bei sehr kleiner Pflanzenware und Liguster bis zu zehn pro Meter. Wichtig ist nun ein regelmäßiger Schnitt. Damit die Hecke nach dem Schnitt sauber aussieht, spannt man am besten vor dem Schnitt eine Schnur. Besonders zu beachten ist der konische Schnitt der Hecke: unten breiter als oben (siehe Abbildung). Das entspricht dem natürlichen Wachstum der Hecke, andernfalls würde sie unten verkahlen oder vom Schnee zerdrückt.

Saubere Rasenkanten ohne krummen Rücken.

Mit der kabelfreien Akku-Grasschere P 800 ST haben Sie in kurzer Zeit mühelos saubere Rasenkanten. Dafür sorgen 10 cm Schnittbreite und ein Scherblatt aus rostfreiem Edelstahl, was besser ist als eine Schutzbeschichtung, die sich abnutzen kann.

Vier aufladbare Nickel-Kadmium-Zellen sorgen für eine lange Schnittzeit (etwa 60 Minuten) und können über das mitgelieferte Ladegerät immer wieder aufgeladen werden. Der Fahrstock mit Ein- und Ausschalter am Handgriff läßt einen die Rasenkanten in aufrechter Haltung bewältigen.

Schnellaustausch-Service: das gibt es nur bei Bosch.

Falls Ihr Bosch-Gartengerät nach der Garantiezeit tatsächlich einmal ausfallen sollte, erhalten Sie kostengünstig ein werkgeprüftes Austauschgerät mit sechs Monaten Garantie.

Bei Ihrem Fachhändler* können Sie alle Bosch-Gartengeräte in die Hand nehmen. Der hat auch die neuen Prospekte mit dem kompletten Gartengeräteprogramm und wird Sie bestens beraten.

*auch in Österreich und der Schweiz

Die wichtigsten Laub- und Nadelgehölze für Formhecken

Weißdorn (Crataegus monogyna), Höhe 100 bis 200 cm, Buschbreite 50 bis 60 cm

Hainbuche (Carpinus betulus), Höhe etwa 200 cm

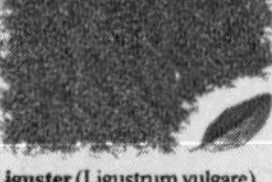
Liguster (Ligustrum vulgare), Höhe 50 bis 200 cm

Feldahorn (Acer campestre), Höhe 300 bis 400 cm

Kreuzdorn (Rhamnus cathar-ticus), Höhe 100 bis 200 cm

Eibe (Taxus), Höhe 150 bis 200 cm

Lebensbaum (Thuja), Höhe 100 bis 500 cm

Scheinzypresse (Chamnaecyparis), Höhe 100 bis 200 cm

Die gebräuchlichsten Schnittformen für Schneidehecken

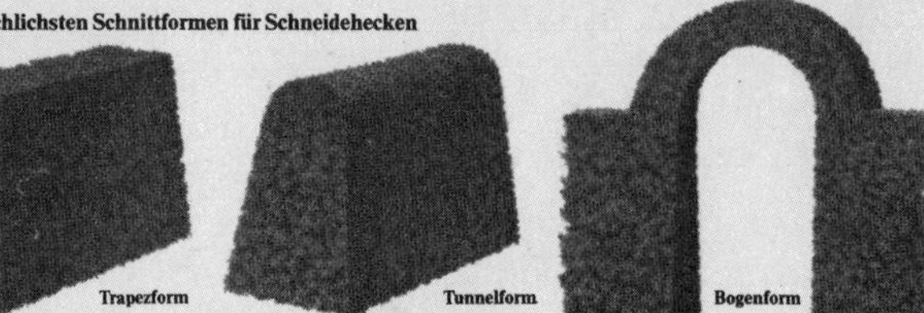

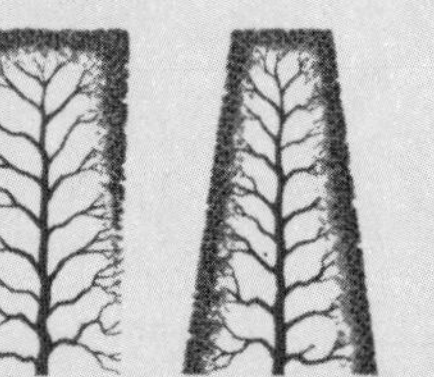
Falsch: Bei Vertikalschnitt verkahlt die Hecke an der Basis.

Richtig: Hecken müssen unten breiter als oben gehalten werden.

Wichtig! Vor dem Schnitt eine Schnur spannen, dann sieht die Hecke nach dem Schnitt sauber aus.

BOSCH
Der Spezialist für elektrische Gartengeräte.

Mehr Freude am Garten kostenlos.
Wir senden Ihnen gern kostenlos die kleine Broschüre „Mehr Freude am Garten", die Ihnen viele nützliche und praxisnahe Hinweise gibt, wie Sie mehr aus Ihrem Garten machen können.
Kleben Sie nur den Kupon auf eine Postkarte, und senden Sie sie an

Bosch-Gartengeräte,
Postfach 6666, 4830 Gütersloh

Name:
Anschrift:

Heckenschere P 801. 42 cm Schnittlänge, 350 Watt. Gegenläufige Messer in Tropfenform. Dauerscharf. Rutschkupplung. Vollisoliert. Schwenkbarer Handgriff.

0522 1 Y&R EW 577

4a

4b

5

IAC Ein Autoradio, das statt schöner Klänge allzu häufig nur hässliche Störgeräusche von sich gibt, kann einem nicht nur das Autofahren verderben, sondern auch die Freude an der Musik.

Deshalb hat Philips die automatische UKW-Entstörung IAC erfunden. Damit werden alle Störgeräusche direkt im Autoradio ausgelöscht, gleichgültig ob sie von Hochspannungsleitungen, Trams, Bogenschweissanlagen, Töfflis oder Eisenbahnen stammen. Bis jetzt gibt es vier Philips Autoradios mit IAC (Interference Absorption Circuit), von Fr. 210.– bis Fr. 875.–

Dass sich mein Autoradio dauernd stören lässt, hat mich jetzt lange genug gestört. Bitte schicken Sie mir Ihre Informationsunterlagen zu einer ungestörten Lektüre.

Name: ____________ IAC

Strasse: ____________

PLZ/Ort: ____________

Coupon einsenden an:
Philips AG, Abt. RGTT, Edenstrasse 20, 8027 Zürich

PHILIPS

6

Press advertisements
Annonces de presse
Zeitungs-Inserate

1a-b Germany
AD Deutscher Sparkasse- und Giroverband, Bonn
AG Langer-Visualisation
DIR/DES Helmut Langer
ILL Marina Langer-Rosa
savings banks, caisses d'épargne, Sparkasse

2 Great Britain
AD Lloyds Bank International
AG Fletcher, Shelton, Reynolds & Dorrell
DIR/DES Andy Arghiron
ILL Greg Bright
COPY Paul Delaney

3 Great Britain
AD National Westminster Bank
AG J. Walter Thompson
DIR/DES Rob Oliver
ILL Michael Williams
COPY David Holmes
bank, banque

4 Switzerland
AD Avis Switzerland
AG Adolf Wirz AG
DIR A. Pfister
DES R. Farinoli
car hire

5a-b Denmark
AD topsikring
AG RT Reklame-tjenesten
DIR Sigurd Christensen (RT)
ILL Bent Rej
COPY Erik Pichard
insurance company, société d'assurance, Versicherungsgesellschaft

6 Great Britain
AD Land of Promise Ltd
AG Your Company By Design Ltd
DIR/DES Derrick Holmes
COPY Derrick Holmes, Elizabeth Neate
property development company

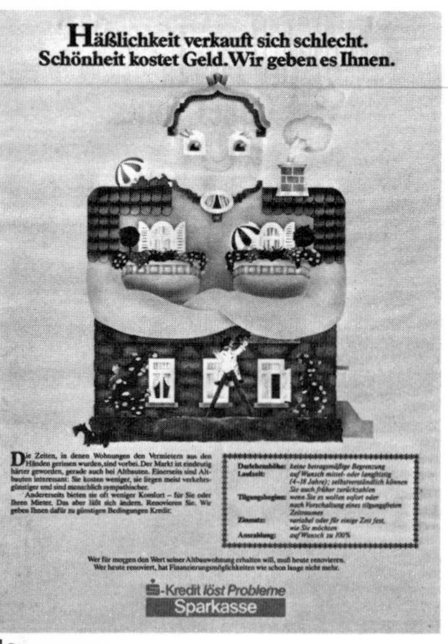

1a

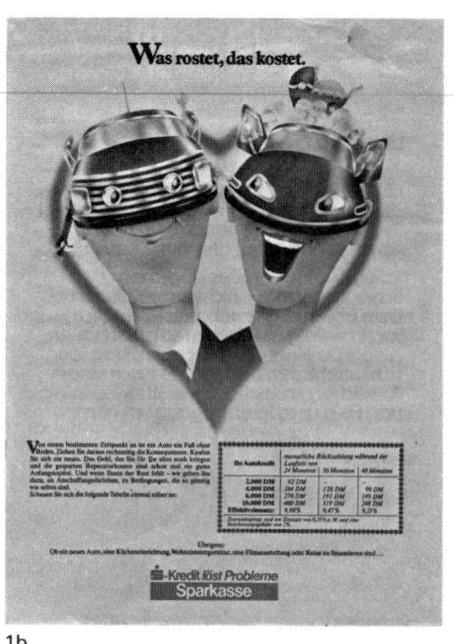

1b

How did three British capital goods manufacturers obtain for their customers over £200,000,000 and over US $200,000,000 for a major development in the Middle East?

Start here.

Or here.

LLOYDS BANK INTERNATIONAL

The international bank that knows its way around the financial maze.

The above project isn't a hypothetical one. It's one that we were involved in from initial brief to completion. However, as you'll appreciate, even if the complexity of the solution could be explained in such a limited space, the confidentiality our clients expect prevents us going into details.

But please, get in touch, and without breaching any confidence, we'll tell you how we helped solve this particular financial problem. And perhaps advise you on any that you might have. By the way, drop us a line if you'd like a solution to the maze.

2

3

4

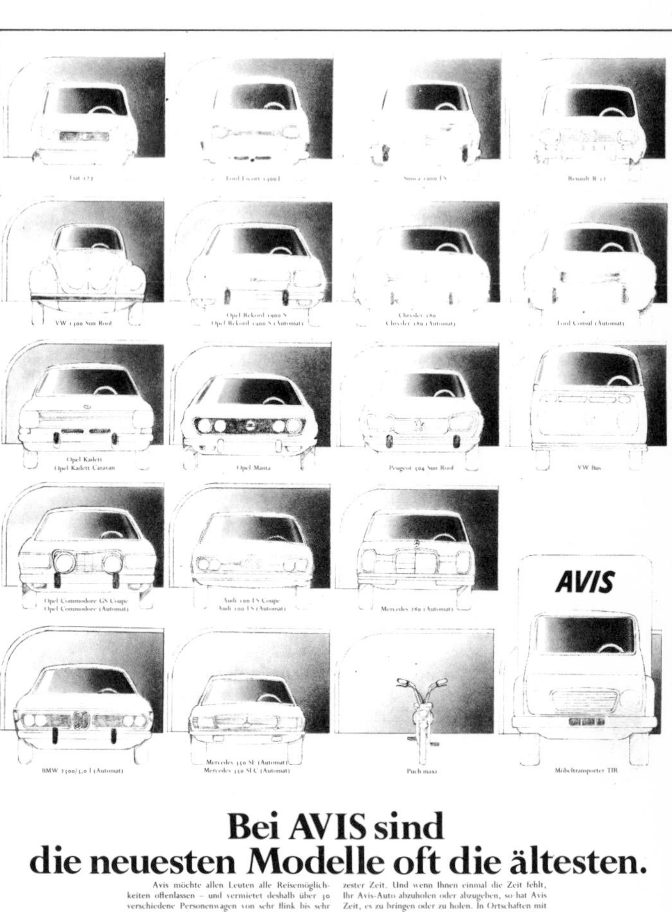

7a-c Great Britain
AD Prime Computer (UK) Ltd
AG Bloy Eldridge
DES Robert Custance
name-building campaign

8 Spain
AD Caja de Ahorros Provincial de Guipuzcoa
AG Nucleo de Comunicacion & Marketing SA
DIR/DES Salvatore Adduci
COPY R. Salcedo, N. Rey
savings bank, caisse d'épargne, Sparkasse

5a

5b

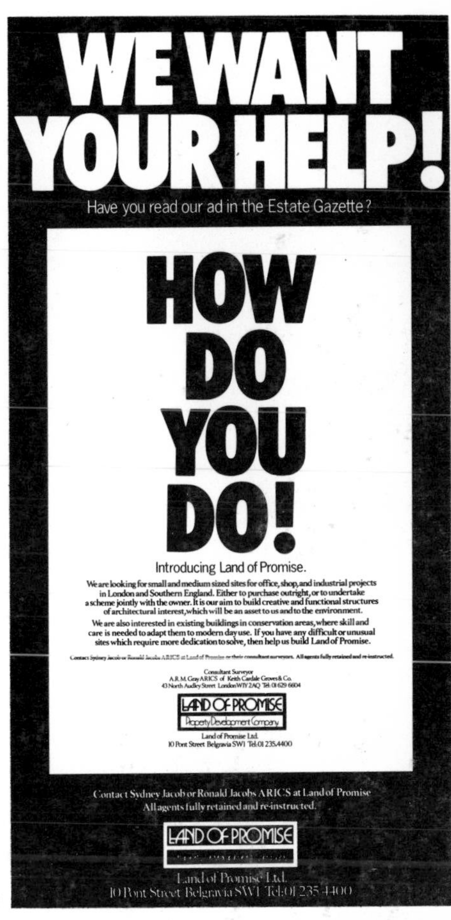

6

7a 7b 7c

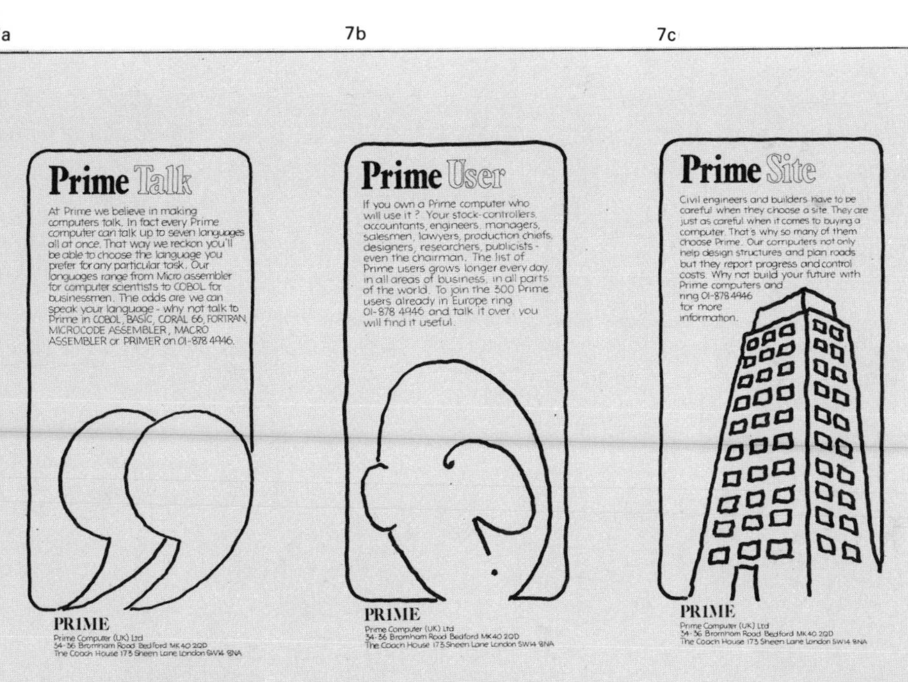

8

Press advertisements
Annonces de presse
Zeitungs-Inserate

1 Israel
AD Tri Wall Pack
AG OK Advertising
DIR Gad Almaliah
ILL Vision Tel Aviv
COPY Dovev Eli
packaging

2 Sweden
AD Sandvik Coromant Sandviken
AG Marknads Team AB
DIR Bengt Wesström
ILL Ture Hadberg
COPY Börje Eklund

3 Switzerland
AD Haass AG Verpackungs-Abteilung
DES Maya Stange ASG
ILL Werner Grüter
aircushions for packaging,
Luftkissenpolster für Transport und Verpackung

4 Canada
AD Dominion Bridge & AMCA
AG Gordon Hill Advertising Ltd
DIR/DES Billy Sharma
ILL Ed Henderson
COPY Russ Showell

5 United States
AD Pertec
AG Boylhart, Lovett & Dean, Inc
STUDIO Dennis S. Juett & Associates Inc
DIR/DES Dennis S. Juett
ILL Dave Holt
COPY Barbara Jones
computer peripheral tape and disk drives

6 Holland
AD IBM Nederland
AG Prad BV
DIR Joop Smit
ILL Mariet Numan
COPY Jolle Westermann
computer

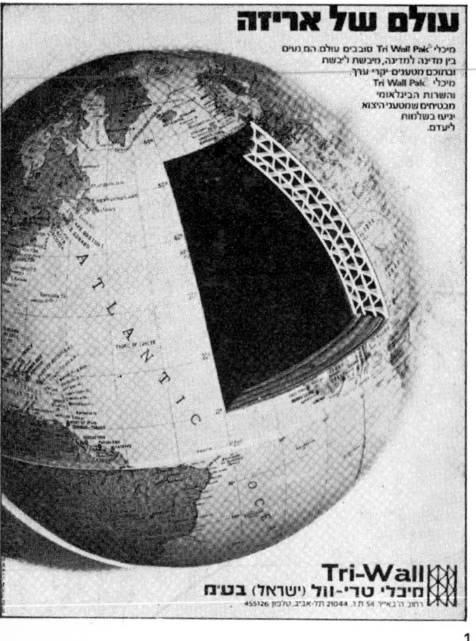

1

2

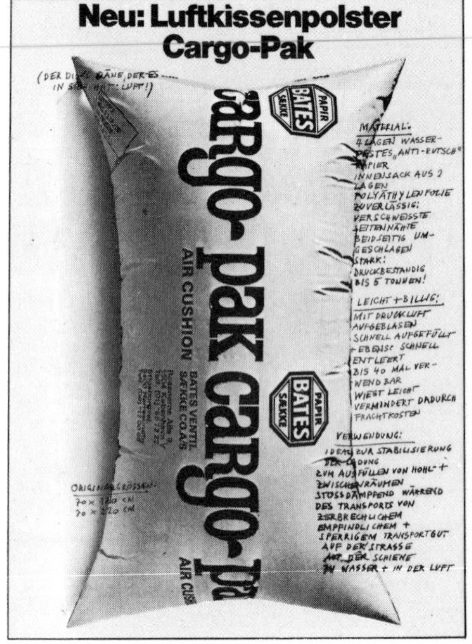

3

4

7 Great Britain
AD Parker Pen Co
AG Collett Dickenson & Pearce
DIR Bob Isherwood
PHO Graham Ford
COPY David Watkinson
Parker Laque ballpoint pens

5

6

7

Punch, June 15 1977

We've a reputation for using old-fashioned methods. This one is 2,200 years old.

There is something most distinctive about our new ball pen on the right.

It has a lacquer finish.

We build up layers of varnish over layers of paint the way the ancient Chinese did; by hand.

As a result, each pen varies slightly from the next, and each takes a long time to make.

We start with coats of paint, possibly three or four. Then we bake them for 2½ hours to a hard shell.

Next, three layers of varnish. These, we bake to form a second, even tougher surface.

Between every coat of paint and each layer of varnish our ladies rub the pen down till it's as smooth as glass, and every bit as shiny.

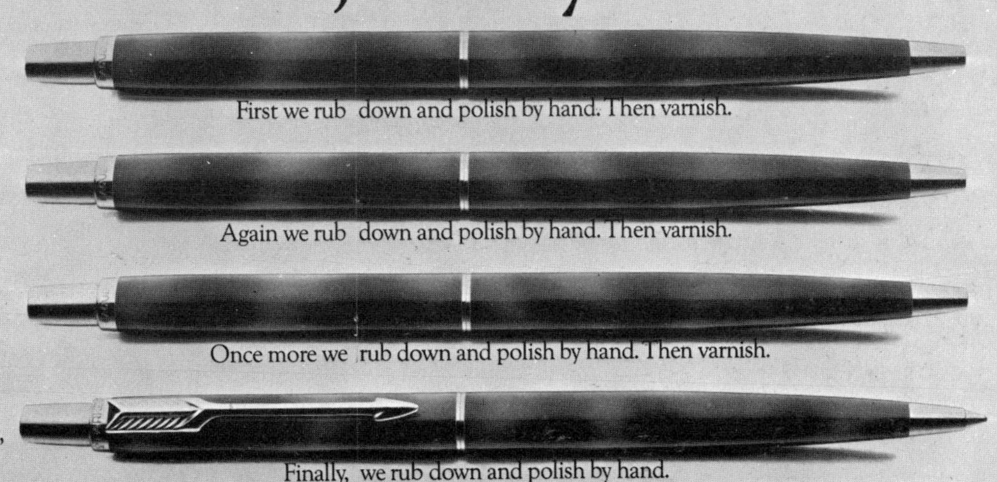

This is always done by hand for the simple reason that no machine can be as sensitive as a woman's touch.

We've called the pen, the Parker Laque. It costs £15.00.*

You may feel that is an outrageous price for a ball pen.

If all you were getting were a ball pen, we would agree with you. PARKER

Press advertisements
Annonces de presse
Zeitungs-Inserate

1 Holland
AD Foundation National Lotto
AG Nationale Publiciteits Onderneming BV
DIR Peter Wagner
DES Jan Voorthuis
ILL Dan Fern
COPY Fred Cante
national lottery

2 United States
AD Johnny Walker
AG Smith Greenland
DIR/DES Stuart Pittman
PHOTO Gervasio Gallardi
COPY Faith Popcorn
whisky

3 Germany
AD Gebr Märklin & Cie GmbH
AG Studio Gerhard Berger
DES Gerhard Berger
ILL Roland Fürst

4 Holland
AD NV Philips' Gloeilampenfabrieken
AG Nationale Publiciteits Onderneming BV
DIR/DES Theo Stradman
ILL Boudewijn Neuteboom

5 Denmark
AD Botex
AG Benton & Bowles AS
DIR/DES John Andersen
ILL Fjeldsted
COPY John Andersen
curtains, rideaux, Vorhänge

6 Great Britain
AD Shell Chemicals (UK) Ltd
AG Leo Burnett Ltd
DIR Chris Baker
DES Julian Graddon
insecticide

1

2

3

7 Germany
AD Druckfarbenfabrik Gebr Schmidt GmbH
AG Olaf Leu Design
DIR/DES Olaf Leu, Fritz Hofrichter
ILL Didi Cromphout, Belgium

4

Danmarks nye gardiner hedder Botex Pioner.

Nu lanceres Botex Pioner. En ny spændende serie gardinstoffer, der går helt nye veje indenfor moderne gardin-design. 36 smukke muligheder designet af Vincent Lerche.
I ren ny uld eller acryl.
Botex Pioner lægger ud med helsider i farver i førende ugeblade og boligtidsskrifter.
Første gang i Bo Bedre 26. august.
De har vel fået Botex Pioner hjem? Ellers er det på høje tid.

Botex. Herning Mekaniske Væveri A/S, Skolegade 75, 7400 Herning – tlf. (07) 12 17 66.

5

IT'S NOT THE ONLY THING WE'LL BE KILLING OFF THIS SUMMER.

Sure, we're good at getting rid of flies.
That's our business.
Last year we outsold all other competitive products three to one.
This year we're going to do even better.
We'll be spending more money on advertising than has ever been spent before.
Using TV and colour ads in the Reader's Digest, Woman, Woman & Home, the Radio Times, the TV Times, and Good House-keeping.
Talking to the people who really matter, housewives.
That's going to mean more brand awareness. Increased sales figures. And soaring profits.
So flies and any would-be competitors beware. You haven't got a chance.

Vapona.

FOR FURTHER INFORMATION CONTACT YOUR VAPONA REP. OR WHOLESALER OR PHONE PETER WHITE AT SHELL CHEMICALS UK LTD., 061-775 2601.

6

7

Prof. Max Lüscher
deutet Farben

Rot wirkt erregend,
aktiv, dynamisch:
Der brave VW-Käfer
wird durch die Farbe Rot
zum rasanten Vehikel.

Bildermacher brauchen
Farbenmacher.
Gebr. Schmidt
Druckfarben

Press advertisements
Annonces de presse
Zeitungs-Inserate

1 Spain
AD Laboratorios Pensa
AG Pharma / Consult SA
DIR/DES Vicente Olmos
ILL Vicente Olmos, Joan Enric
pharmaceuticals

2 Spain
AD Grupo
AG C. Rolando & Asociados
DIR C. Rolando
DES Roberto Dosil
ILL D. Melgarejo, R. Dosil, C. Rolando
advertising agency

3 Spain
AD Hoechst
AG Soley / Torrecilla / Minerva
DIR Soley, Torrecilla
DES M. Torrecilla
veterinary pharmaceuticals

4 United States
AD Medalist Industries, Inc
AG The Haas Company Ltd
DIR/DES Jim Finnerty
ILL Ferderbar Studios
COPY Mike McFarland
athletic uniforms

5a-b United States
AD Dividend Industries Inc
AG Gauger Sparks Silva
DIR/DES (a) Walter Sparks
(b) David Gauger
COPY Larry Silva
housing developer

1

2

3

4

What a difference!

The first American basketball team clad in khaki and wool took to the court at Springfield College in 1891. They needed a fellow on a ladder to retrieve the balls from the baskets after a score. The game has changed a lot since then, and Medalist Sand-Knit has helped make the difference.

With Medalist Sand-Knit basketball uniforms, the choice is yours. Choose from the finest quality selection of style, color, fabric and cut available in America today. And because of this custom quality, Sand-Knit uniforms will still be in the game long after others have been relegated to the practice courts. Whether you're buying for High School, College or Pros, it makes sense to buy Sand-Knit.

Call toll free today 800-558-9858 for the name of your nearest Medalist Sand-Knit dealer, and find out what a difference Sand-Knit can make for your teams. (In Wisconsin call collect (414) 271-8186.) Or write us direct at 290 Junction Street, Berlin, WI 54923 for free full color catalog.

Medalist SAND-KNIT
290 Junction Street
Berlin, Wisconsin 54923

© Copyright Medalist Industries 1977

6a-b United States
AD Wilkes Bashford
AG Gauger Sparks Silva
DIR/DES (a) Walter Sparks
(b) David Gauger
ILL Peter Ogilvie
COPY Larry Silva
men's clothing store, magazin de vêtements d'homme, Herren moden

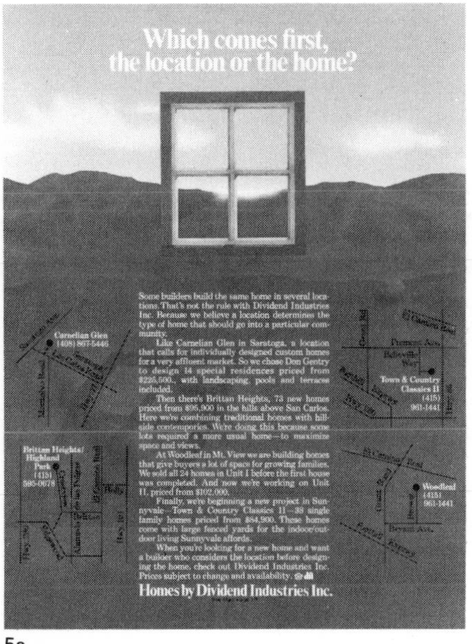

5a

Last year, when many builders were biting their nails, we had our best year ever. Here's why.

We specialized. Our philosophy has always been based on discovering a need and then building quality homes that are sensible additions to a specific community. So you won't find Dividend Industries Inc. building 300 mass produced homes, but you will find them building 4 in Los Gatos, 10 in Los Altos and 24 in Mt. View.

Our record is distinctive. In fact, House & Home Magazine ran a feature article on it in their June issue. Our product is directed to people who can afford a luxury home priced from the mid 80's to over $200,000.

Mt.View

Twenty-four spacious homes at Woodleaf is Mt. View at its best. Choose from a 3 bedroom home with master retreat to a 5 bedroom home with separate den. Woodleaf was designed for an indoor/outdoor lifestyle with large fenced lots, service bars, plumbed gas for an outdoor barbecue and 3 car garages. Priced from $94,900. Call 961-1441.

San Carlos

Highland Park, 25 single family homes high on the hills above San Carlos with spectacular views to the East and West. The homes are available in a selection of 6 floorplans with 3-5 bedrooms, 2-3 baths, two fireplaces, deluxe kitchens, wet bars, tiled Roman tub/showers, large laundry rooms and 2 or 3 car garages. Highland Park is located at the North end of Crestview Drive off Brittan. From $97,900. Call 595-0678.

Los Altos

Ensenada Oaks, 10 outstanding homes at a very desirable address. All homes are on large fenced lots with 3-5 bedrooms plus den, 2½-3 baths, two fireplaces and wet bars. Plus the special Epicurean kitchen with Thermador double ovens (one self-cleaning), Jenn Air Space Range, Waste-King dishwasher and disposer and In-Sink-Erator trash compactor. Priced from $104,950. Call 961-1441.

Los Gatos

In a quiet, secluded area of Los Gatos there's Longmeadow, 4 luxury homes designed for an exciting lifestyle. These homes feature 4-5 bedrooms plus den, fireplaces, gourmet kitchens, large homesites, 3 car garages and many more details and amenities. Located at the end of Longmeadow Drive. From $139,950. Call 961-1441.

Saratoga

The ultimate in luxury—Carnelian Glen—14 individually designed homes in Saratoga. Each home is a statement of its own with careful attention to architectural style, construction and detail. Special materials, swimming pools, landscaped gardens, walkways, terraces, marquees and atriums serve to accentuate the individual architecture of each home. Carnelian Glen features distinctive residences for individuals who seek and can afford the very best. Carnelian Glen is located off the Saratoga/Los Gatos Road across from the entrance to the Villa Montalvo. From $180,000. Call 247-1088 for an appointment.

Next year.

We're already planning ahead. We have 6 homes under construction in Alamo, 49 homes planned for Saratoga, 38 lot line cluster homes in Palo Alto and 63 homes in the San Carlos Hills.

If you're looking for a new home from an established, successful developer, consider Dividend Industries Inc. Our offices are at 3600 Pruneridge in Santa Clara, (408) 247-1088. Prices are subject to change and availability.

See Map Pages 8 & 10

44

San Carlos
Mt.View
Los Altos
Los Gatos
Saratoga

5b

6a

6b

Press advertisements
Annonces de presse
Zeitungs-Inserate

1 France
AD Société Chamar
DIR/DES Gilbert Petit
department store, Warenhaus

2 Israel
AD Israel Export Institute
DIR/ILL Ben Lam

3 Israel
AD Can-Can
AG Karmon
DIR Y. Molcho
ILL Ben Lam
panty hose, Strumpfwaren

4 Israel
AD Lodgia
AG Arieli Adv Ltd
DIR/DES Dali Bahat
ILL Yona Flink
socks, chaussettes, Socken

5a-b Canada
AD Cutex Cosmetics
AG Burns, Cooper, Donahue, Fleming & Co
DIR Terry Isles, McCann Erikson
ILL Heather Cooper
cosmetics

6 France
AD Maxime Delrue
AG J. Walter Thompson SA
DIR/DES Nicole Fabrice
ILL Morris Smith
COPY Thelma Volkman
orange juice, jus d'orange

7a-b Brazil
AD Cianê Co
AG Bureau Técnico de Publicidade BTP Ltda
DIR Jose Agel Kropivka
ILL Miro
COPY Liliana Barabino
fabrics, tissus, Stoff

2

3

4

Shades of things to come.
We're very proud of our new frosted shades. Not just because they're new and ultra-contemporary. But because we can offer them to you at a sensible price. And you'll find that besides being super to look at, the new frosted shades (and all our other Cutex colours) have actually been improved. So they represent more than beautiful colours, they mean a whole new Cutex. For today and especially tomorrow.
The new Cutex Frosted Shades have arrived.

5a

Let your hands come out of their shell.
Think of the soft shimmer that you see when a sea shell is held to the light, and you will begin to realize what Cutex can now do for your hands. For our new opaline shades have arrived and each captures the enchanting, subtle sheen of a pearl, a shell or an opal. And only Cutex can offer you so many shades to choose from, at such a sensible price. The new Cutex opalines.
The new Cutex Opaline Shades have arrived.

5b

TROPICANA
GRAND CRU DE FLORIDE
TROPICANA
Nous pressons. Vous versez.

6

7a

Há 70 anos estamos vivendo juntos e eu nunca disse que te amava. Desculpe.
Este é um caso de amor muito antigo entre Cianê e a mulher brasileira.
Ele sempre trabalhou duro para dar a melhor qualidade, as cores mais modernas e as estampas mais sofisticadas, para transformá-la numa das mulheres mais elegantes do mundo. E como ele ficava feliz quando ela se olhava no espelho e sorria!
Afinal, era por sua causa que ela estava tão bonita. E por incrível que pareça, talvez por excesso de humildade ou por timidez, ele nunca teve coragem de contar a sua vida para ela. Nem mesmo seu nome.
Mas isso não podia continuar assim.
Um tecido que há 70 anos é um dos maiores líderes do mercado, cujas fábricas fazem parte de um conglomerado de mais de 20 empresas e que é considerado um dos maiores experts em moda no Brasil, só poderia ter muito orgulho da sua história. Por isso, o tecido Cianê resolveu se declarar publicamente à mulher brasileira.
Afinal, nunca é tarde para revelar um grande amor.
Mesmo que seja aos 70.
Cianê
O tecido que você sempre usou e nunca soube.
CIANÊ COMPANHIA NACIONAL DE ESTAMPARIA

7b

Eu sempre fui usado por você e você nunca me chamou pelo nome.
Se era para impressionar a namoradinha nova, lá estava ele transformado na camisa mais charmosa do mundo. Se era pra badalar o cliente, nada melhor que aquela calça com a caída impecável que só ele sabia dar.
Sempre incógnito e silencioso, há 70 anos ele vem se deixando usar pelo homem brasileiro. E nem sequer um agradecimento.
Sempre oferecendo sua qualidade, suas cores modernas, suas estampas sofisticadas e sua profunda experiência em moda masculina, sem nunca ser reconhecido.
Mas já é hora de conhecer esse amigo pelo nome: Cianê.
Tecido Cianê.
A partir de hoje, ele tem certeza de que será chamado assim.
Afinal, ninguém deve esquecer o nome de um amigo.
Cianê
O tecido que você sempre usou e nunca soube.
CIANÊ COMPANHIA NACIONAL DE ESTAMPARIA

Press advertisements
Annonces de presse
Zeitungs-Inserate

1a-b Switzerland
AD Atlantis Hotel AG
AG Adolf Wirz AG
DIR A. Bosshard
DES R. de Wijs
ILL A. Bosshard
hotel

2 Turkey
AD Anka
AG San Grafik
DIR/DES Mengü Ertel
newsagency, Agence de Presse, Presse ageutur

3a-b United States
AD Asylum Records
AG E/A Records
DIR (a) Anne Garner
(b) Tony Lane
ILL (a) Norman Seeff
(b) Bob Meyers
record, disque

4a-b Hong Kong
AD Hong Kong Land
AG Clic Studios Ltd
Chi Fu Fa Yuen new town construction company

5 Spain
AD Chasyr 1879 Assegurances
AG Mass-Media
DIR Pere Ariño
DES E. Gandara, P. Ariño
Insurance company celebrating the first Catalan periodical since the Spanish Civil War

6a-b Switzerland
AD Sabez
AG Gisler & Gisler
DIR/DES Erich Hartmann
COPY Peter Schulz
bathroom, salle de bain, Badezimmer

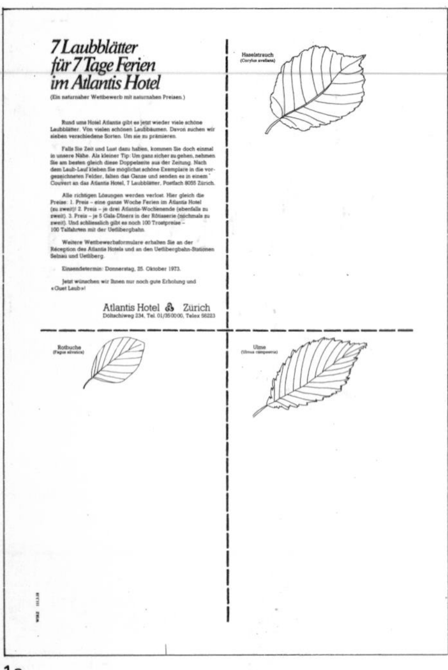

1a

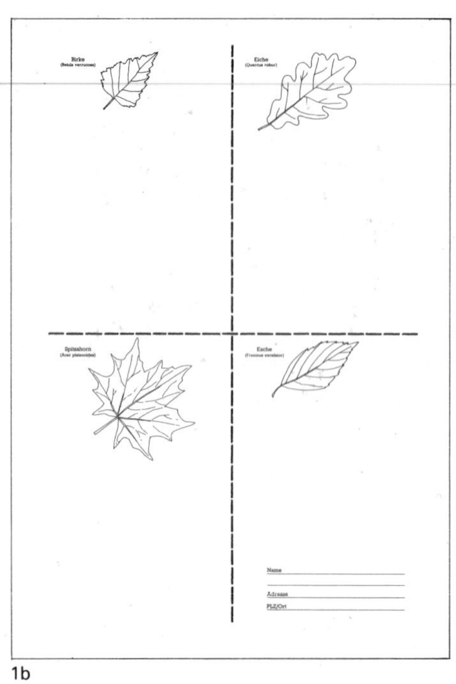

1b

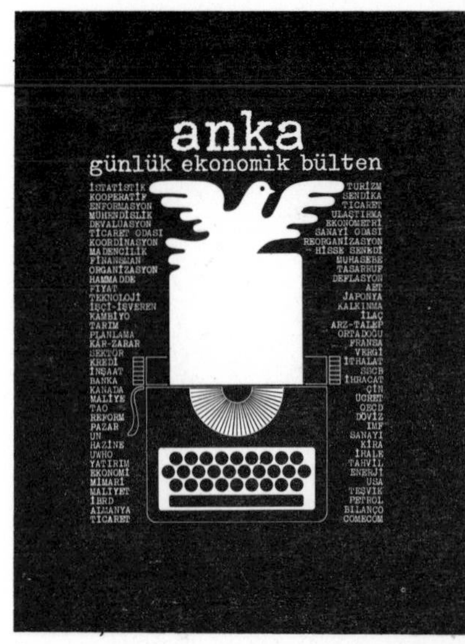

2

3a

HAUNTING...

"COYOTE" (E-45377) YOU'LL HEAR IT, LONG AFTER YOU HEAR IT.
JONI MITCHELL'S NEW SINGLE FROM THE ALBUM, HEJIRA. ON ASYLUM RECORDS.

3b

TOM WAITS · SMALL CHANGE

TOM WAITS, WHO SINGS OF WAITRESSES', STRIPPERS, AND OLD CARS, OF DOWN AND OUTS WHO ARE INTO MUSCATEL AND GIN, AND OF LATE NIGHTS AND SMOKEY BARROOMS IS BACK WITH SMALL CHANGE HIS FOURTH ALBUM ON ASYLUM RECORDS. WAITS' MUSIC IS A LESSON IN REALITY WITH ITS BLUESY, JAZZY AND COOL PRESENTATION OF PAIN, POVERTY, AND PERVERSION. SMALL CHANGE, A SMALL PRICE TO PAY FOR A CONTEMPORARY TALENT.

PRODUCED BY BONES HOWE FOR MR. BONES PRODUCTIONS, INC.

THE PIANO HAS BEEN DRINKING... NOT ME! THE PIANO HAS BEEN DRINKING!!

OF DOLLARS CAN'T CHANGE THAT. SMALL CHANGE GOT RAINED ON WITH HIS OWN 38

UR-GH-H-H HM-M-M-M

I CAN'T WAIT TO GET OFF WORK & MY BABY,

Small Change · Tom Waits

tom waits nighthawks at the diner

AVAILABLE ON ASYLUM RECORDS & TAPES.

asylum

7 Germany
AD Max Bruestle
AG Volker Zahm Werbung
DES Barbara Buchwald
COPY M. Bruestle
ready-to-wear fashions

4a

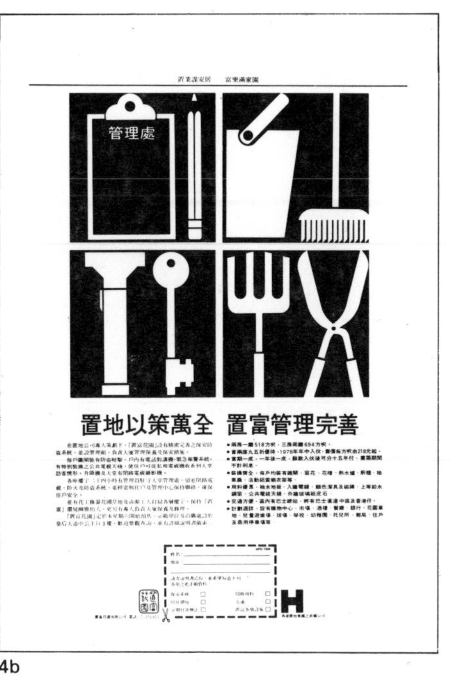

4b

5

6a

6b

Aktion gegen langweilige Badezimmer

z.B.
ein fröhlicher Duschvorhang

damit Sie nach Herzenslust spritzen können.

In unseren Ausstellungsräumen finden Sie alles, was auch Ihr Bad schöner machen kann.

sabez

Kreuzstrasse 54, 8008 Zürich
Tel. 01/47 35 10

7

Bookjackets
Chemises de Livres
Buchumschläge

1 Switzerland
AD Kunst Kreis Luzern
DES Hans Erni
ILL Hans Erni
series of monographs

2a-b Hungary
DIR István Balogh
ILL István Orosz
insect alphabeth

1

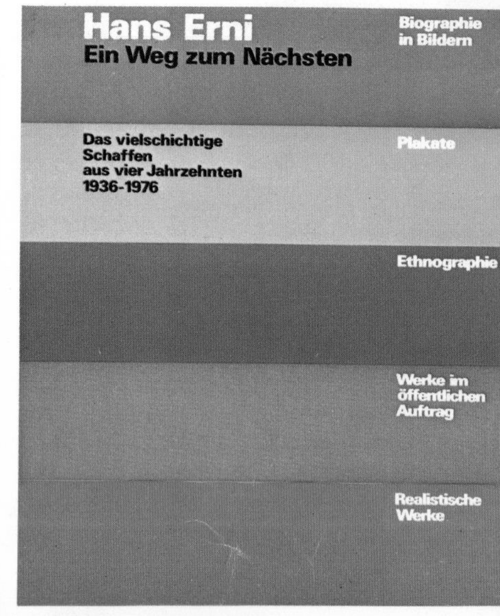

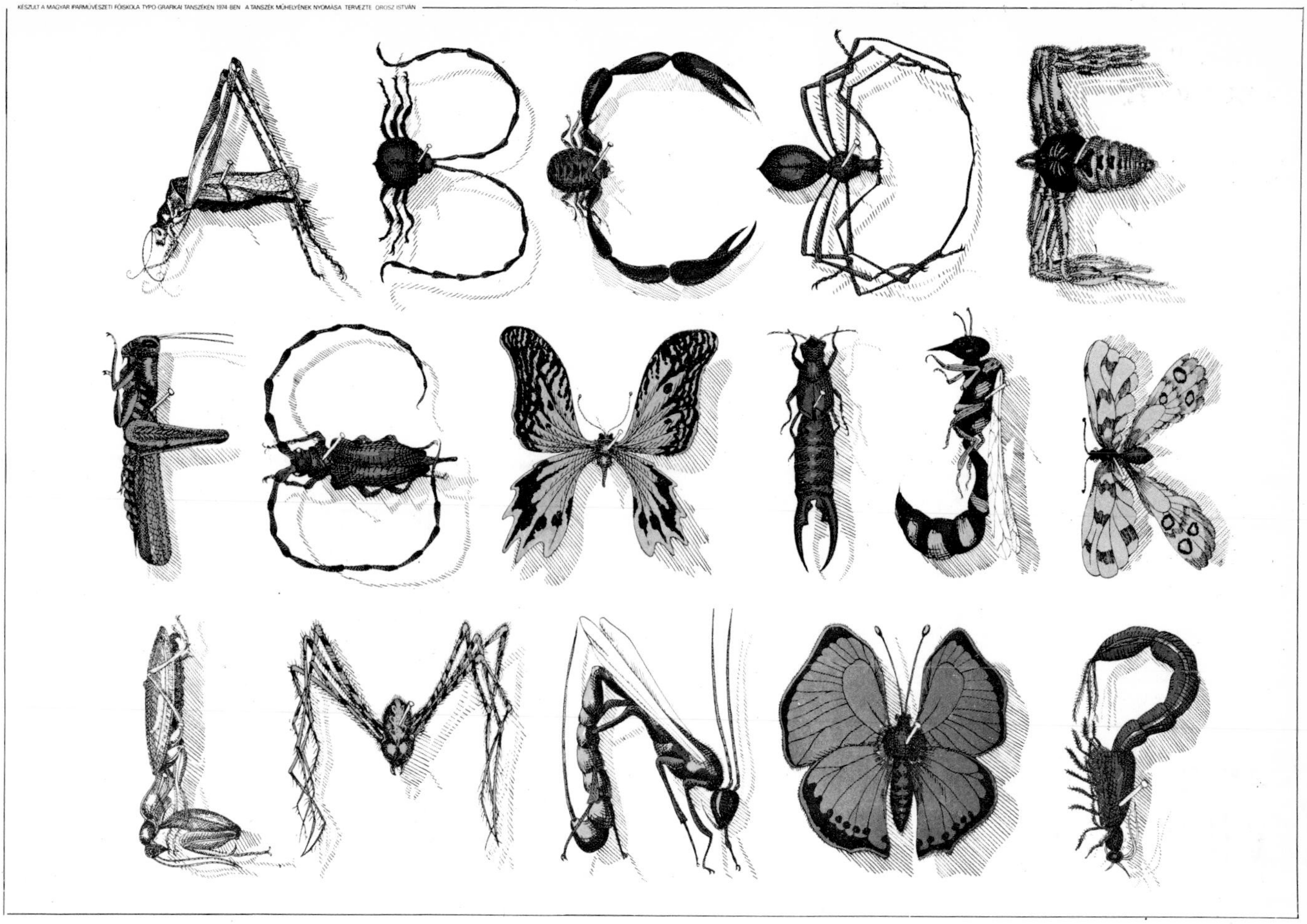

KÉSZULT A MAGYAR IPARMŰVÉSZETI FŐISKOLA TYPO-GRAFIKAI TANSZÉKÉN 1974-BEN A TANSZÉK MŰHELYÉNEK NYOMÁSA TERVEZTE OROSZ ISTVÁN

2a

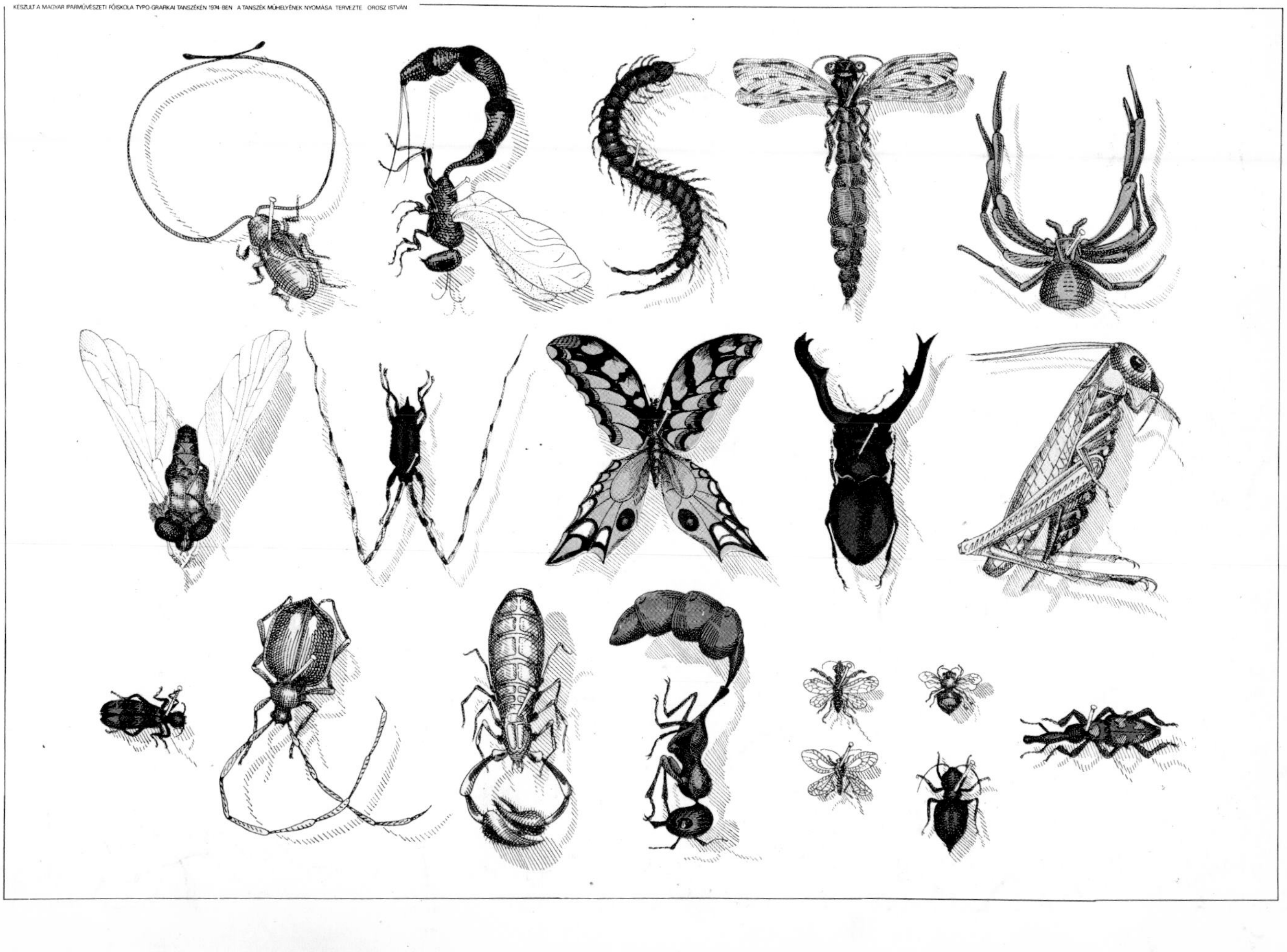

KÉSZULT A MAGYAR IPARMŰVÉSZETI FŐISKOLA TYPO-GRAFIKAI TANSZÉKÉN 1974-BEN A TANSZÉK MŰHELYÉNEK NYOMÁSA TERVEZTE OROSZ ISTVÁN

2b

Typefaces
Caractères
Schrifttypen

1a-c Great Britain
AD/AG Face Photosetting
DIR Michael Chave
DES Patricia Cutler
(a) 'Bellini Original'
(b) 'Futura Demi Bold Script'
(c) 'Roller'

2 United States
AD Photo-Lettering
AG Stano & Sweeny
DIR/DES Nicholas M. Stano
new alphabet design

3 France
AD Hollenstein
ILL Jean Alessandrini
typeface '1900'

4a-b Brazil
AD Mecanorma
DES Hans J. Donner, Sylvia Trenker
typefaces

5 Germany
AD Mecanorma, France
AG Zembsch Werkstatt
DIR/DES Dieter Zembsch
new typeface

6 Japan
AD Type Bank
AG T. Degro
DES Masakatscu Suga
new typeface

ABCDEFGHIJKLMNOPQRSTUVWXYZÆŒ

abcdefghijklmnopqrstuvwxyzæœøß

£1234567890 &.:;,"''"!?()-

ABCDEEFGHIJJKLMNOPQRSTUVWXYZ

abcdefghijkklmnopqrrsstuvwxyz

£1234567890&&.,:;""–"!?()æœøßÆŒØ

ABCDEFGHIJKLMNOPQRSTUVWXYZ

abcdefghijklmnopqrstuvwxyz

£1234567890&.,:;""-!?()

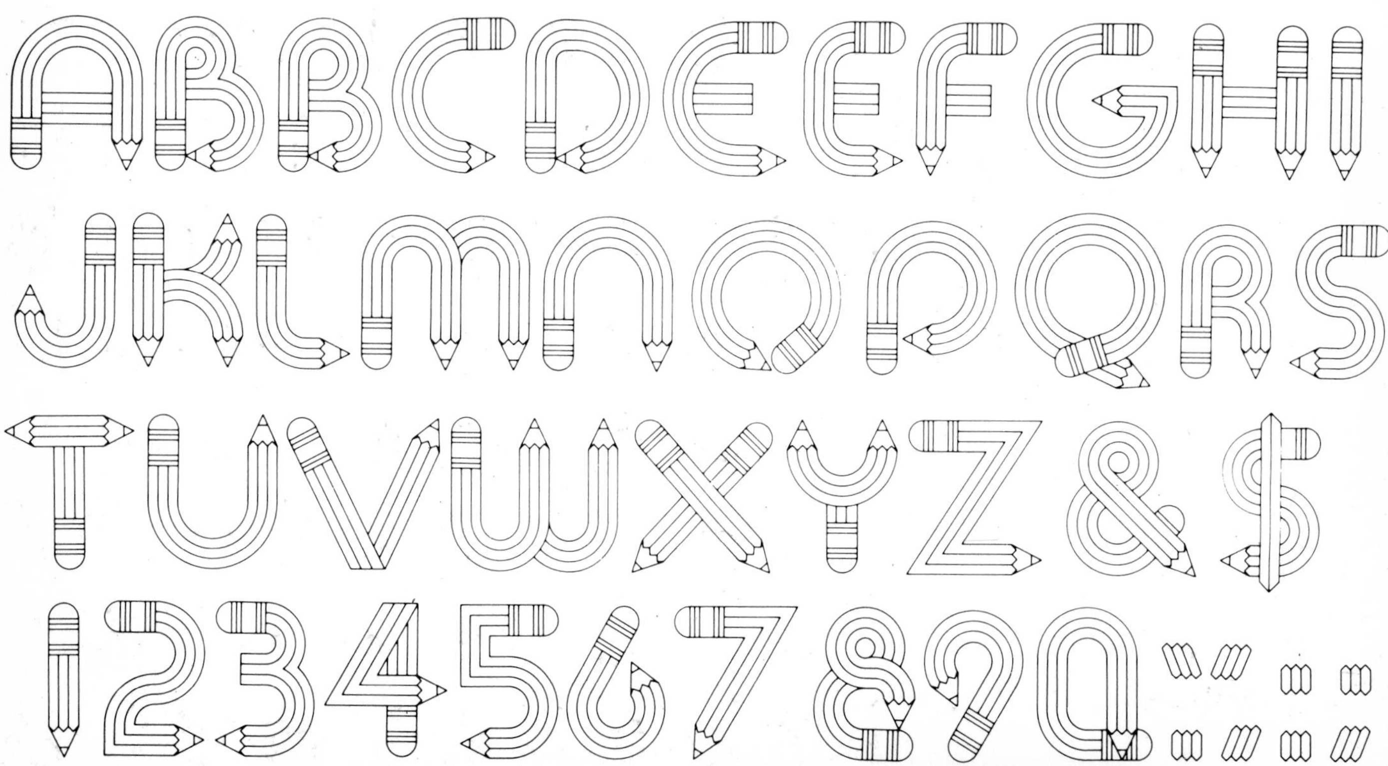

ABCDEFGHIJKLMNOPQRSTUVWXYZ&.

abcdefghijklmnopqrstuvwxyz?!

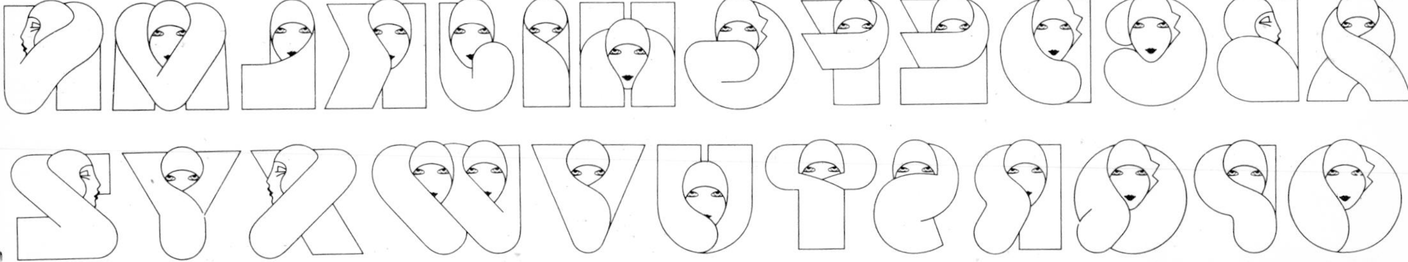

AA BCDEFGHIJKLMNOPQR

STUVWXYZ 1234567890.

$ÇØ! &%£ ?(:) ÆŒç_

AABCDEEF
FGGHHIJKLLLM
MNOOPQ
QURRSSTTUV
VVWIYYZ
ÆŒUE
!?&$;.,()//&

abcedeef
flggghhijklm
nopqrsstatt
tuzuvvvvwxyy
zA1122345
678890O

あいうえおかきくけこさ
しすせそたちつてとなに
ぬねのはひふへほぱぴぷ
ぺぽまみむめもやゆよら
りるれろわをんゞー｜ぁ
ぃぅぇぉゃゅょゎっ;:、。„”
= ॥ ∷ ∴ ‥ ・・― ¡ ～ ∫ ¥ ”
1234567890O

Typefaces
Caractères
Schrifttypen

1a-c Italy
AD Nebiolo SpA
AG (b, c) Giob
DIR/DES (a) Pino Tovaglia
(b, c) R. Del Sordo,
G. Berlinghieri
typefaces

2a-b Germany
AD Deutsche Letraset GmbH
DES/ILL Christof Gassner
COPY Gunther Kopp, Reinhold Jakob
art material

3a-d Germany
AD/AG H. Berthold AG
DIR Götz Gunnar Görissen
DES Wolfgang Schulze
typefaces

4a-c Germany
AD Heinz Knauer
DES Dietrich K. Fröbisch
typefaces

4d Germany
AD Heinz Knauer
DES Dieter K. Fröbisch
COPY Gerd A. Schuster, London
Christmas present

1a

1b

1c

2a

4 1976 ART MATERIAL MAGAZIN LETRASET

LetraTime

13 neue Typen von Letraset

2b

5/1976 ART MATERIAL MAGAZIN LETRASET

LetraTime

Letra SchriftFamilien Chronik

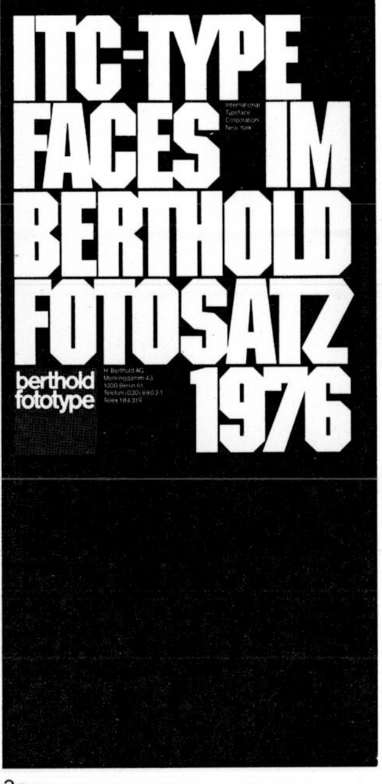

3a

3b

abcdefghijklmnopqrstuvwxyz
ABCDEFGHIJKLMNOPQRSTUVWXYZ
1234567890(&.,:;!?'''''-—*$¢%)

26
good
reasons
to use
Newtext
Reg. Italic

Excellence in typography is the result of nothing more than an attitude. Its appeal comes from the understanding used in its planning; the designer must care. In contemporary advertising, the perfect integration of design elements often demands unorthodox typography. It may require the use of compact spacing, minus leading, unusual sizes and weights; whatever is needed to improve appearance and impact. Stating specific principles or

Excellence in typography is the result of nothing more than an attitude. Its appeal comes from the understanding used in its planning; the designer must care. In contemporary advertising, the perfect integration of design elements often demands unorthodox typography. It may require the use of compact spacing, minus leading, unusual sizes and weights; whatever is needed to improve appearance and impact. Stating specific principles

3c

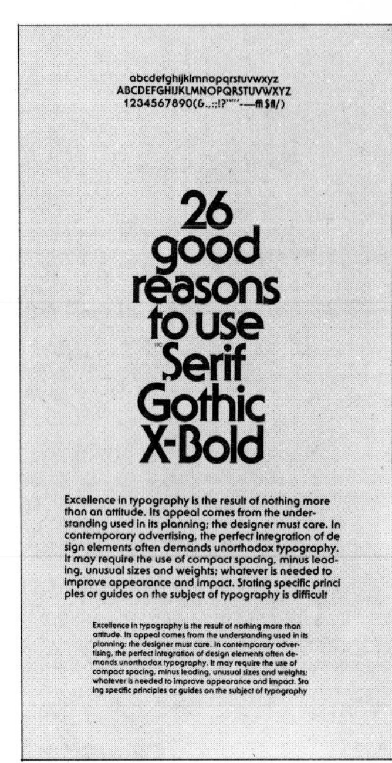

3d

4a

LOVE LANE

4b

Eine schmale verkümmerte Gasse zwischen vorgestreckten Hinterhöfen, leicht ansteigend, halb erdrückt, ihr Beginn kaum eine Lücke zwischen den Häusern der Thomas Street, London S. E. 18. Aber der Name stimmt. Da steht es. Love Lane. Drei Meter hohe, in Stufen ansteigende, verputzfleckige Ziegelmauern auf beiden Seiten, schartige Flaschenscherbengebisse auf ihren Kronen, dornige Stacheldrahtverhaue, verbeulte Wellblechflächen in kaltem Blaugrün.

4c

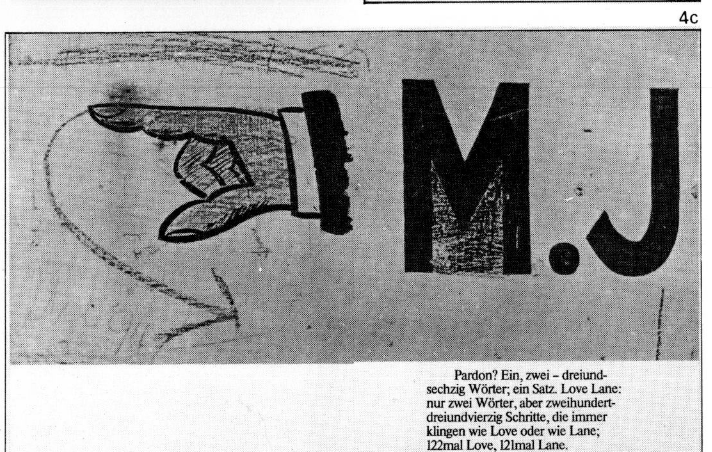

Pardon? Ein, zwei – dreiundsechzig Wörter; ein Satz. Love Lane: nur zwei Wörter, aber zweihundertdreiundvierzig Schritte, die immer klingen wie Love oder wie Lane; 122mal Love, 121mal Lane.

4d

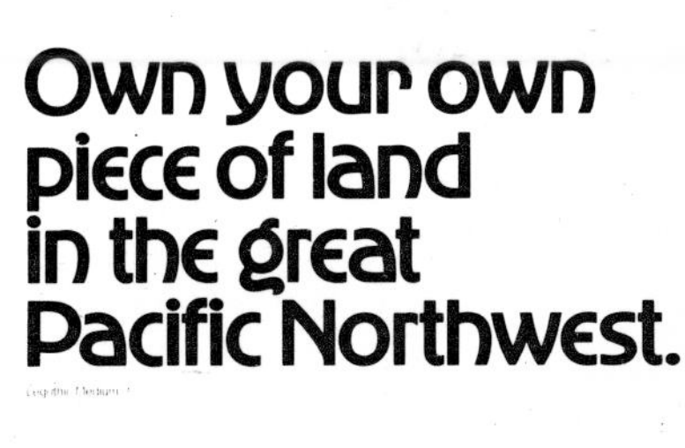

"I
WISH"

Send for this
free booklet
full of very
expensive
ideas.

Century Schoolbook Open

Century Schoolbook Heavyweight

Bookjackets
Chemises de Livres
Buchumschläge

1 Great Britain
AD Penguin
AG Pentagram
DIR Alan Fletcher
DES Julia Alldridge

2 Great Britain
AD Penguin
AG Pentagram
DIR/DES Mervyn Kurlansky
ILL John Stone

3 United States
AD Scholastic Book Publishers
AG Barnett/Goslin/Barnett
DIR/DES Dennis Barnett

4a-c Spain
AD Alianza Editorial SA
DES Daniel Gil

5 Brazil
AD Círculo do Livro SA
DES Alfredo Aquino

6 Norway
AD Gyldendal Norsk Forlag
DIR/DES Peter Haars

7 Germany
AD Rowohlt Taschenbuchverlag
AG Ziegenfeuter
DIR M. Waller
DES Dieter Ziegenfeuter

8 Spain
AD Circuló de Lectores SA
DES Javier Noguera

9 Sweden
AD GLA forlag
DES Stellan Kristenson

1

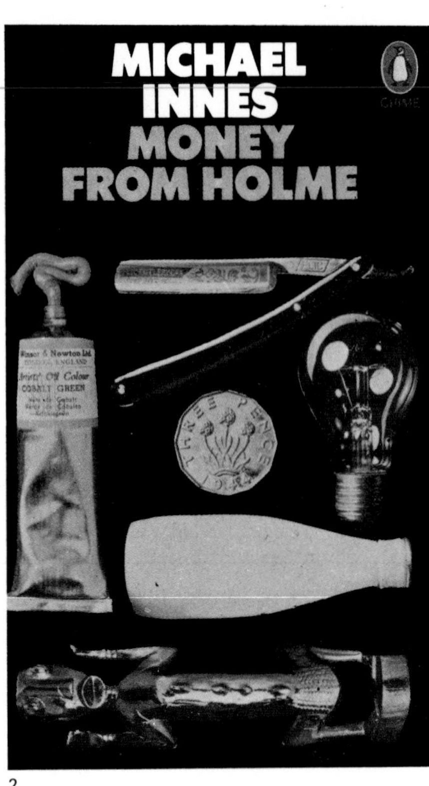

2

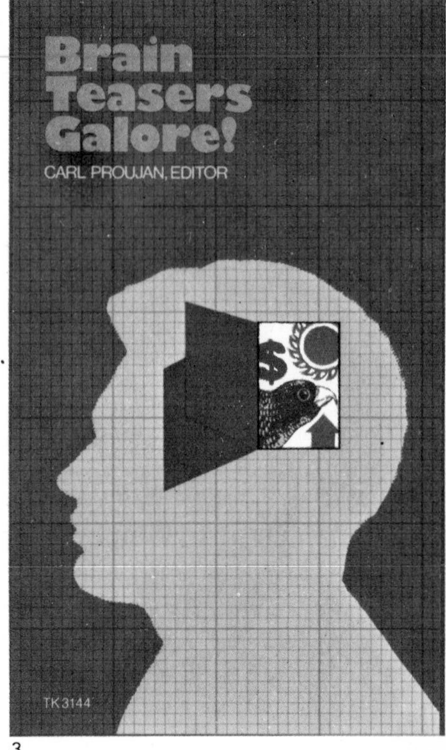

3

4a
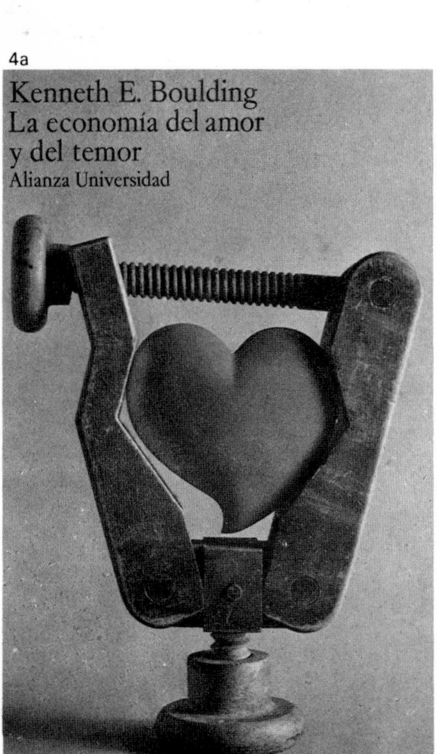

4b
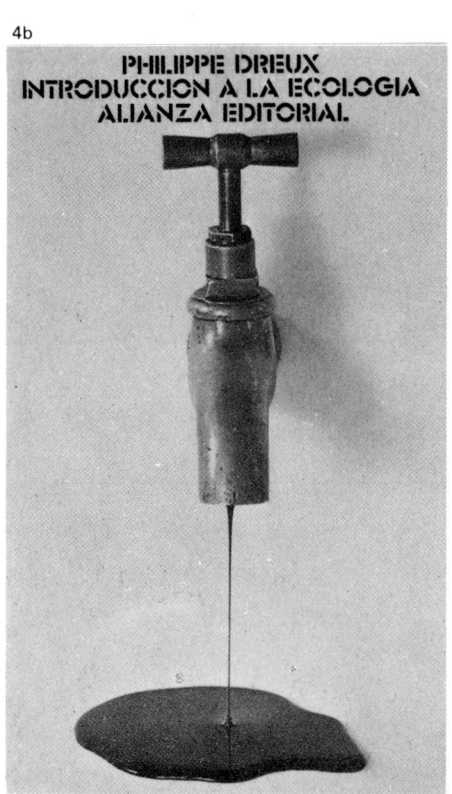

4c

10 Italy
AD Editoriale Bari
AG Studio de Liso
DIR/DES Geppi de Liso
ILL Dicandia-Marangio

5

6

7

8

9

10

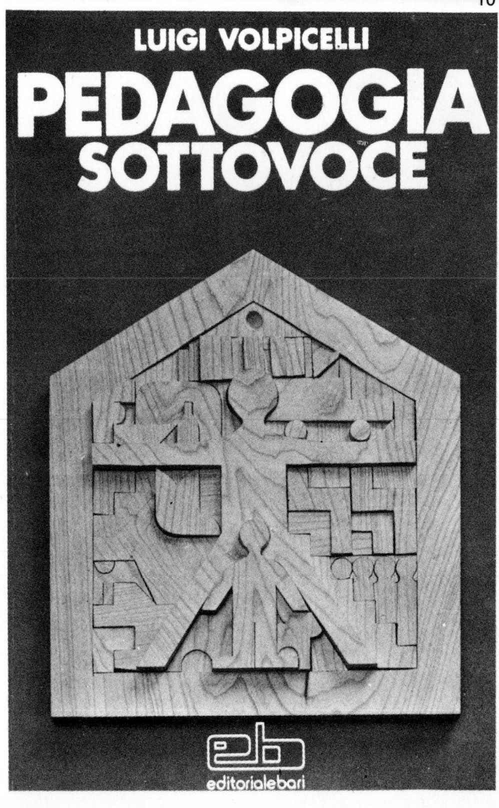

Bookjackets
Chemises de Livres
Buchumschläge

1 Great Britain
AD Robson Books
ILL Shelagh McGee

2 Great Britain
AD Transworld Publishers
DIR John Munday
DES Denise McAllister
ILL Rowan Barnes Murphy

3 Australia
AD Cassell Publishers, Australia
DES Jack Larkin

4a-b Italy
AD Nicola Zanichelli SpA
ILL Sergio Salaroli

5 Hungary
AD/AG Móra Ferenc
DES László Réber

6a-b United States
AD Scholastic
DIR Skip Sorvino
DES (a) Penny Coleman
(b) Martha Savitzky
ILL (a) Lionel Kalish
(b) Jared Lee

7 Great Britain
AD Frederick Warne
ILL Agnes Molnar

1

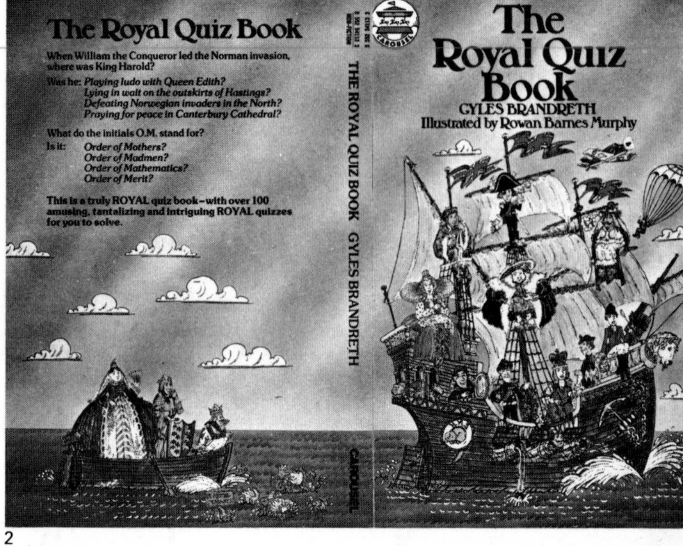

2

3

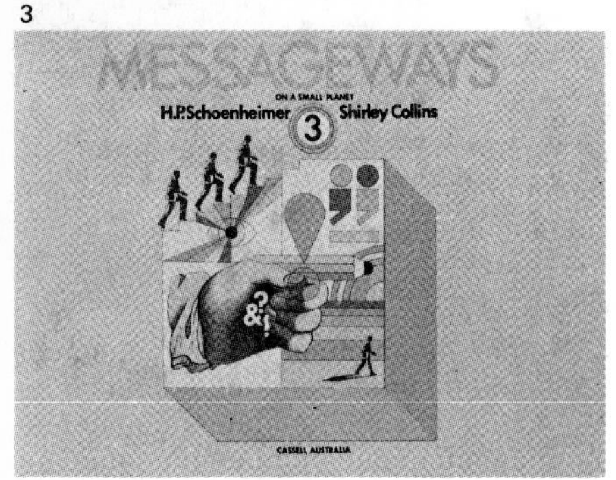

4a

4b

5

6a

6b

8 Italy
AD Giulio Einaudi
DES Cristina Lastrego, Francesco Testa

9 Germany (DDR)
AD Verlag Junge Welt Berlin
DES Christina Petzak
ILL Egbert Herfurth

10 Great Britain
AD Macmillan Education
ILL Ron van der Meer

11 Great Britain
AD Robson Books
ILL John Astrop

12 Great Britain
AD Transworld Publishers Ltd
AG Roman, Moira Buj
DIR John Munday
DES/ILL Roman Buj

13 France
AD Bayard Presse
DES Martin Berthommier

14 Switzerland
AD Diogenes Verlag
AG/DES Walter Grieder

15 Turkey
AD Akbank
AG San Grafik
DIR/DES Leyla Ugansu
children's theatre

16 Germany
AD Heinmük-Verlag
ILL Eva-Maria Ott-Heidmann

7

8

9

10

11

12

13

14

15

16

Bookjackets
Chemises de Livres
Buchumschläge

1 Holland
AD Kluwer Technische Boeken
AG I.D. Unit
DES Robert Schaap

2a-b United States
AD Simon & Schuster
AG Barnett/Goslin/Barnett
DIR Frank Metz
DES (a) David Barnett, Charles Goslin
(b) David Barnett

3a-c Hungary
AD Corvina
Photo Károly Gink

4 United States
AD Franklin Watts Inc
DIR Judi Mills
DES Frances Jetter

5 France
AD Cal
AG Primart
DIR/DES Ulrich Meyer

6a-b Great Britain
AD Weidenfeld & Nicholson
DIR Behram Kapadia
DES (a) James Campus
(b) Grant Bradford
ILL (a) Honeysett
(b) Colleen Payne

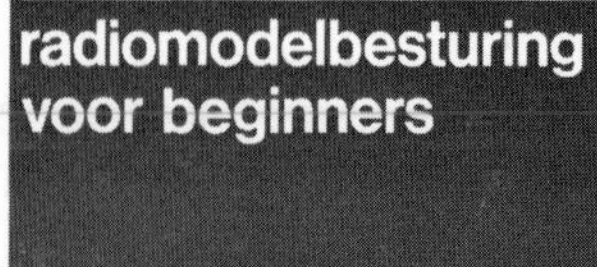

1

2a

The latest Sunday collection! A feast of solving for the ardent puzzler and the neophyte...
CROSSWORDS FROM THE TIMES
Series 30
Fifty extra-tantalizing puzzles especially selected from the famous Sunday New York Times Magazine feature for their debut in book form and edited by MARGARET FARRAR
$2.95

2b

3a

3b

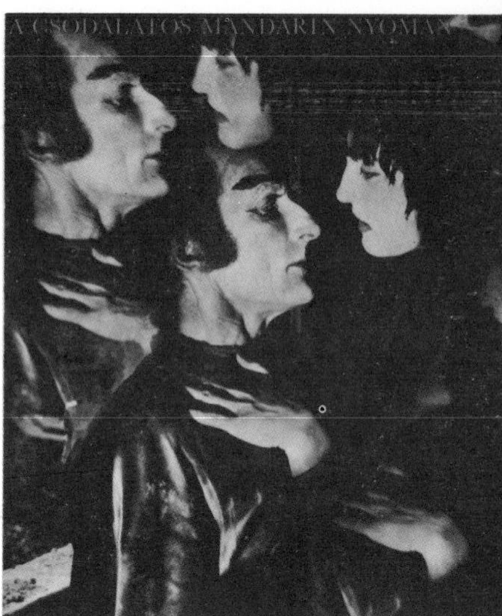

3c

4

5

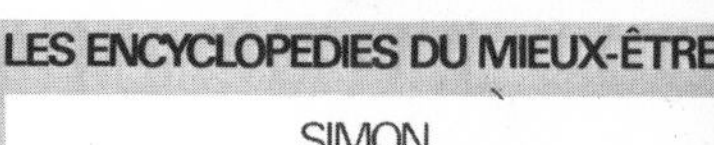

7a-b Italy
AD Arnoldo Mondadori
AG Servizio Grafico Editoriale
DIR Bruno Binosi
DES Ferruccio Bocca

8a-b Great Britain
AD Oxford University Press
DIR/DES Arthur Lockwood
ILL (a) Mike Abrahams
(b) Geoffrey Drury

9 Turkey
AD Dergah publishing company
DIR/DES Bülent Erkmen

10 Italy
AD Arnoldo Mondadori Editore
AG Servizio Grafico Editoriale
DIR Bruno Binosi
DES Ferruccio Bocca

11 Australia
AD Macmillan Publishers Australia
DES Jack Larkin

12 Germany
AD Presse und informationsamt des Landes Berlin
DIR Wolfgang Kruse
DES Martin Wilke

13 Germany
AD Fischer Taschenbuch Verlag
AG Studio Laeis
DIR/DES Christoph Laeis

6a

6b

7a

7b

8a

8b
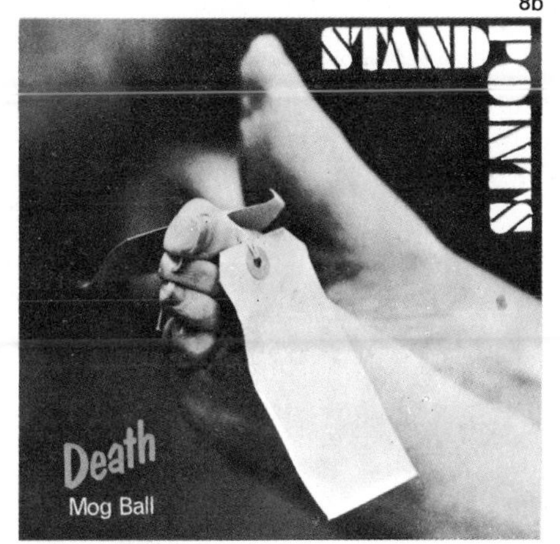

9
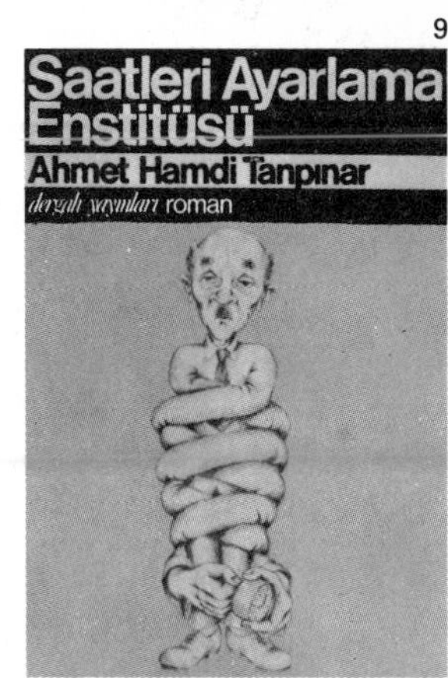

10
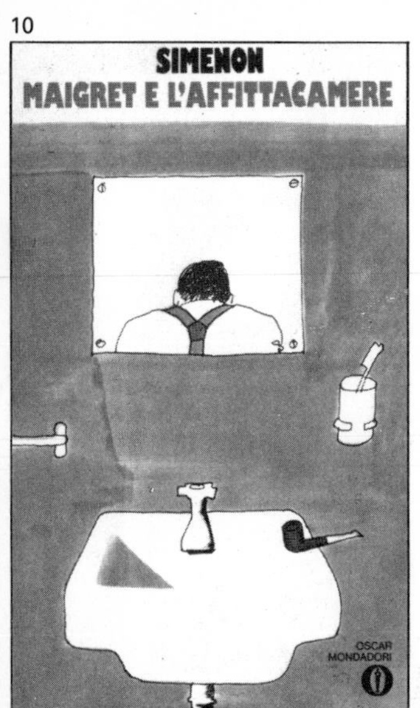

11

12
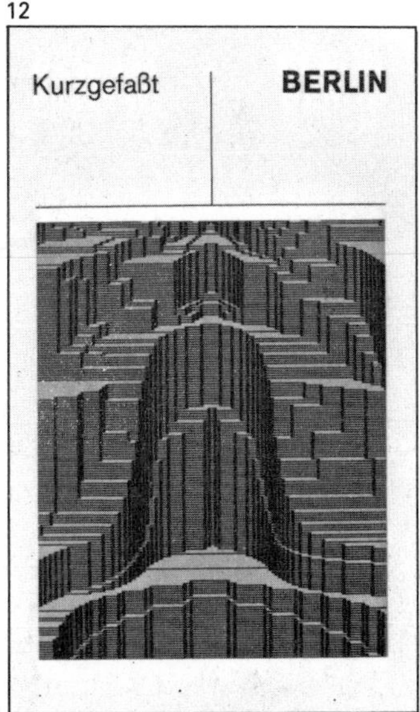

13

Bookjackets
Chemises de Livres
Buchumschläge

1 France
AD AGEP
DIR Francisco Hidalgo
DES Gerard Gagnepain
PH Francisco Hidalgo
Book of Paris, cover illustration

2 Great Britain
AD Hodder & Stoughton
AG Tony Page Associates
DIR/DES Tony Page

3 United States
AD Houghton Mifflin Co
AG Wendell Minor Design
DIR Louise Noble
DES Wendell Minor

4 Germany
AD C. Bertelsmann Verlag
AG Zembsch Werkstatt
DES Dieter Zembsch

5 Germany
AD Büchergilde Gutenberg
DES Michael Mathias Prechtl

6 Spain
AD Granica Editor
AG C. Rolando & Asociados
DIR C. Rolando
DES C. Rolando, Marta Rourich

7 Great Britain
AD Ebury Press
DIR Derek Morrison
DES Richard Tilley

8 Great Britain
AD Robson Books Ltd
DES Harold King

1

2

3

4

5

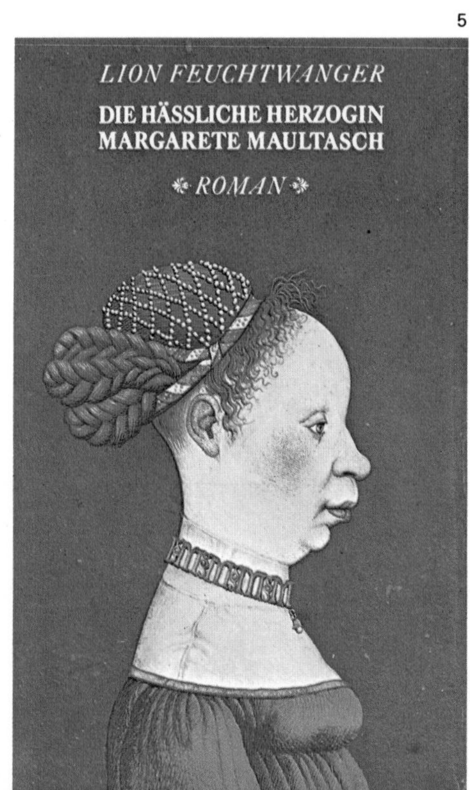

6

9 Holland
AD Rijksmuseum Kröller-Müller
DES Pieter Brattinga

10 Yugoslavia
AD Institute for Psychology of the Faculty of Philosophy Beograd
AG Studio Structure
DIR Masic Slobodan
DES Masic Saveta, Masic Slobodan
ILL Nikolic Branislav

11 Great Britain
AD Martin Robertson
AG Your Company By Design Ltd
DIR/DES Derrick Holmes

12 France
AD Librairie Eugène Belin
AG Atelier de creation Belin
DIR Mario Pasini
ILL Roger Blachon

7

8

9

10
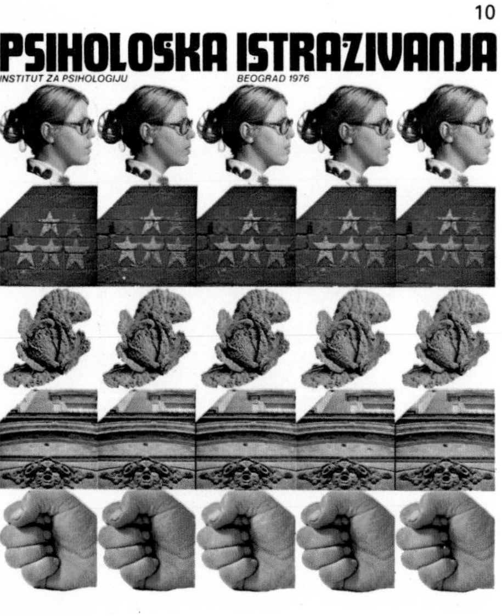

11

12

Bookjackets
Chemises de Livres
Buchumschläge

1 France
AD Librairie Eugène Belin
AG Atelier de créations Belin
DIR Mario Pasini
DES Roland Leygue

2 Finland
AD Otava
AG Ateljee Omppu
DIR/DES Osmo Omenamäki

3 United States
AD Scholastic Book Publishers
AG Barnett/Goslin/Barnett
DIR/DES Dennis Barnett

4 Switzerland
AD International Montreux Festival
AG Publicité Bornand + Gaeng
DIR/DES Bruno Gaeng
ILL Giuseppe Pino, Milan

5 Italy
AD Zanichelli Editore
DES Cristina Lastrego, Francesco Testa

6a-b Norway
AD (a) Norske Bokklubben
(b) Gyldendal Norsk
DES Hans Jørgen Toming

7a-d France
AD (a) Folio, (b, c) Promesses,
(d) Editions la Noria
ILL Jean Alessandrini

8a-b Great Britain
AD Boosey & Hawkes
AG Pentagram
DIR Mervyn Kurlansky
DES Mervyn Kurlansky, Jane Parnaby
ILL Anna Pugh

9 France
AD Publications Paul Montel
DES/ILL Gilbert Petit

1

2

3

4

5

6a

6b

7a

7b

7c

7d

8a

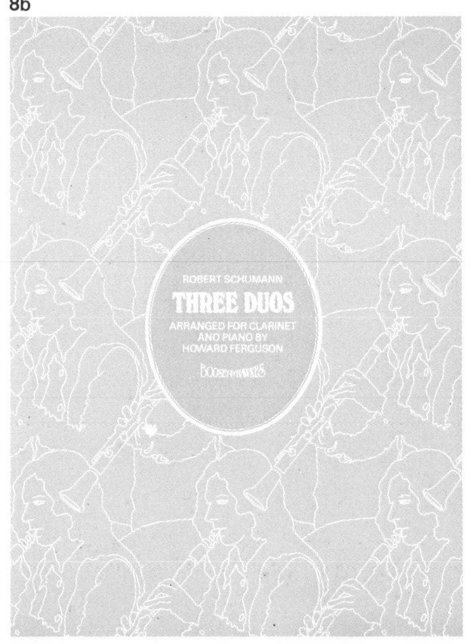

8b

9

Postage-stamp designs
Dessins de-Timbres -poste
Briefmarken Entwürfe

1a-c Sweden
AD Royal Swedish Post Office
DES Dahlbäck & Berglund

2a-h Sweden
AD Royal Swedish Post Office
DES (a) Birgitta Lundberg
(b) R. Holmquist
(c,d) O. Sörling
(e) Nisse Zetterberg
(f) Kerstin Abram Nilson
(g) P. A. Persson
(h) Jan Magnusson

3 Australia
DES Bruce Weatherhead

4 Czechoslovakia
DES Klaus Ensikat,
Engraver L. Jirka

5a-c Switzerland
DES (a) Walter Haettenschweiler
(b) Kurth Wirth
(c) Bornand & Gaeng

6 Japan
DES Takashi Shimizu

7a-b Israel
DES E. Weishoff

8 Brazil
DES Ari Fagundez

9 Jersey
AG Crown Agents
DES Jennifer Toombs

1a

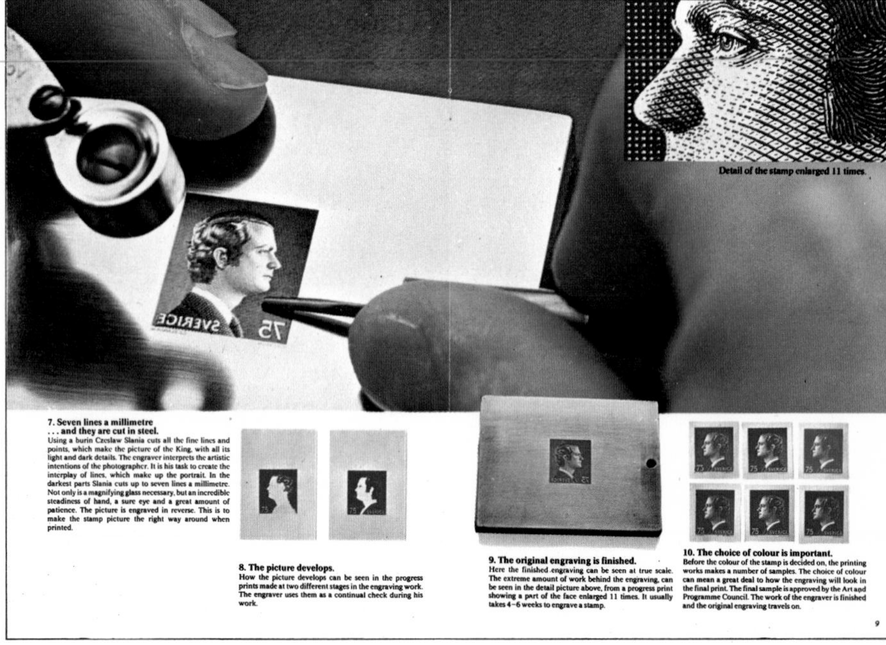

Detail of the stamp enlarged 11 times.

7. Seven lines a millimetre ... and they are cut in steel.
Using a burin Czeslaw Slania cuts all the fine lines and points, which make the picture of the King, with all its light and dark details. The engraver interprets the artistic intentions of the photographer. It is his task to create the interplay of lines, which make up the portrait. In the darkest parts Slania cuts up to seven lines a millimetre. Not only is a magnifying glass necessary, but an incredible steadiness of hand, a sure eye and a great amount of patience. The picture is engraved in reverse. This is to make the stamp picture the right way around when printed.

8. The picture develops.
How the picture develops can be seen in the progress prints made at two different stages in the engraving work. The engraver uses them as a continual check during his work.

9. The original engraving is finished.
Here the finished engraving can be seen at true scale. The extreme amount of work behind the engraving, can be seen in the detail picture above, from a progress print showing a part of the face enlarged 11 times. It usually takes 4–6 weeks to engrave a stamp.

10. The choice of colour is important.
Before the colour of the stamp is decided on, the printing works makes a number of samples. The choice of colour can mean a great deal to how the engraving will look in the final print. The final sample is approved by the Art and Programme Council. The work of the engraver is finished and the original engraving travels on.

9

1b

1c

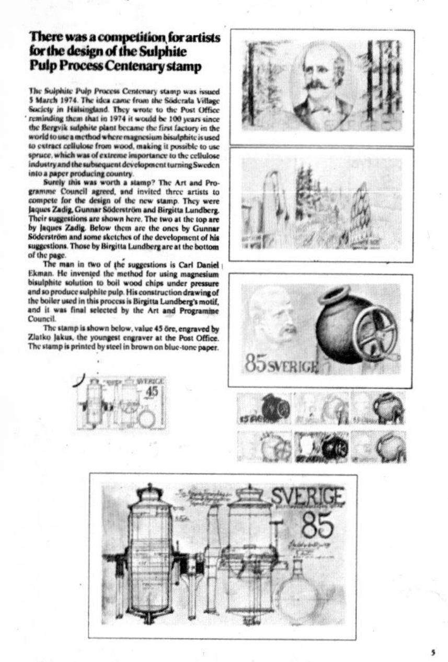

There was a competition for artists for the design of the Sulphite Pulp Process Centenary stamp

The Sulphite Pulp Process Centenary stamp was issued 5 March 1974. The idea came from the Söderala Village Society in Hälsingland. They wrote to the Post Office reminding them that in 1974 it would be 100 years since the Bergvik sulphite plant became the first factory in the world to use a method where magnesium bisulphite is used to extract cellulose from wood, making it possible to use spruce, which was of extreme importance to the cellulose industry and the subsequent development turning Sweden into a paper producing country.

Surely this was worth a stamp? The Art and Programme Council agreed, and invited three artists to compete for the design of the new stamp. They were Jaques Zadig, Gunnar Söderström and Birgitta Lundberg. Their suggestions are shown here. The two at the top are by Jaques Zadig. Below them are the ones by Gunnar Söderström and some sketches of the development of his suggestions. Those by Birgitta Lundberg are at the bottom of the page.

The man in two of the suggestions is Carl Daniel Ekman. He invented the method for using magnesium bisulphite solution to boil wood chips under pressure and so produce sulphite pulp. His construction drawing of the boiler used in this process is Birgitta Lundberg's motif, and it was final selected by the Art and Programme Council.

The stamp is shown below, value 45 öre, engraved by Zlatko Jakus, the youngest engraver at the Post Office. The stamp is printed by steel in brown on blue-tone paper.

85 SVERIGE

SVERIGE 45

SVERIGE 85

5

2a 2b 2c 2d 2e 2f 2g 2h

0 Malta
ES Anthony de Giovanni

1 Israel
ES A. Kalderon

2a-b Belgium
ES (a) M. H. Binneweg
(b) M. A. Pasture

13a-c Netherlands
DES (a) Otto Treumann
(b) Gratama, De Vries, Van der Toorn
(c) Gerrit Noordzij

14 Czechoslovakia
DES K. Svolinsky

15 India
DES Benoy Sarkar

96-97

3

4

5a

5b

7

8

5c

6

9

10

11

12a

12b

13a

13b

14

15

13c

Postage-stamp designs
Dessins de Timbres-poste
Briefmarken Entwürfe

1 Belgium
DES J. de Vos

2 Bangladesh
DES A. F. Karim

3a-c Pakistan
DES (a) Mian Mohammad Sahib
(b) Adil Salahuddin
(c) Mukhtar Ahmed

4 Malaysia
DES MAB Studios

5 India
DES Benoy Sarkar

6 Swaziland
AG Crown Agents
DES Jennifer Toombs

7 Brazil
DES Aluisio Carvao

8 Indonesia
DES Masino Nsd

9a-c Portugal
DES (a) Jorge Vidal
(b,c) Antonio Garcia

10 Belgium
DES Malvaux Studio

11 Denmark
DES Dan Sterup

12a-b Netherlands
DES (a) Donald Patiwael
(b) Gratama de Vries/
Van der Toorn

13 India
DES Benoy Sarkar

14 Bulgaria
DES Lyudmil Chechlarov

15 Czechoslovakia
DES J. Liesler

1

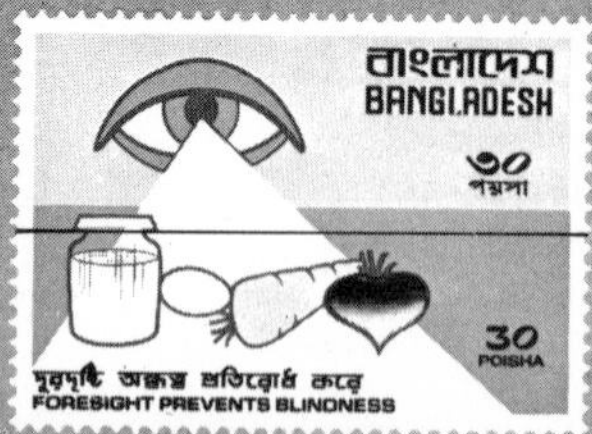

2

3a

3b

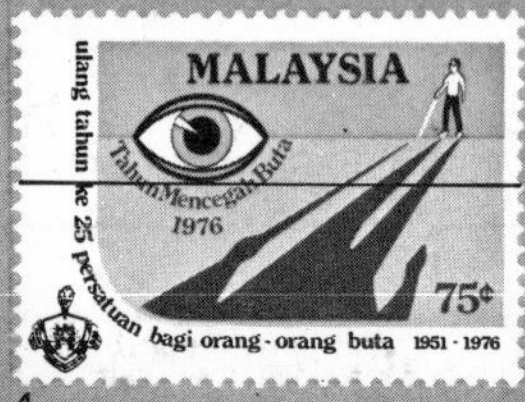

4

5

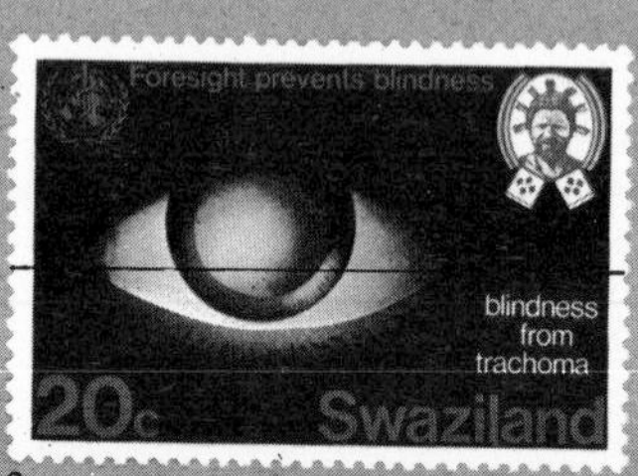

6

3c

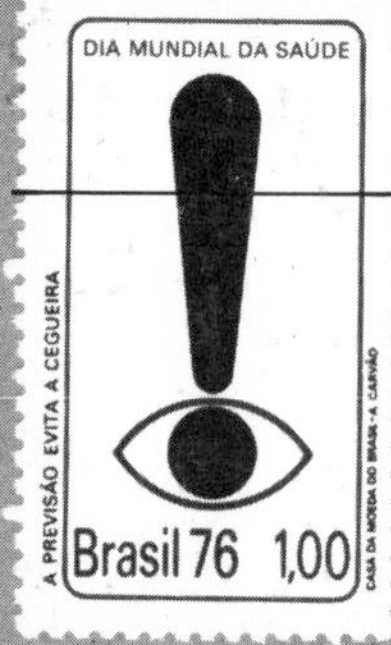

7

8

9a

9b

9c

10

11

12a

12b

13

14

15

16

16 Turkey
DES Namik Bajik

Black and African Festival of Arts

17 Ghana
AG Crown Agents
DES Rena Femesy

18 Mauritius
AG Crown Agents
DES B.G. Studios

19 Nigeria
AG Crown Agents
DES O. I. Oshiga

20 Guyana
AG Crown Agents Stamp Bureau
DES P.A.D. Studio

Popular Art

21 Papua New Guinea
AG Crown Agents
DES R. Bates

22a-b Solomon Islands
AG Crown Agents
DES John Cooter

23 Gilbert Islands
AG Crown Agents
DES John Cooter.

24 Hong Kong
DES Tao-Ho

25a-b St. Lucia
DES Inter-Governmental Philatelic Corp.
DES Waddington Studios

26a-b Mauritius
AG Crown Agents
DES John Waddington Studios

27a-b Trinidad & Tobago
DES/AG Crown Agents

28 Isle of Man
AG Crown Agents
DES J. H. Nicholson

29 South Georgia
DES John Waddington Studios

30a-b Poland
DES St. Malecki

31a-b Bulgaria
DES Stefan Kantchev

Postage-stamp designs
Dessins de Timbres-poste
Briefmarken Entwürfe

1 Brazil
DES Ari Fagundez

2a-b Botswana
AG Crown Agents Stamp Bureau
DES (a) R. M. Baylis
(b) M. F. Bryan

3 Bahamas
AG Inter-Governmental Philatelic Corporation
DES Pad Studio

4 Republic of Korea
DES Ahn Sung Kyung

5a-d Lesotho
DES Dick Findlay

6a-b Bulgaria
DES Lyudmil Chechechlarov

7a-b Gibraltar
AG Crown Agents
DES A. G. Ryman

8a-b Republic of South Africa
DES Dick Findlay

9a-b Jamaica
AG Crown Agents
DES John Cooter

10a-b Antigua
AG Intergovernmental Philatelic Corporation
DES Vasarhelyi

11 Norfolk Island
AG Crown Agents
DES Brian Hargreaves

12a-b Ethiopia
DES Rogale Belachew

13a-b, 15 Grenada
AG Inter-Governmental Philatelic Corporation
DES Waddington Studios

14a-b Japan
DES Wokana Emori

1

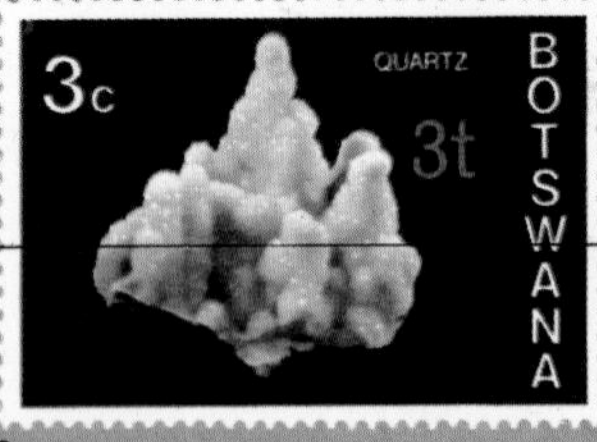

2a

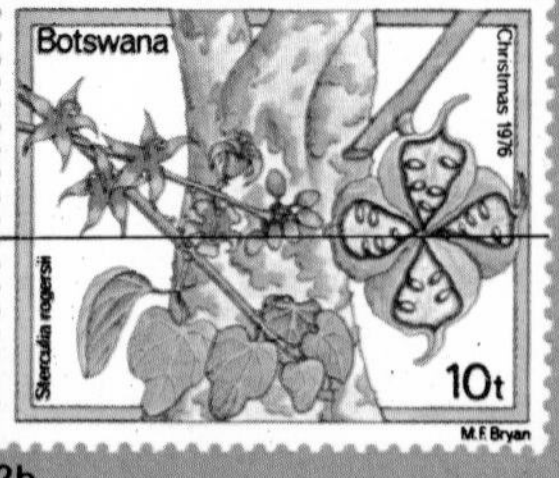

2b

3

4

5a

5b

6a

6b

7a

The Red Admiral
(Vanessa atalanta)
This butterfly is very common and widespread all over the Rock, appearing in early February and very often seen during the whole year. It is one of the species of the large family Nymphalidae.

7b

8a

8b

9a

9b

10a

10b

11

12a

12b

13a

13b

16 Czechoslovakia
DES J. Balaz

17 Gambia
AG Crown Agents Stamp Bureau
DES Gordon Drummond

18a-b Liechtenstein
DES Louis Jaeger

19 Antarctic Territory
AG Crown Agents
DES John Cooter

20 Kenya
AG Crown Agents
DES Adrienne Kennaway

21 Antigua
AG Intergovernmental Philatelic Corporation
DES Gordon Drummond

22 Dominica
AG Intergovernmental Philatelic Corporation
DES Gordon Drummond

23 India
DES Benoy Sarkar

24 Pakistan
DES Adil Salahuddin

25a-b Jersey
DES Jennifer Toombs

26 Israel
DES J. Ferguson

27 Guinea
DES Oswald Adler

Postage-stamp designs
Dessins de Timbres-poste
Briefmarken Entwürfe

1a-c Brazil
DES (a) Ari Fagundez
(b, c) Martha Poppe

2 Sultanate of Oman
AG Crown Agents
DES Vic Whiteley Studio

3 United Arab Emirates
AG Crown Agents
DES Al Muharraqi

4a-b Czechoslovakia
DES A. Strnad

5 Republic of Korea
DES Chun Hee Han

6 India
DES Benoy Sakar

7a-d Israel
DES Weishoff Studios

8 Nauru
AG Inter Governmental Philatelic Corporation
DES Julian Vasarhelyi

9 Jamaica
AG Crown Agents
DES Clive Abbott

10, 19 Samoa I Sisifo
AG Inter Governmental Philatelic Corporation
DES Clive Abbott

11a-e Germany
DES (a) Heide Holzing
(b, c) Hella and Heinz Schillinger
(d) Gunter Jacki
(e) Prof. Albrecht Ade

12a-b Hungary
DES Janos Kass

13 Bolivia
DES Ari Fagundez

1a

1b

1c

2

3

4a

4b

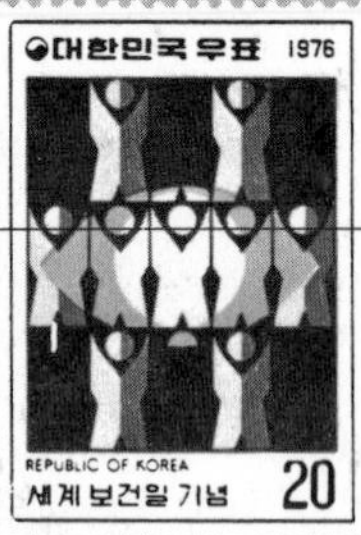
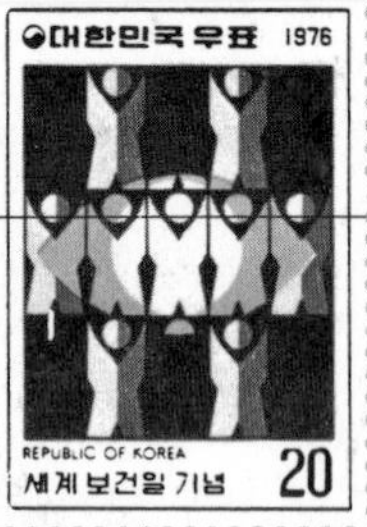

5

6

7a

7b

7c

7d

8

9

10

14a-b Vietnam
DES (a) Nguyen Van Ri
(b) Nguyen Nguyen

15a-b Republic of South Africa
DES Jeremy Sampson
ILL John Maskew

16 Hong Kong
DES Jennie Wong

17 Mauritius
AG Crown Agents
DES John Waddington

18 Austria
DES E. Freund

20 Bulgaria
DES H. Hristov

11a

11b

12a

12b

11c

11d

11e

14a

14b

13

17

18

15a
15b
16

19

20

Trademarks
Marques
Schutzmarken
Letterheads
en têtes
Briefköpfe

1 Germany
AD Sozialdemokratische Partei Deutschlands (SDP)
AG ARE Kommunikation
DES Helmut Schmid
COPY Hubert Maessen
election campaign

2 Great Britain
AD/DES Anthony D. Forster · self-promotion, typo-lettering service

Und so sollen die Werbemittel aussehen, die von den verschiedenen Herstellern angeboten und produziert werden.

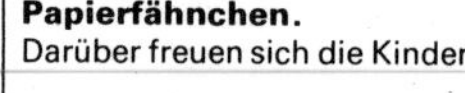

Papierfähnchen.
Darüber freuen sich die Kinder.

Schlüssel-anhänger.
Mit Kampagnen-Zeichen und Kanzler Helmut Schmidt.

Krawatte.
Macht jedem Krawatten-Muffel endgültig den Garaus.

Schirm.
Bei Regen: Regenschirm.
Bei Sonne: .... ja, genau.

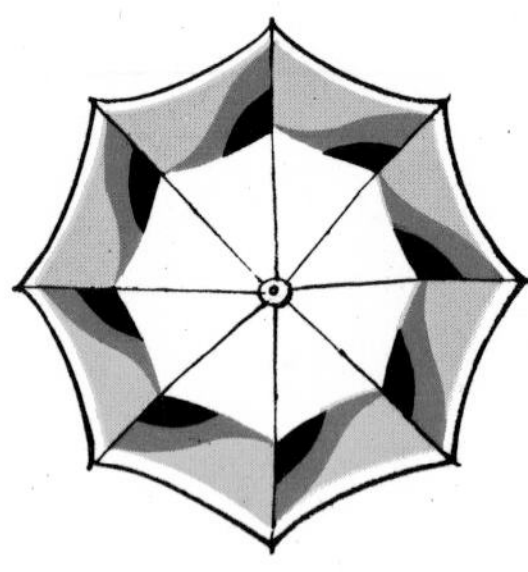

Trimm-Ball.
Damit bleibt man in Form.
Übrigens: Ein gutes Geschenk für Sportvereine im Wahlkreis!

Sonnenblende.
Damit laufen Kinder den ganzen Sommertag Reklame.

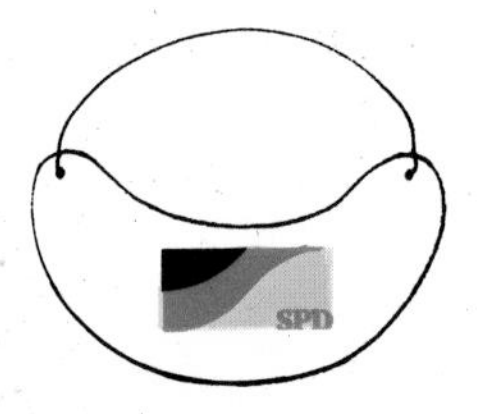

Windmühlchen.
Darüber freuen sich die Kinder auch.

Mütze.
Praktischick.
(Darüber freuen sich nicht nur Kinder.)

Schiebe-Puzzle.
Für garantiert lange Beschäftigung mit unserem Wahlkampfzeichen.

Luftballon.
Nett, aber keinesfalls symbolisch zu sehen.

Spielkarten.
Aus einem einfachen Skatblatt werden 32 Trümpfe.

Schlüsselbundtäschchen.
Hat man immer bei sich.

Bikini.
Wird der Knüller der Saison.

Badetuch.
So schön, daß man sich am liebsten danebenlegt.
Größe: 70 x 140 cm.

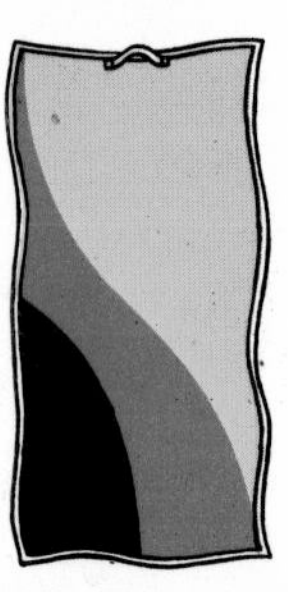

"blitz"
Royal Northern College of Music
Rogue
Boutique
Brown Street
off Market St.
Manchester 1
061 834
8710
NOAH'S ARK
Wine List
Artistic Framing Limited
Le Café Corfu
Jackie Phillips
The Empire Line
Hedda Gabler
H. Ibsen
The Zenith
6
Happy New Year
kelley's eye
abel
forster
H. Wills Ltd.
Paulette
Jewellery
14 Linda Drive
Hazel Grove
Cheshire
061-483 2981
Merry Xmas
Prospectus
Blue Future Sky Light Show
The President's Trophy
The WOOD
GUIPHALL BANQUET
16
After sixteen
What do I want to be
Where shall I go
How can I decide
New Look
Neville
Menu
Letter
Edgar Allen Poe

1 Hong Kong
AD De Santis Internation Co Ltd
AG Kinggraphic
DIR Hon Bing-Wah
DES So Man-Yee

6 Canada
AD Hôtel Méridien
AG Guillon/Designers Inc
DIR/DES Frédéric Metz
restaurant

2 United States
AD HBK, Inc
AG Gauger Sparks Silva
DIR Walter Sparks
DES Walter Sparks, David Gauger
ILL Walter Sparks, Roger Takiguchi
COPY Larry Silva
frozen yougurt refreshment bar

7 Great Britain
AD Wembley Conference Centre
AG Design Research Unit
DIR/DES Richard Dragun
'1926' restaurant

3 South Africa
AD Marina da Gama
AG Unimark International, Johannesburg
DIR/DES Arie J. Geurts
marina complex

8 United States
AD Biltmore Hotel
AG John Follis & Associates
DIR John Follis
DES T. Wayne Hunt
ILL Chuck Schmidt
restaurant

4 South Africa
AD Escape Magazine
AG Grapplegroup CJA
DIR Richard Ward, Roy Clucas
DES Richard Ward

9 Austria
AD Roland Rapp
AG Watzlwork
DES Peter Watzl
do-it-yourself supplier

5 United States
AD Arista Records/Suzi Quatro
AG Promedeus Arts
DIR Bob Heimal
DES Steven Bernstein
'Rock' singer

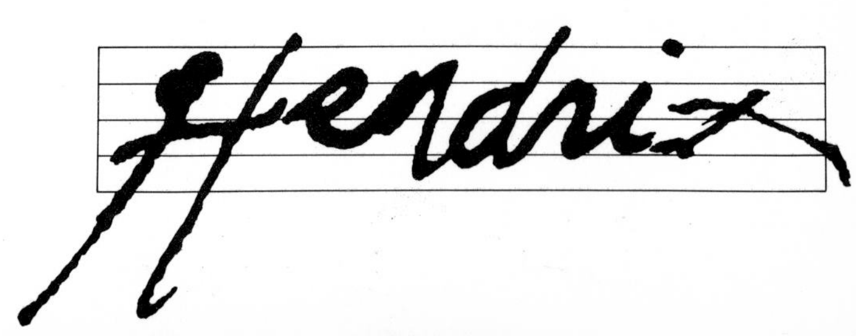

10 Spain
AD Musidora Films
DES Fernando Medina
Hendrix film

11 Great Britain
AD Borregard
AG Lock/Pettersen Ltd
DIR/DES Tor Pettersen
paper manufacturer, papier

16 Great Britain
AD Horburys
AG John Nash
DES Malcolm Smith
doors and door furntiures, portes, Türen

12 Mexico
AD Seccional SA
AG Laboratorio de Diseno y Mercadotecnia
Carton y Papel de Mexico
DIR/DES Graham Edwards
COPY 'Norden'
furniture, Meubles, Möbel

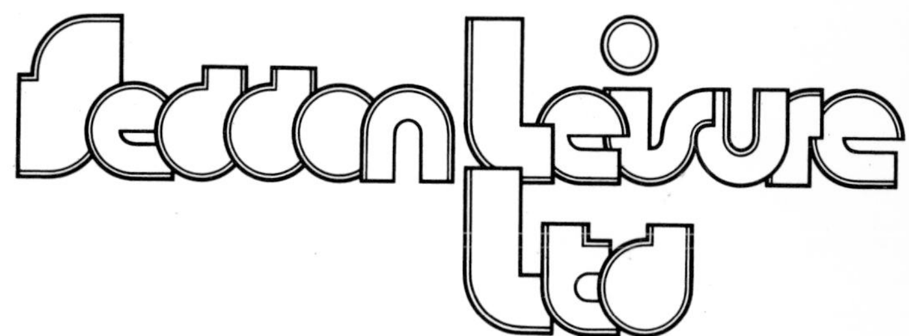

17 Great Britain
AD Seddon Leisure Ltd
AG Derek Forsyth Graphics Ltd
DES Adrian Williamson

13 Great Britain
AD Alleycat
AG Ron Ellis Design
DIR/DES Ron Ellis
boutiques

18 France
AD Tourisme et Travail
DIR Michele Droneau, Danièle Itasse
DES Jean Larcher
travel

14 Austria
AD Terra
AG Vorarlberger Graphik
DES Othmar Motter
COPY Linus Gebhardt
building company, entrepreneur en bâtiment, Wohnbaugesellschaft

19 Spain
AD Empesa
AG/DES Enric Huguet
Bathroom installations, installations

20 Spain
AD Bagoa
AG Estudi Ariño
DES Pere Ariño
restaurant

15 Spain
AD De Felipe Sempere, electropist
AG/DES Jose Ros Gonzalez
air brush, Aerograph

Trademarks
Marques
Schutzmarken

1 United States
AD Board of Jewish Education of Chicago
AG Visual Design Center, Inc
DIR Don Levy
DES Jerry Cain, Don Levy
ILL Roy Kawamoto

6 India
DES Sudarshan Dheer
Tantrik symbol

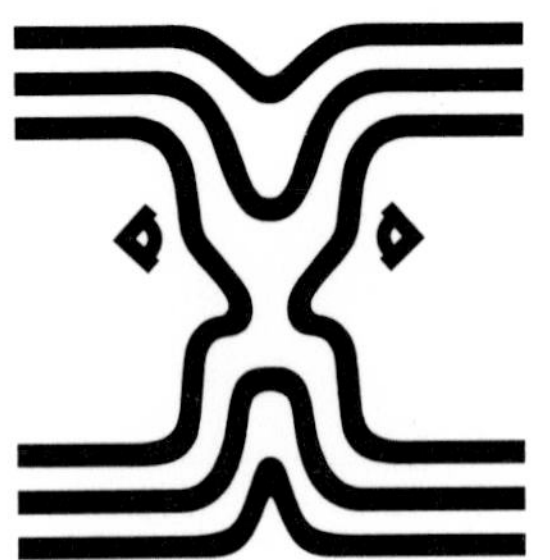

2 United States
AD Hypnosis Training Institute
AG Zahor Design Inc
DIR/DES D. Bruce Zahor

7 Bulgaria
AD Bulgarian Television
DES Nikola Petrov Nikolov
tv

3 France
AD Lita Perfumes, USA
AG Garamond
DIR R. C. Garamond
DES Jacques Nathan-Garamond
perfumes, parfums

8 Mexico
AD Mexican Citrus Growers Association
AG Laboratorio de Deseno y
Mercadotecnia — Carton y Papel de Mexico
DIR/DES Pancho Guitierez

4 Italy
AD Armando Curcio Editore
DES Vittoria Antinori
publishers

9 Mexico
AD Playschool Kindergarten
AG/DES Arie J. Geurts

5 Bulgaria
DES Stephan Kantscheff
health organization

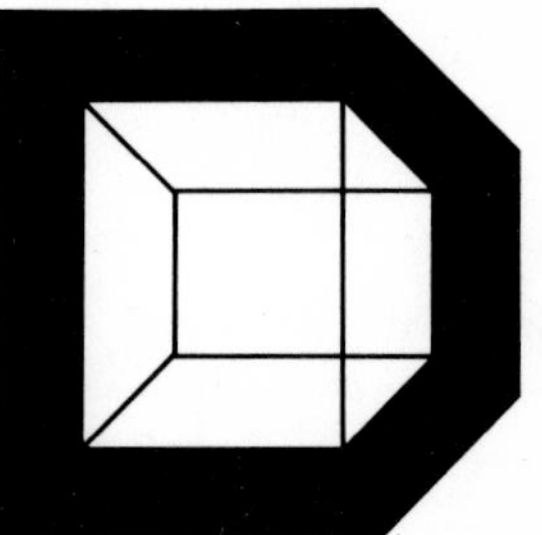

10 Germany
AD Dimo Wehner Industriemonsage
DES Ludvik Feller
interior architecture

11 Great Britain
AD Hutchinson Publishing Group Ltd
AG Hans Schleger & Associates
DIR Hans Schleger
publishers

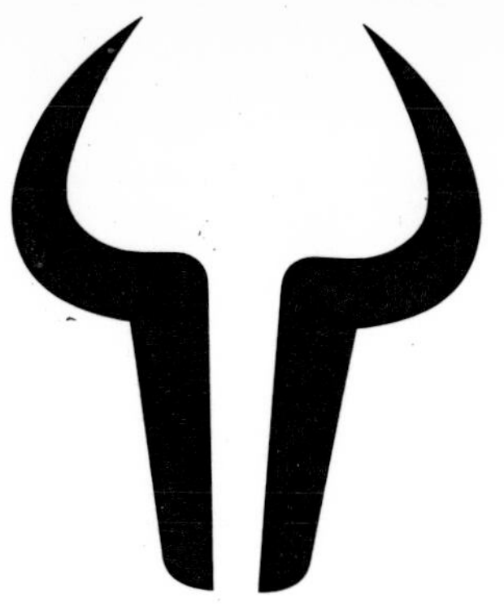

16 Germany
AD Edition 9
AG Studio für Grafik Wieland Schütz
DIR/DES Wieland Schütz

12 Turkey
AD LASSA Lastik Sanayi ve Ticaret AS
DIR/DES Bülent Erkmen
car tyres

17 Japan
AD Isetan Dept Store
AG Nippon Design Center
DIR Kenzo Nakagawa
DES Kenzo Nakagawa, Hiro Nobuyama
umbrella, parapluies, Regenschirme

13 Italy
AD Azienda Soggiono e Turismo Isole Eolie
AG Castellano & Co Associati
DIR/DES Mimmo Castellano
corporate image

18 Italy
AD Ediltur Valorizzazioni turistiche
AG Studio de Santis
DIR/DES Alfredo de Santis
tourism

14 Hungary
AD Hungexpo
DIR/DES Nándor Szilvásy
international toy exhibition, exposition international de jouets

19 Great Britain
AD Eisenmann & Co Ltd, Bowman Harris
AG Trickett & Webb Ltd
DIR Lynn Trickett, Brian Webb
DES Lynn Trickett, Brian Webb, Andrew Thomas
toys, jouets, Spielzeuge

15 Italy
AD Maria Imperio
AG Studio de Liso
DIR Geppi de Liso
DES Lilli de Liso
furniture store, magazine de meuble

20 Spain
AD Universidad Politécnica de Barcelona
AG E studio Ariño
DIR Pere Ariño
DES Eduardo Gandara
world conference on mathematics

Trademarks
Marques
Schutzmarken

1 Great Britain
AD Geoffrey Tucker Ltd
DES Kenneth Hollick
public relations

6 United States
AD Kentuck Electric Steel Co
AG David E. Carter Corporate Communications
DIR/DES David E. Carter
steel manufacturer, aciferie, Stahlwerk

2 Germany (DDR)
AD Verband Bildender Künstler der DDR
DES Axel Bertram
exhibition of art

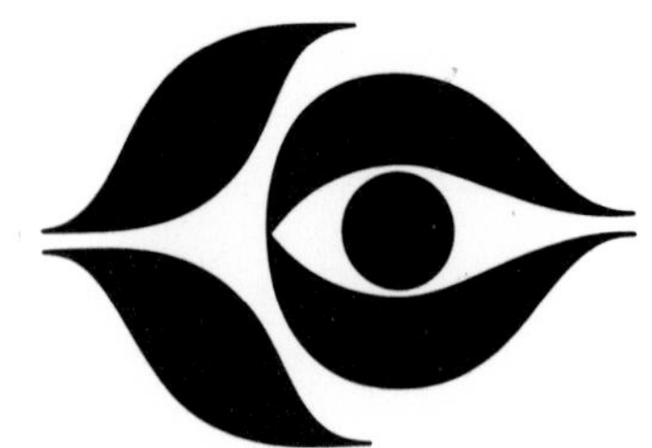

7 United States
AD Flextech Oil Pipe (Holdings) Ltd
AG Devonshire Studios
DIR Mike Conrad
DES Mike Conrad, Dave Teece
flexible oil pipes

3 South Africa
AD Romatex Ltd
AG Jeremy Sampson Associates (Pty) Ltd
DIR Jeremy Sampson
DES Marlene Blomerus
commercial carpeting, tapis industriel, indstirelle Teppiche

8 Great Britain
AD London Celebrations Committee for the Queen's Silver Jubilee
AG Guyatt/Jenkins Ltd
DIR Nicholas Jenkins
DES Prof. Richard Guyatt
Queen's silver jubilee

4 Great Britain
AD Alterego
AG Robin Bath Design
DIR Edmond Swain
DES Robin Bath
computers

9 Great Britain
AD Boulogne Chamber of Commerce and Industry, France
DIR/DES Stan Krol
Boulogne port,

5 United States
AD Teachers College Press
AG Ner Beck Design
DIR/DES Ner Beck, Richard Florschutz
educational research programme

10 United States
AD Lincoln Community Center
AG Bob Coonts Design
DIR/DES Bob Coonts
cultural events building, centre pour les évènements culturels

11 United States
AD The Wurlitzer Company
AG The Design Partnership
DIR Jack Weiss
DES Randi Robin

12 Belgium
AD/AG Aid
DIR/DES Luk Vangheluwe
advertising ideas design

13 Austria
AD Schneiderbauer
AG watzlwork
DES Peter Watzl

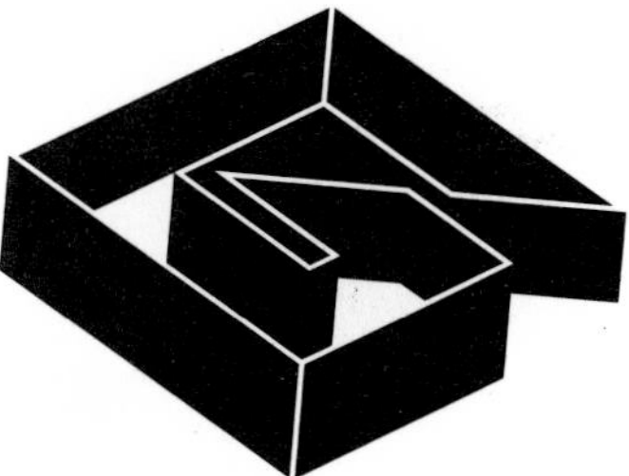

14 Great Britain
AD Peter Green
AG Gavin Healey Design
DES Gavin Healey

15 United States
AD/AG Gianninoto Associates, Inc
DIR John DiGianni
self-promotion

16 Germany
AD/DES Herbert Wenn
designers self-promotion

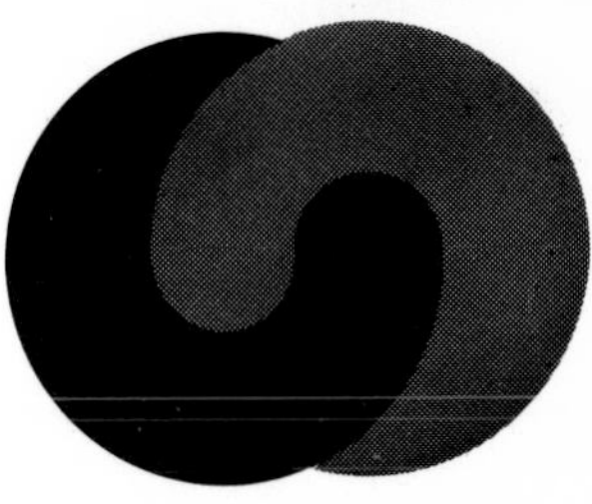

17 Austria
AD Ochsner & Sohn
AG Watzlwork
DES Peter Watzl

18 France
AD Arbed, Belgique
AG Garamond
DIR R. C. Garamond
DES Jacques Nathan-Garamond

19 Finland
AD Tanhuvaaran Urheiluopisto
AG Zetterborgs
DIR/DES Bror B. Zetterborg
women's sports institute

20 Hong Kong
AD Pansonic Ltd
AG 3A Publicity 'n Promotions
DIR/DES Michael Miller Yu
recording studio

Trademarks
Marques
Schutzmarken

1a-b Sweden
AD Twilfit
AG Studio Gunnar Sörman
DES Gunnar Sörman
ILL Göran Phil
fashions, modes, mode

2a-b United States
AD Industria Italiana Petroli Genoa, Italy
AG Landor Associates

3a-c Denmark
AD Bellacenter
AG Folkmar Roll Graphic Designer
DES Folkmar Roll
exhibition centre

4 United States
AD W. R. Grace & Co
AG George Tscherny, Inc
DIR/DES George Tscherny
ILL John T. Hill

5a-c Canada
AD LaCité
AG Guillon/Designers Inc
DIR Laurent Marquart
DES Frédéric Metz

6a-b Hong Kong
AD The Manila Peninsula Hotel
AG Design Development
DIR Peter Chancellor
DES (a, b) Peter Chancellor
(c) Chiu Wing Wah . Michelle Shek

1a

1b

2a

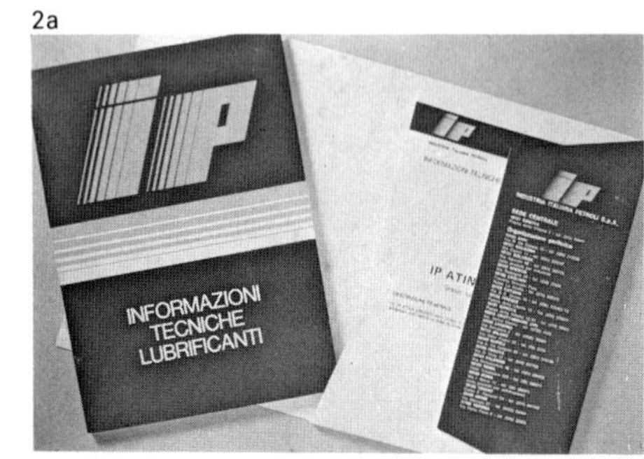

2b

3a

3b

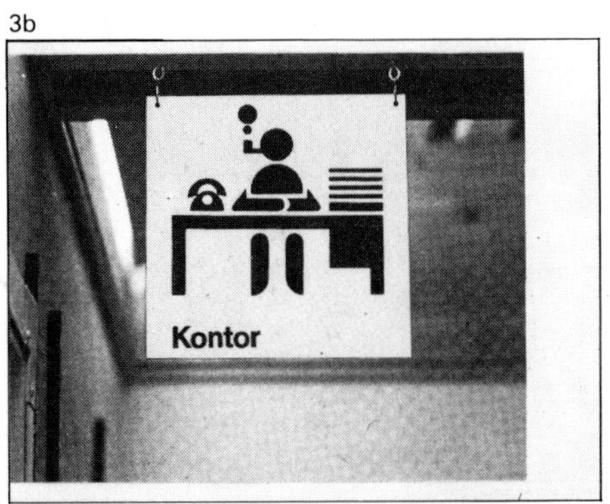

3c

4

5a

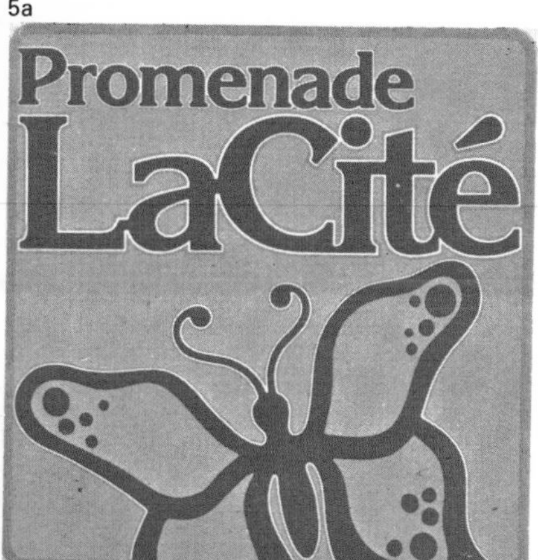

5b

5c

6a

6b

6c

Letterheads
en têtes
Briefköpfe

1 Great Britain
AD/DES Alan Dempsey
designer's own stationery

2 Great Britain
AD/DES Len Payne
designer's own stationery

3 United States
AD Hamoor Communications
AG/DES Joe Scoresone

4 Spain
AD Paste-Up
AG C. Rolando & Asociados
DIR/ILL C. Rolando
paste-up studio

5 Canada
AD Canadian Psychological Consultants
AG Harry Agensky Design
DIR/DES Harry Agensky

6 Great Britain
AD Charles Letts & Co Ltd
AG W. M. de Majo Associates
DIR/DES W. M. de Majo
diary and address book publishers, maison d'edition pur les journaeaux et les carnets d'adresses

7 Spain
AD Pauimentos Mata
AG/DES Francesi Guitart
filing

8 Spain
AD Granica Editor
AG C. Rolando & Asociados
DIR C. Rolando
DES C. Rolando, Maria Rourich
book publisher, maison d'edition, Verlagsbuchhandlung

9 Iran
AD Dalami Company Ltd
AG Publiciteam
hi-fi equipment

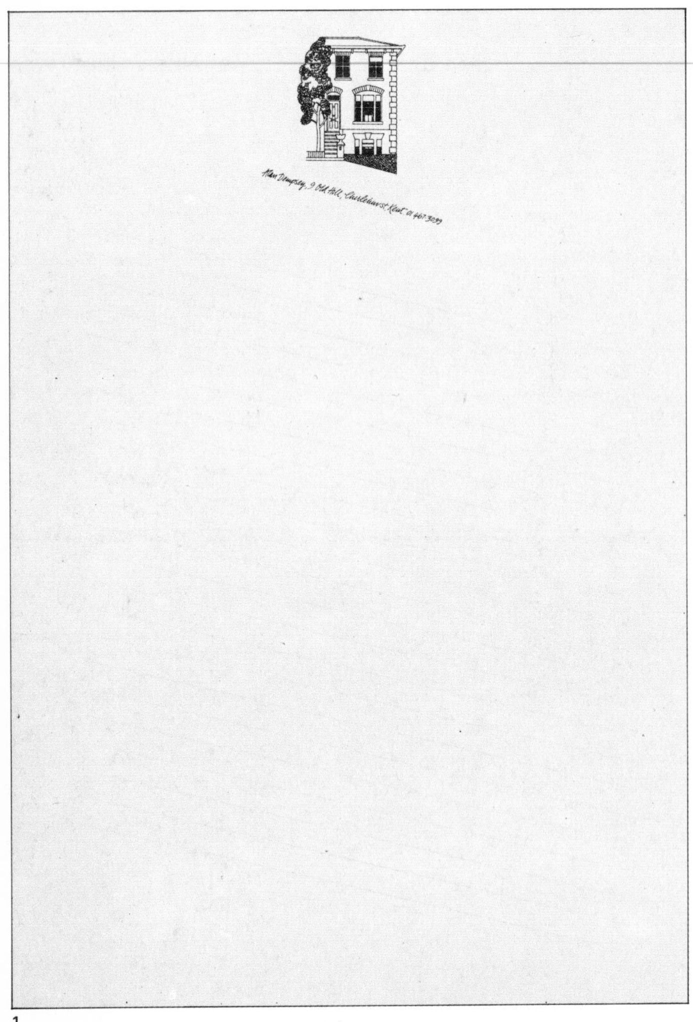

1

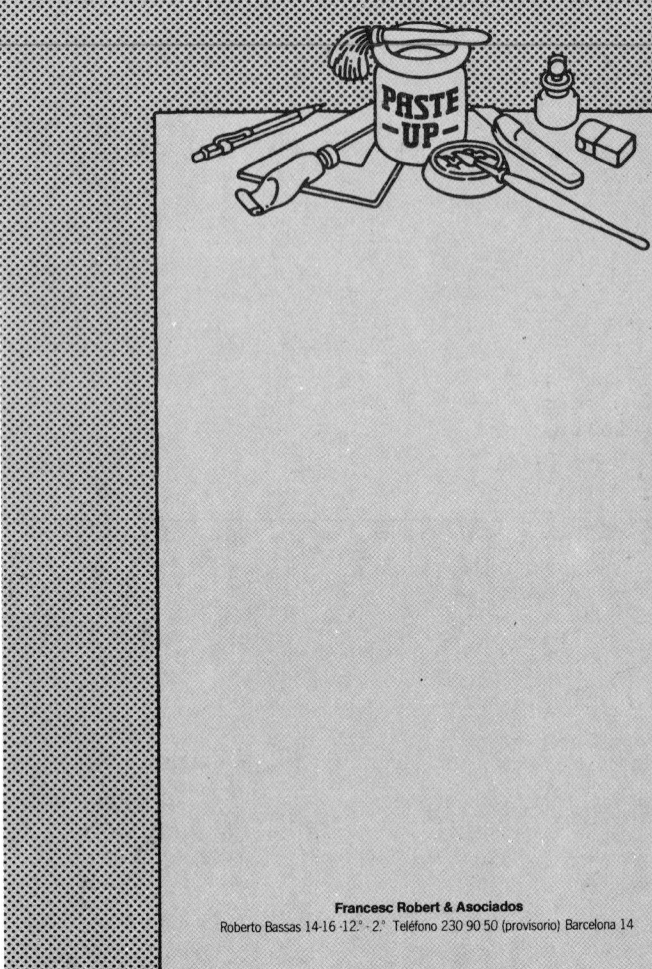

4

2

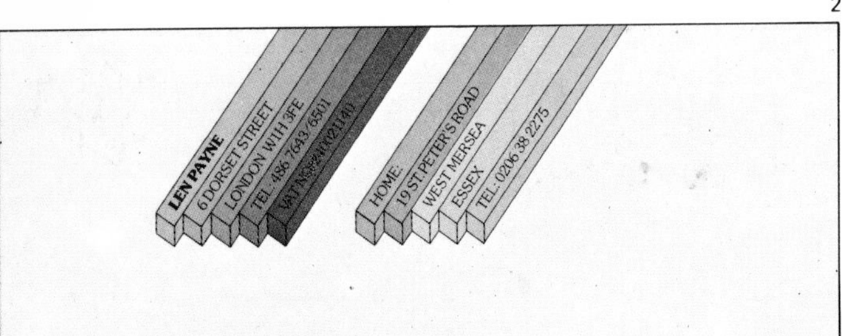

5

3

10 Great Britain
AD Stephen Lewis
AG John Harris Design Partnership
DIR John Harris
DES Sylvia Sims
gift and furniture shop, boutique

11 Holland
AD De Leeuw Jellema
AG Weda
DES Theo de Witte

12 Great Britain
AD Henry Jones
AG Trickett & Webb Ltd
DIR/DES Lynn Trickett/Brian Webb
stationery range for porcelain shop

7

8

Granica Editor SA

10

11

Projektontwikkelingsmij.
Projektgroep Noord BV

projektgroep noord

Gorredijk Badweg 42
Postbus 83 Tel. 05133-2175

Friesland Bank Leeuwarden
Rek.nr. 29.82.54.514

9

DALAMI CO. LTD.
P.O. Box 44.1357
No. 6 Third Street
Avenue Kouh-e Nour
Avenue Takht-e Tavous
Tehran Iran
Tel: 628716 620516.620197
Telex: 213364 CMET—IR

12

HENRY JONES (CHINA AND GLASS) LIMITED
79 HIGH STREET. MARLOW SL7 1AB. TELEPHONE MARLOW 72838-9

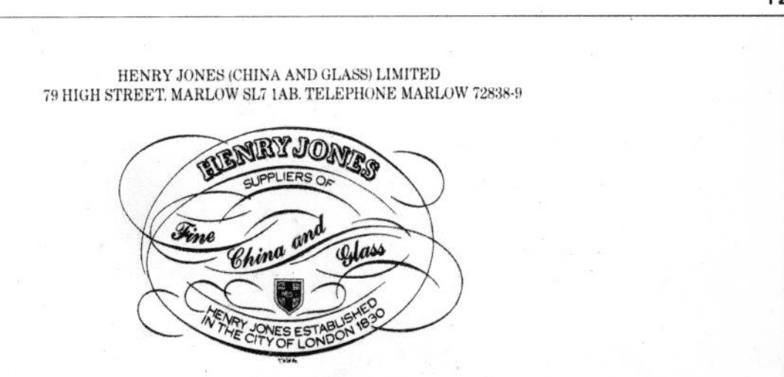

Letterheads
en têtes
Briefköpfe

1 Great Britain
AD Ian Atkinson
AG Graphic Partners
DES Kenneth Craig
stationery for studios in Edinburgh and Paris

2 Great Britain
AD Woodbridge & Evergreen
AG Forth Studios
DIR/DES Peter Lloyd
timber companies, charpente, Holz

3 Great Britain
AD Fred To Solar Powered Aircraft Developments
AG Pentagram
DIR John McConnell
DES Howard Brown
solar powered aircraft

4 United States
AD The Media Shop
AG/DES Joe Scorsone
COPY Bob Lazar
multi-media shows

5 Spain
AD Romvaldo Salcedo Real
DIR/DES Salvatore Adduci
ILL Fernando de Bustos

6 Great Britain
AD Scantest
AG The Buchanan Company
DIR/DES Michel H. G. Huet

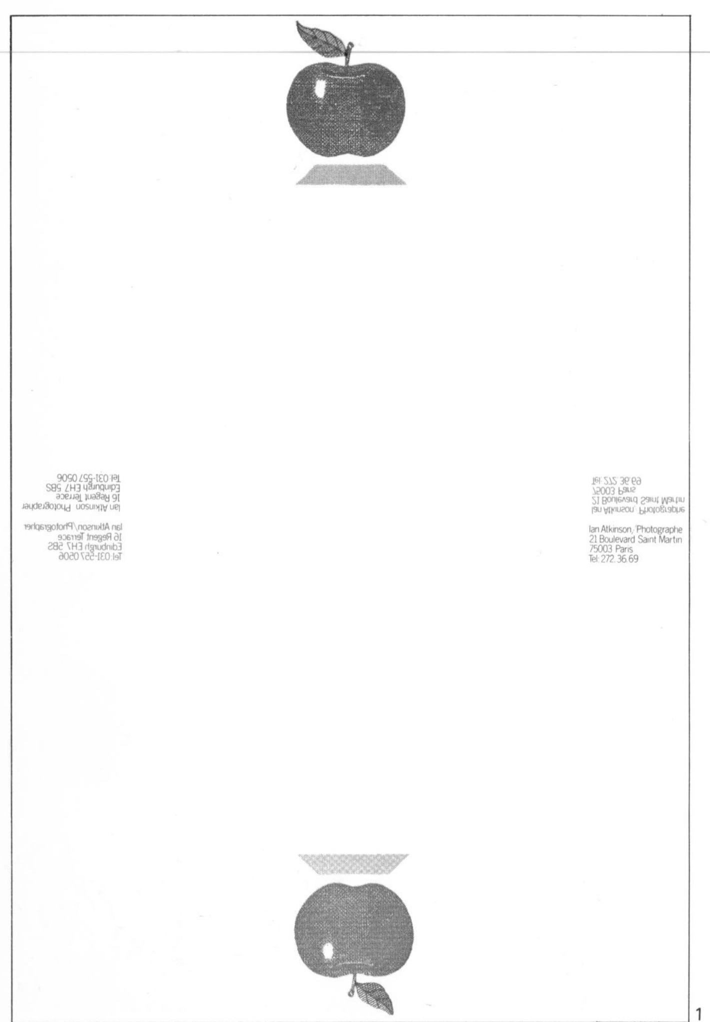

1

4

2

5

3

6

7 Hong Kong
AD/AG Graphic Communication Ltd
DIR/DES Henry Steiner
Dragon Year stationery

8 Great Britain
AD Vintage Type Supplies Ltd
AG Chris Keeble, Studio D
DIR/DES Chris Keeble

9 Mexico
AD Green Plant Thumb Service
AG/DES Arie J. Geurts

10 South Africa
AD/AG Grapplegroup CJA (Pty) Ltd
DES Kenny Saint, Roy Clucas

11 Switzerland
AD Organisation De Mercurio
AG Publicite Bornand + Gaeng
DIR/DES Bruno Gaeng
hotel

12 Finland
AD City tourist office of Lahti
AG Lahti Mainos Oy
DIR/DES Jori Svärd

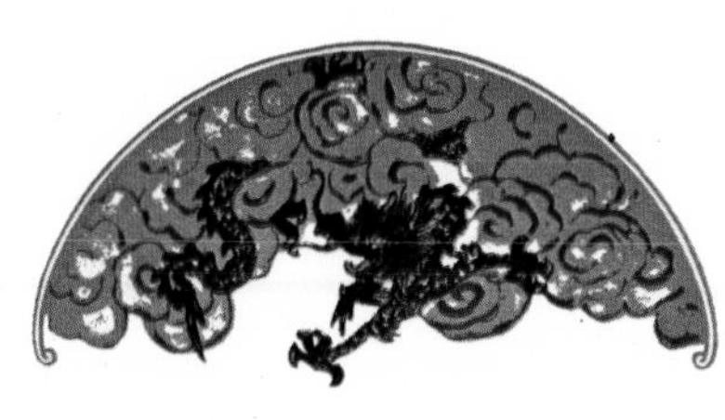

Graphic Communication Ltd.
6th floor, Printing House, 6 Duddell Street, Hong Kong phone: 5-230101 cable: Graphicom Hongkong

7

10

8

VINTAGE TYRE SUPPLIES LTD

11

9

Stefano Cacace

Green Plant Thumb Service

(213) 874-0800
(213) 653-9486
806 North Alfred
West Hollywood
California 90069

12

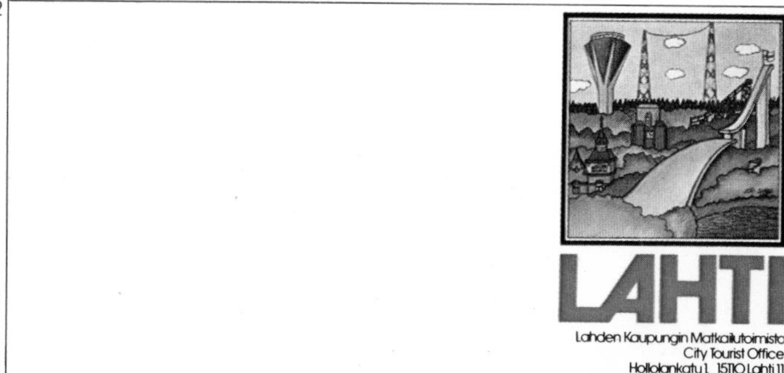

Letterheads
en têtes
Briefköpfe

1 Great Britain
AD/AG Tony Page Associates
DES Tony Page

2 Hong Kong
AD/AG Fritzy Design
DIR/DES Fritz Wong

3 United States
AD Eye/Spectacles & Contacts
AG Sam Smidt Associates
DIR/DES Sam Smidt

4 United States
AD Dellen Publishing Company
AG Gauger Sparks Silva
DIR/DES Walter Sparks
publisher, maison d'edition, Verlagsbuchhandlung

5 Iran
AD Ghotb Livestock and Citrus Industry
AG Publiciteam
livestock and citrus farm, ferme a betail et citron,

6 United States
AD The Drain Surgeon
AG Wayne Hunt Graphic Design
DIR/DES T. Wayne Hunt
plumbers, installateur

7 Great Britain
AD Theo Crosby
AG Pentagram
DIR/DES Alan Fletcher
ILL David Pearce
designer

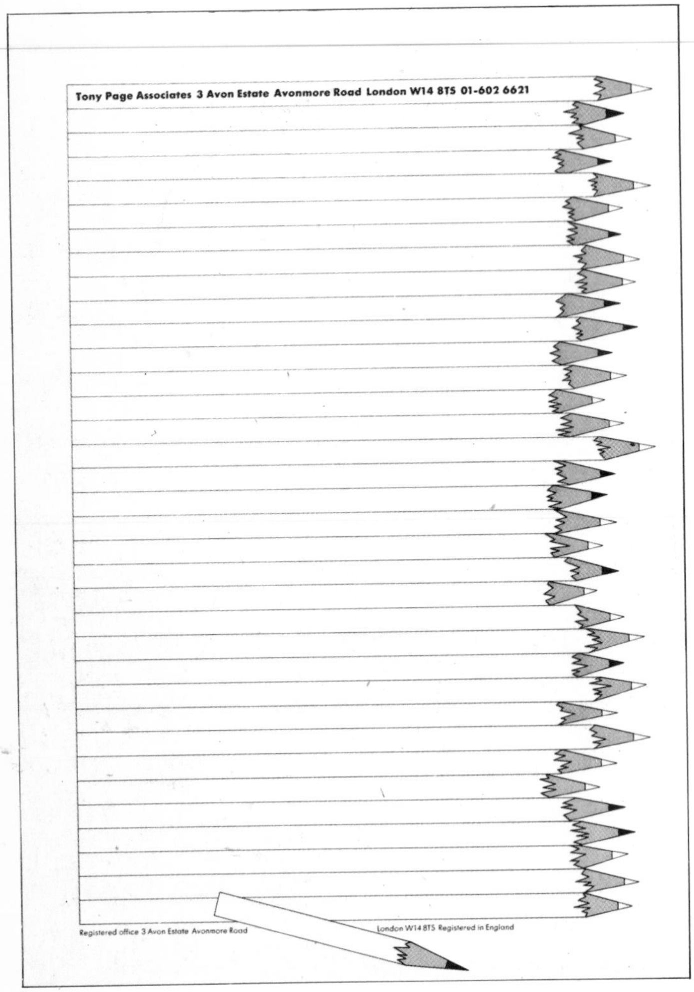

Tony Page Associates 3 Avon Estate Avonmore Road London W14 8TS 01-602 6621

Registered office 3 Avon Estate Avonmore Road London W14 8TS Registered in England

1

DELLEN PUBLISHING CO.

1441 Van Ness
San Francisco
Calif. 94109
415-673-3603

Dellen
Publishing
Company
1441 Van Ness
San Francisco
Ca. 94109

4

5

Fritzy Design
FritzyDesign
1002 Kuala Lumpur
Finance Commercial Building
88-98 Des Voeux Road
Central Hong Kong
Telephone 5 441258

2

6

3

8 Great Britain
AD Mack-Brooks Exhibitions Ltd
DES Gina & Sidney Day
ILL Sidney Day
exhibition designers

9 Sweden
AD 'Troldungen'
AG Niels Christensen Reklam
DIR/DES Niels Christensen
children's clothes dealer, vêtements d'enfants, Kinderkleidung

10 Italy
DES Rinaldo Cutini
designers

11 Brazil
AD Rosenlandia Brinquedos Ltda
DES Suzana Fonseca d'Arinos Silva

12 Great Britain
AD/AG Monaghan & Beard
DES Mike Monaghan, Pete Beard

THEO CROSBY RIBA FSIA
TOWER 3
WHITEHALL COURT
LONDON SW1A 2EL
TELEPHONE 01·930 3160

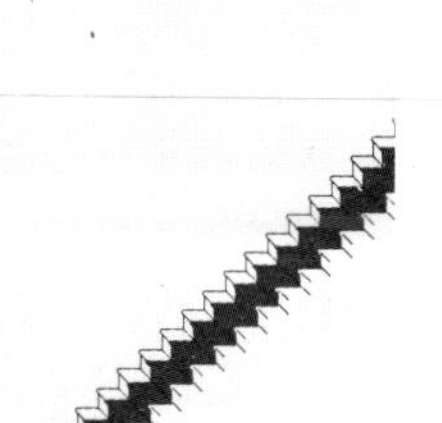

7

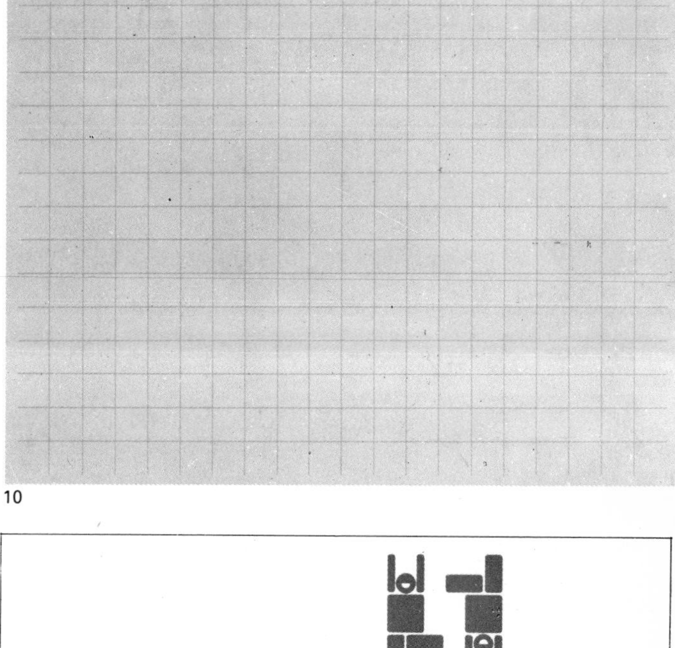

10

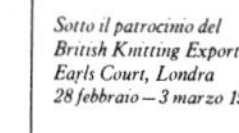

Fiera internazionale della Maglieria

Sotto il patrocinio del
British Knitting Export Council
Earls Court, Londra
28 febbraio – 3 marzo 1977

Mack-Brooks Exhibitions Ltd
62-64 Victoria Street, St Albans
Hertfordshire AL1 3XT Inghilterra
Telefono: St Albans 63213
Telegramma: Macbrooks Stalb
Telex: 266350

8

Rozenlandia Brinquedos Ltda.

11

9

specialforretningen

i smart børnetøj!

AALBORG DEN:

DERAS REF.:
(YOUR REF.)

VOR REF.:
(OUR REF.)

12

MONAGHAN BEARD
DESIGN · ILLUSTRATION
AND ANIMATION

1a-b Great Britain
AD Sopad, France
AG Cato Johnson
DES Roger Harris
chocolate sardines

2a-b France
AD Peroche
AG Mafia (Maime Arnodin, Fayolle,)
International, Associés
fashion, modes

1a

1b

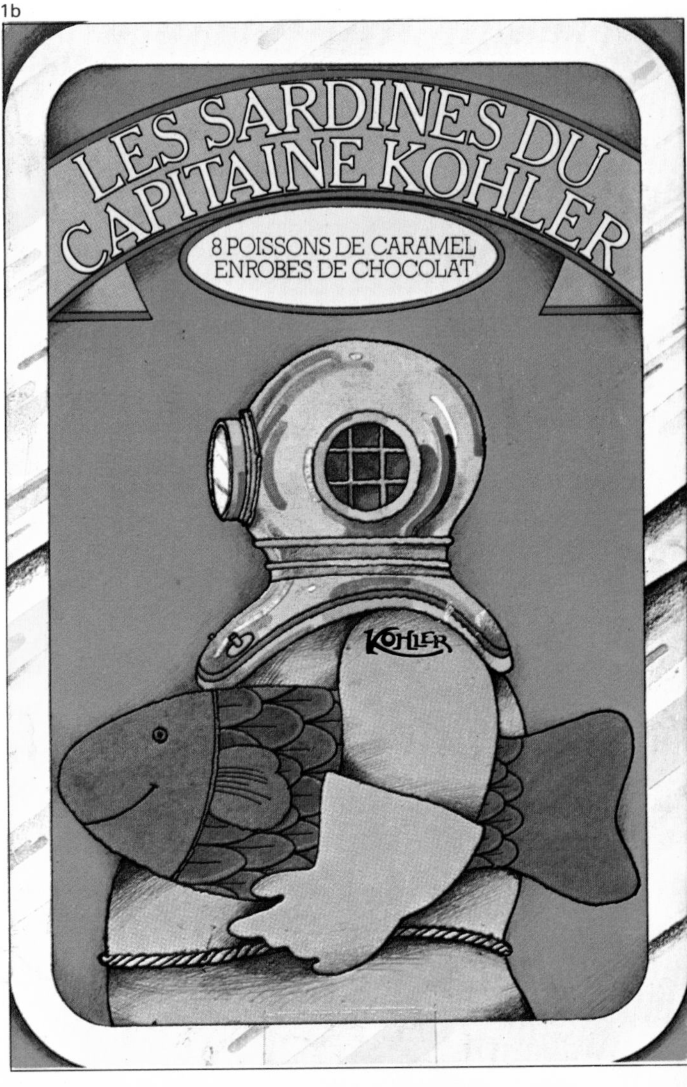

120-121

peroche

2

Packaging
Emballages
Verpackungsgestaltung

1a-d Great Britain
AD Marks & Spencer
AG David Tyrell & Associates
DIR Sally Lee
DES David Tyrell
ILL (a) John Ireland
(b-d) David Tyrell
(a) bread, pains, Brot
(b-d) biscuits, Keks

2 Great Britain
AD Halbeath Inns Ltd
AG Thyne Design Studio
DIR/DES Richard Drayson
frozen foods, surgelés, tiefgefrorene Lebensmittel

3 United States
AD Oroweat Foods Company
AG Richard C. Runyon Design
DIR Richard C. Runyon
DES Julie Morris, Richard C. Runyon
bread, pain, Brot

4 Finland
AD Paasivaara-Yhtymä Oy
AG Lintas
DIR/DES Bror B. Zetterborg
concentrated fruit juice bricks, jus de fruit concentre, verdichter Obstsaft

5a-c Denmark
AD FDB (Danish Cooperative Wholesale Soc.)
AG RT
DIR Jørgen Madsen
DES (a) Birgit Christiansen
(b) Ingerlill
(c) Jørgen Madsen
(a) gelatine, (b) meat recipe book, recettes pour la viande, Fleisch-Rezepte (c) juice cartons, cartons à jus, Kartons für Saft

6 Israel
AD Shemen Industry Ltd
DIR/DES A. Kalderon
washing powder, poudre de lessive, Waschpulver

1a

2

1b

3

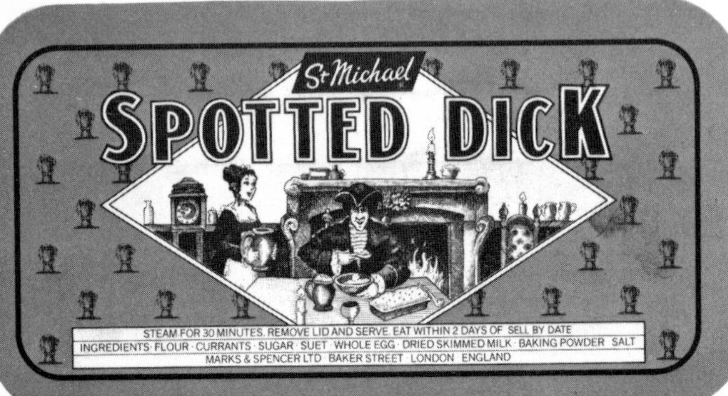

1c

4

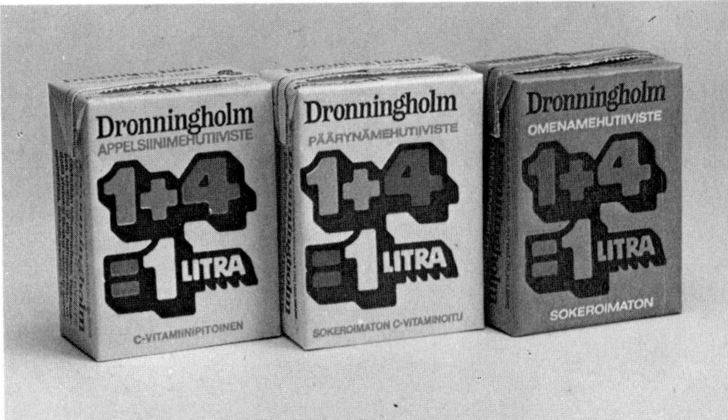

1d

7 Hong Kong
AD Pacific Biscuit & Confectionery Co Ltd
AG Graphic Communication Ltd
DIR/DES Henry Steiner
biscuits, Keks

8 Denmark
AD Carno Denmark
AG SB Grafisk Design
DIR/DES Søren Balle
Conserves

5a

5b

5c

6

7

8

Packaging
Emballages
Verpackungsgestaltung

1 Holland
AD/AG Prad BV
DIR Joop Smit
DES Huib Ebbinge
COPY Jan van der Molen
change of address (Beethovenstraat)

2 Czechoslovakia
AD Supraphon - Prag
DIR Miloš Pokora
DES Ladislav Rada

3 Finland
AD Loverecords Company
DES Piotr Tomaszewski

4a-c Great Britain
AD CBS Records
DIR Roslan Szaybo
DES (a) Glen Travis, Barry Bloomfield
(b) Keith Davis
(c) Michael Farrell

5 Japan
AD CBS Records
DIR/DES Tadanori Yokoo

6 Germany
AD/AG Ariola-Eurodisc GmbH
DIR/DES Manfred Vormstein

7 Israel
AD CBS Records
AG David Tartakover Graphic Design
DIR/DES David Tartakover
ILL Gerard Alon

8 Belgium
AD Unidisc
AG Edi 2
ILL Meirens Lieve

9 Germany
AD/AG Ariola-Eurodisc GmbH
DIR/DES/ILL Manfred Vormstein

1

2

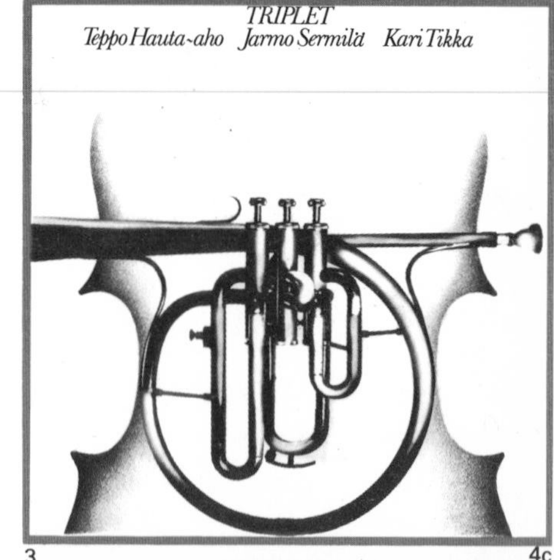

3

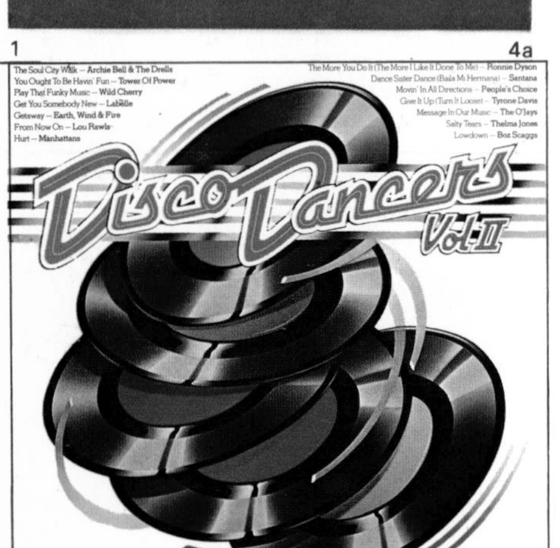

4a

4b

4c

5

Nick Barbarossa's
Disco Strings
STARS, STRIPES AND STRINGS
Red River Story
Sad Sweet Dreamer
Barefoot In The Rain
Moving Like A Superstar
Rainbow u. a.
STEREO

6

CBS
Matti
Caspi

7

8

Strawinsky
PETRUSCHKA
Beethoven
Sonate in D
op. 10/3
Grigorij
Sokolow
Piano
STEREO

9

JACQUES DOUAI
au clair de la lune savez-vous planter les choux
il etait un petit navire il etait une bergere
nous n irons plus au bois
malbrough s en va t en guerre
frere jacques le chevalier du guet
la mere michel le roi dagobert
j ai du bon tabac cadet roussel
sur le pont d avignon la bonne aventure
il court, il court le furet
DISC

Packaging
Emballages
Verpackungsgestaltung

1 United States
AD Venture Foods Inc
AG Roberts P. Gersin Associates Inc
DIR Louis Nelson
DES Paul Hanson
yogurt, yaourt

2 United States
AD Brown & Williamson Tobacco Corp
AG Gianninoto Associates, Inc
DIR John DiGianni
tobacco, tabac

3 Great Britain
AD The Ravenhead Company Ltd
AG Ad Graphics Ltd
DIR Ken Brown
DES Brian Davis
ILL David Lawson
glassware, verrerie, Glas

4 Finland
AD Suomen Vanutehdas-Finwad Ltd
AG Advertising Agency Erva-Latvala
DIR/DES Nuuska Varjus
sanitary towels, serviettes hygiéniques, Monatsbinden

5 Bulgaria
DES Cyril Gogov
matches, allumettes, Streichhölzer

6 Israel
AD Lodzia
AG A. Degani & E. Kürti
DES Alona Degani, Esther Kürti
children's socks, chaussettes d'enfants, Kinder-Socken

1

2

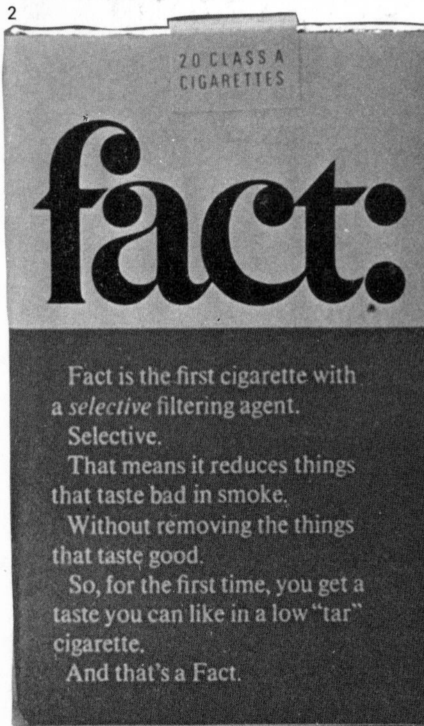

3

4

5

6

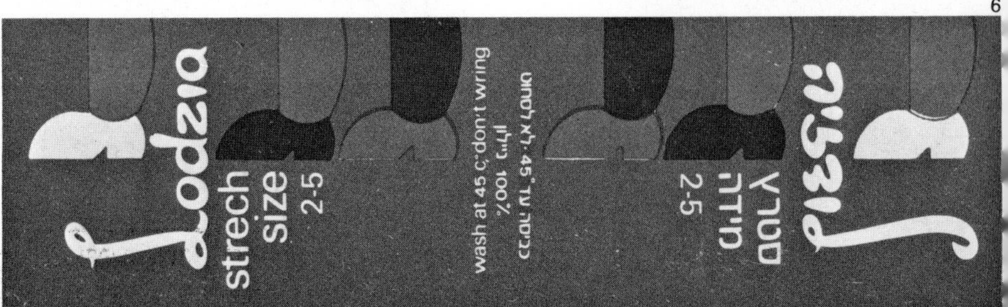

7 France
AD Shell
AG Publicem
DIR Serge Defradat
ILL Jean Claverie

8 France
AD Bergougnan
AG Publicem
DIR Serge Defradat
ILL Jean Claverie
hosepipe, matériel d'arrosage,
Wasserschlauch

9 Brazil
AG PAZ Propaganda
DIR/DES Oswaldo Miranda (Miran)

10 Italy
AD Gruppo Visconti di Modrone
AG Studio Mastellaro & Agenzia Associati
DIR Mario Dagrad, Alfredo Mastellaro
DES Alfredo Mastellaro

11 Austria
AD Chic Gasfeuerzeuge
AG watzlwork
DIR/DES Peter Watzl
ILL Raimund Mayerhofer
COPY Peter Watzl
lighter-gas can, boîte de gaz pour briquets,
Gaspatrone für Feuerzeuge

7

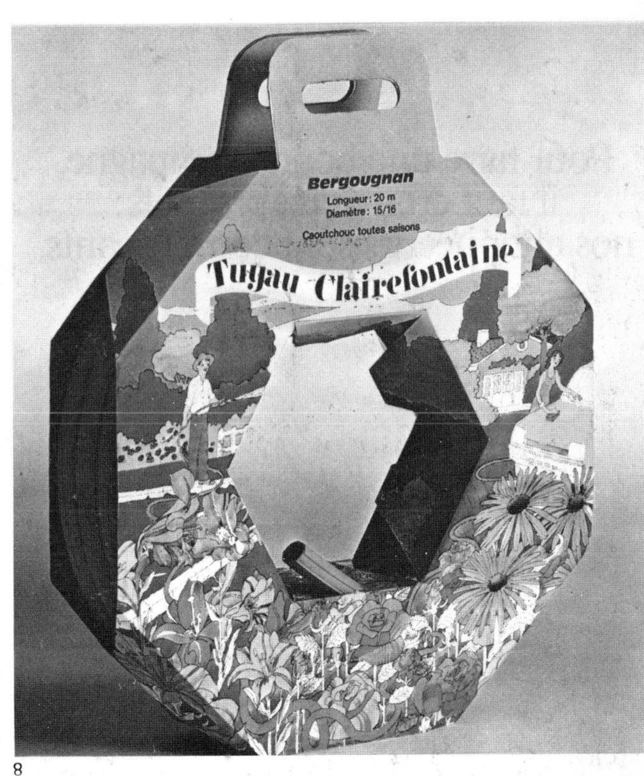

8

9

10

11

Packaging
Emballages
Verpackungsgestaltung

1 Australia
AD Grosby
AG Fountain, Huie
DIR/DES Ted Blackall
sports shoes, souliers de sport, Sport-Schuhe

2 Australia
AD National Chemical Products Pty Ltd
AG Cato Hibberd Hawksby Design Pty Ltd
shampoo

3 Great Britain
AD Calypsa Coffee Company
AG John Harris Design Partnership
DIR/DES John Harris
tea, thé, Tee

4 South Africa
AD Adcock Ingram SA (Pty) Ltd
AG Grapplegroup CJA (Pty) Ltd
DIR/TYPOGRAPHER Jilly Clucas
deodorant

5 South Africa
AD Southern Cross Importers
AG Patricia Frost Graphic Design
DIR/DES Patricia Frost
muesli

6 Italy
AD Bassetti SpA
AG Studio Mastellaro
DIR/DES Alfredo Mastellaro
ILL Antonio dal Santo

7 South Africa
AD Carmel
AG Patricia Frost Graphic Design
DIR/DES Patricia Frost
pickles

8 Germany
AD Mouson Cosmetic Co
DIR/DES Peter Schmidt
mens toiletries, savons, toilettenartikel

9 United States
AD Oroweat Foods Company
AG Richard C. Runyon Design
DIR Richard C. Runyon
DES Julie Morris, Richard C. Runyon
muffins, petits pains mollets, Teegebäck

1

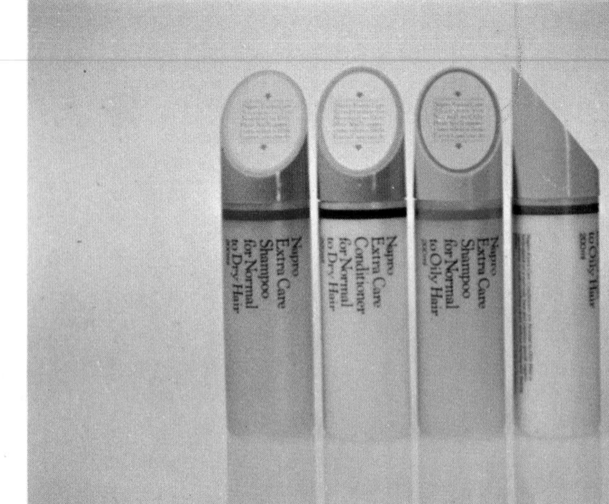

2

3

4

5

6

10 United States
AD Brown Company
DIR Robert Stoming

11 Italy
AD Pierrel SpA
AG Studio Mastellaro
DIR/DES Alfredo Mastellaro
ILL Paolo Guidotti

12 Australia
AD J. C. Holmes Pty Ltd
AG Cato Hibberd Hawksby Design Pty Ltd
disposable dinnerware, service de table, plastisches Esszeug

7

8

9

10

11

12

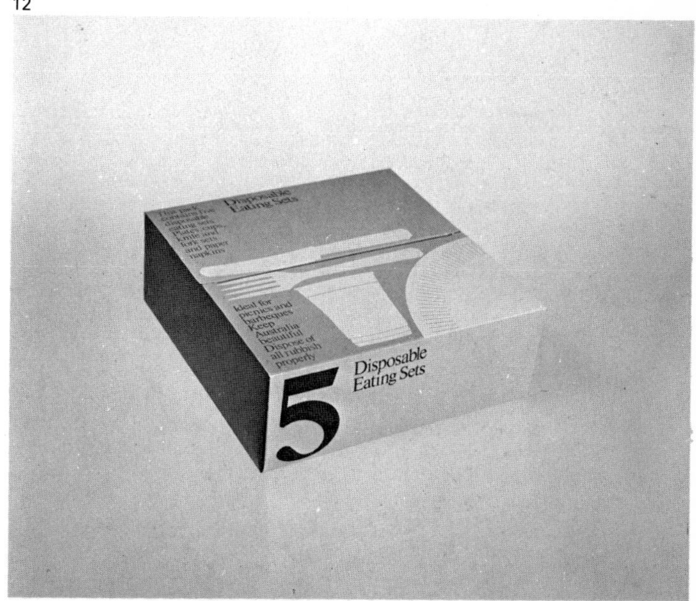

Packaging
Emballages
Verpackungsgestaltung

1 Great Britain
AD Integrity Foods
AG Design for Print Ltd
DIR/DES Gus Hunnybun
traditional country wine, vin, Wein

2 Australia
AG Wynn Winegrowers Pty Ltd
AG Les Mason Graphic Design
DIR/DES Les Mason
wine, vin, Wein

3 Holland
AD J. A. Verbund BV
AG Prad BV
DIR Joop Smit
ILL Kees de Kiefte
wine, vin, Wein

4a-b United States
AD (a) Pepsi-Cola Company
(b) Monsieur Henri Wines
AG Pepsi-Cola Company
DIR (a) Sondra Scarzafaua
(b) Sondra Scarzafaua, Nancy Krieger
DES (a) Sondra Scarzafaua
(b) Calvin Valensi
(a) diet Pepsi, Pepsi de regime, (b) wine, vin, Wein

1

2

3

4a

4b

5 Great Britain
AD Saccone & Speed Ltd
AG The Pack Design Company
DIR/DES John Castle
economy French wines

6 Italy
AD Vimcola Lippolis
AG Studio de Liso
DIR Geppi de Liso
DES Lilli and Geppi de Liso
wine, vin, Wein

7 Great Britain
AD Coca-Cola Company
AG Devonshire Studios
DIR/DES M. Conrad
soft-drink

8 United States
AD Aguas de Tehuacan SA, Mexico
AD Gianninoto Associates Inc
DIR John DiGianni
soft drinks, boissons non alcooliques, alkoholfreies Getränk

9 Great Britain
AD Ringnes Brewery Oslo
AG John Harris Design Partnership
DIR/DES John Harris
beer, Bière, Bier

10 Great Britain
AD Dema Glass Ltd
AG David Harris Consultant Design
DIR/DES David Harris
ILL Theo Cockerell
glassware, verrerie, Glas

5

6

7

8

9

10

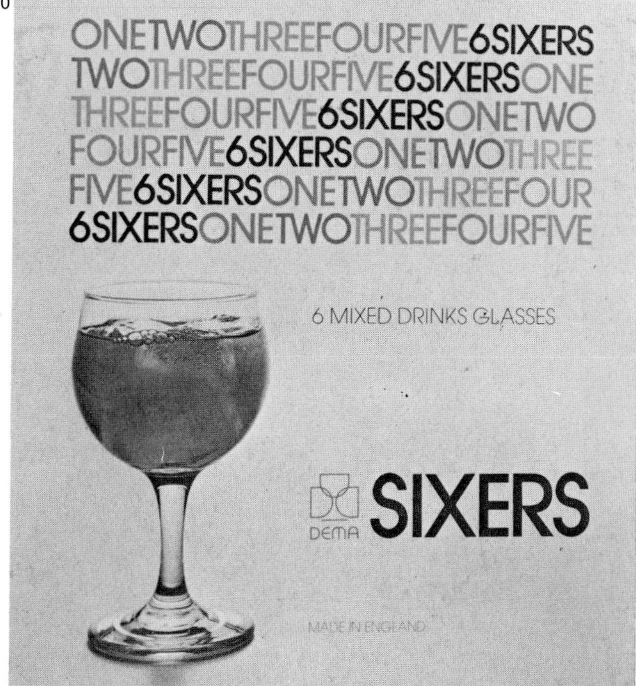

Packaging
Emballages
Verpackungsgestaltung

1 Australia
AD Beecham Australia Pty Ltd
AG Beard Benton & Bowles Pty Ltd
DIR Les Mason Graphic Design
DES Les Mason
pharmaceuticals

2 Germany
AD Germania Backmittel
DES Erich Unger
baking aids, Backmittel

3 Italy
AD Pierrel Spa
AG Studio Mastellaro
DES Alfredo Mastellaro
ILL Occhio Magico

4 Germany
AD Dralle
DES Peter Scmhidt
pharmaceuticals

5 Mexico
AD Pfizer SA
AG Young & Rubicam SA
DIR Justo Somonte
DES Sergio Martinez
ILL Erick Schwartz
COPY Enrique Delgado
antibiotics

6a-b Great Britain
AD Scottish Fine Soaps
AG Russell Design Association
ILL Ilana Richardson
soap, savon, Seife

1

2

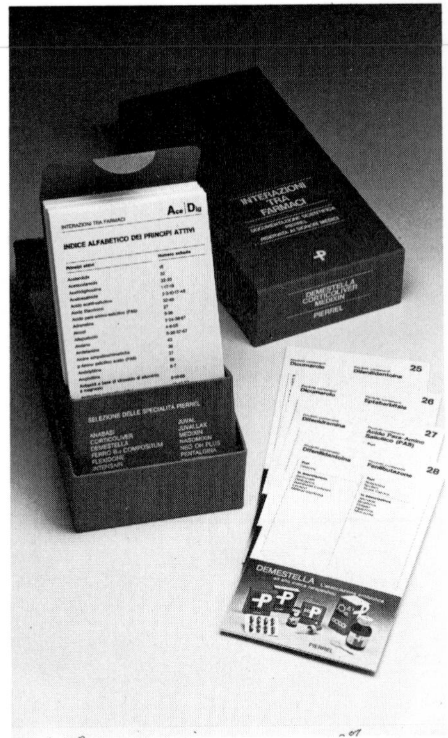

3

4

7 South Africa
AD Parke-Davis
AG Derek Spaull Graphics
DIR/DES Derek Spaull
pharmaceutical — tonic

8 Mexico
AD Parera SA
AG Laboratorio de Diseno y Mercadotecnia — Carton y Papel de Mexico SA
DIR Arie J. Geurts
DES Graham Edwards
ILL Enrique Bostelman
cosmetics

9 United States
AD National Semiconductor Corporation
AG Ken Parkhurst & Associates Inc
DIR Ken Parkhurst
DES Jean-Claude Muller
electronic kits

10 Spain
AD Laboratorios F. Bonet
AG Diseño y Creacion Grafica
DIR/DES Andres Puech
pharmaceuticals

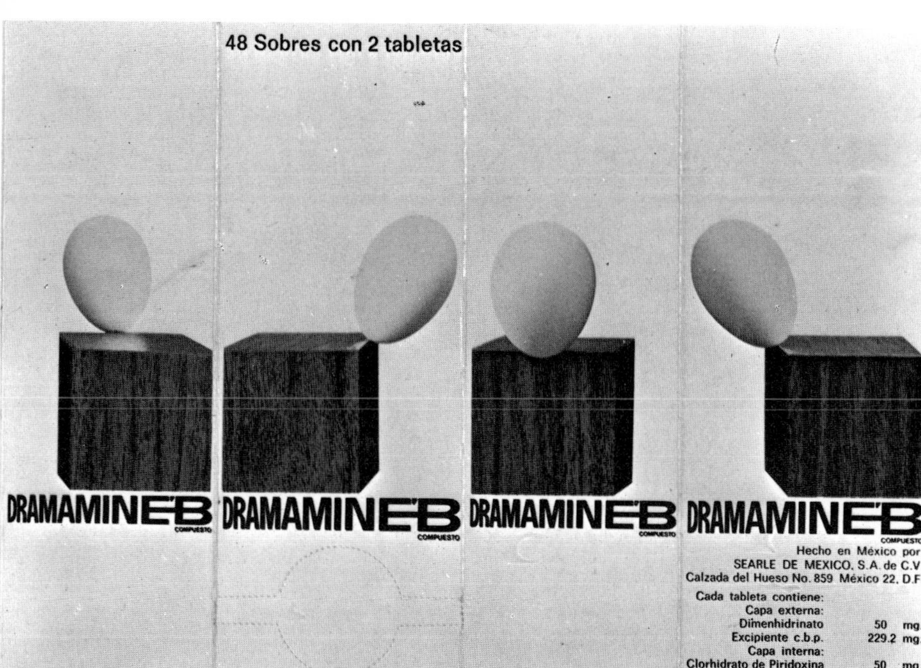

5

6a

Scots Pine
Natural beauty soap
Net Weight 3½oz.
6b

7

8
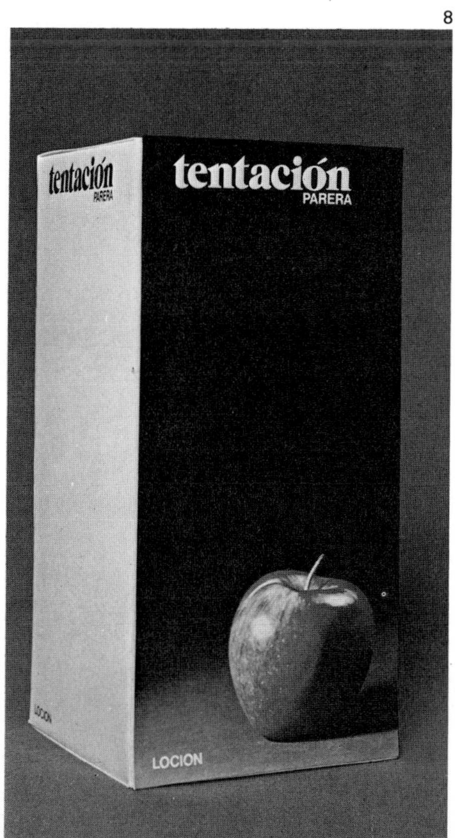

9
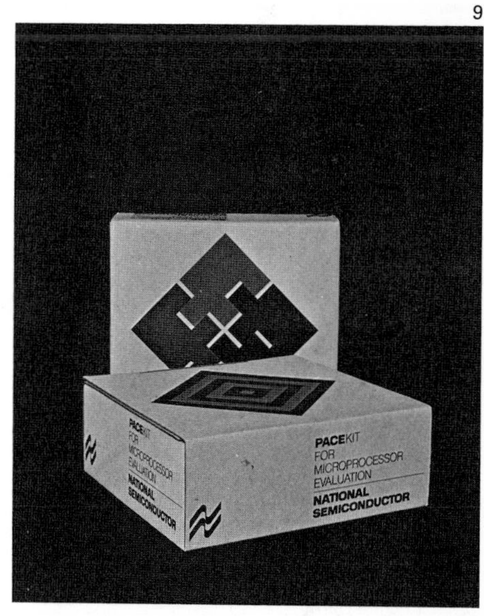

10

Packaging
Emballages
Verpackungsgestaltung

1 Great Britain
AD Black & Decker Ltd
AG Peter Proto Associates
DIR Peter Proto
DES Jon Bodsworth, Peter Proto
home storage system

2 Great Britain
AD Europlastics
AG Trickett & Webb Ltd
DIR Lynn Trickett, Brian Webb
DES Lynn Trickett, Brian Webb, Andrew Thomas
toy, jouet, Spielzeug

3 Denmark
AD Lego
DES Graphic Designer Folkmar Roll
ILL Jørgen Jørgensen
COPY Carl Gyllenhoff
Lego toy packages

4 Spain
AD CECSA
AG Publicidad Mediterranea
DIR Ramiro Sebura
DES Enrique Fernandez
ILL Jose Pallarés
COPY Pedro Nagore
radio

5 Denmark
AD Forlaget Audio AS
AG SB Grafisk Design
DIR/DES Søren Balle
ILL John Fowlie
gramophone pick-up

6a-e Israel
AD Orda Industries Ltd
AG A. Degani & E. Kürti
DES Alona Degani, Esther Kürti
children's puzzles, devinettes pour enfants, puzzle für Kinder

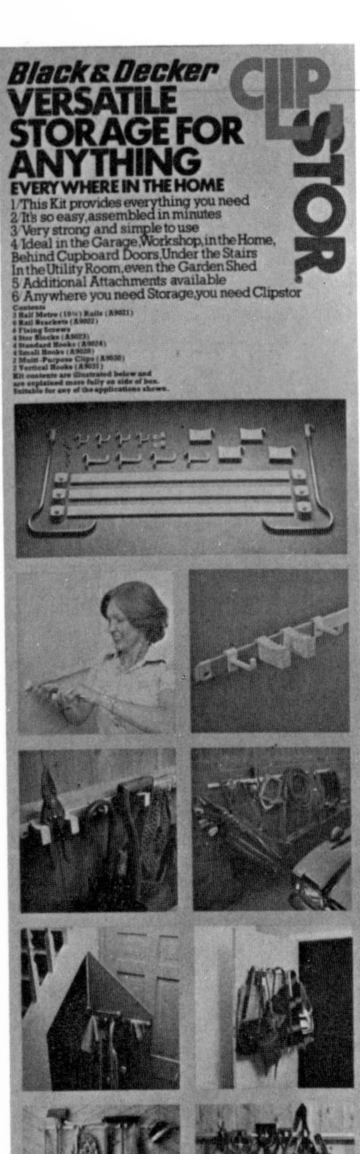

1

2

3

4

am rensearm

5

JEUX NATHAN
FERNAND NATHAN
AUTOPUZZLE
5
• un puzzle en bois à construire
• des roues à monter sur un châssis pour faire une auto à rouler
une autopuzzle qui roule
à partir de 3 ans

6a

6b

1 2 3 4 5 6 7 8
Collectionnez ces 8 modèles qui s'accrochent les uns aux autres

6c

6d

6e

Packaging
Emballages
Verpackungsgestaltung

1 Canada
AD The Eddy Match Co.
AG Burns, Cooper, Donoahue, Fleming & Co Ltd
DIR Robert Burns
DES Dawn Cooper Tennant
household wood and book matches, alumetltes, Zündhötzer

2 Great Britain
AD Habitat
AG Conran Associates
DES Gavin Clive-Smith
hot air balloon, Montgolfier, Heissluftballon

3 India
AD Bata India Ltd
AG Bata Studio
DIR/DES Binay Saha
sports shoes, souliers de sport, Sportsschuhe

4 Spain
AD Podium
DES Jaime Rasqui Llorce
plastic wood

5 Taiwan
AD Chunter Souvenir Shop
AG Tico Graphic Printing Co
DIR/DES Mei-Chung Tsen
souvenir shop

6 Great Britain
AD Coo-Var Ltd
AG Eurographic Ltd
paints and protective treatments, peintures, Farben

7 Switzerland
AD Auer Bittmann Soulié AG
DES Maya Stange ASG
Laboratory supplies

8 Austria
AD Castka Handschuhgeschäft
AG watzlwork
DIR/DES Peter Watzl
gloves, gants, Handschuhe

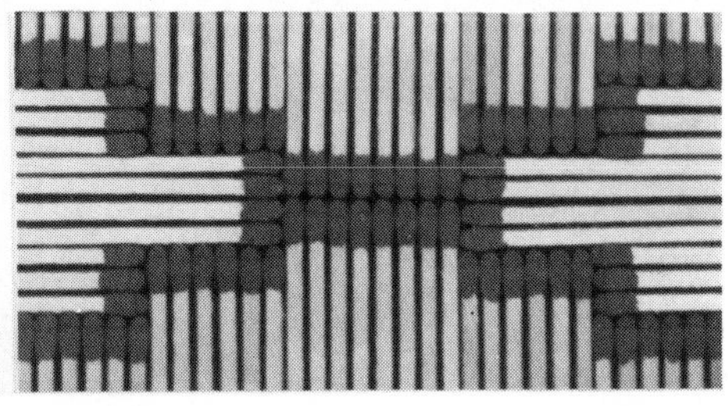

1

2

3

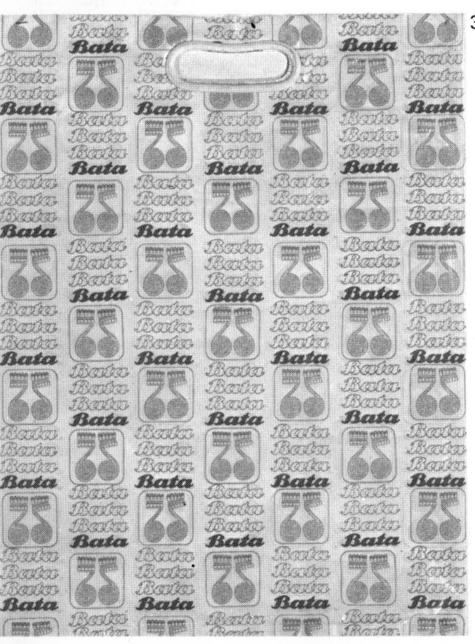

4

5

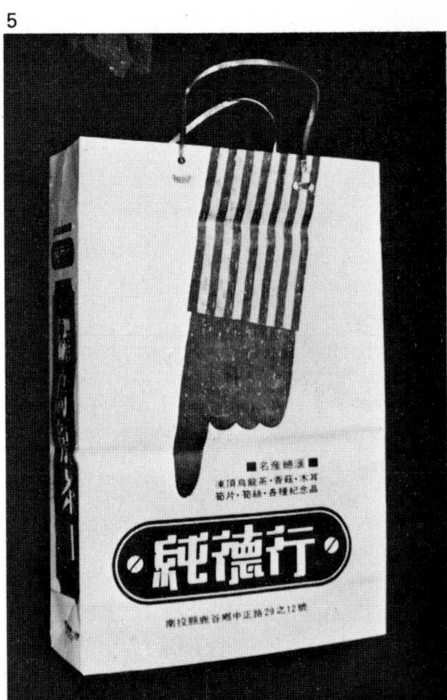

9 Brazil
AD Lafepe Laboratório
AG Cunha Lima e Associados Ltda
DIR Guilherme Cunha Lima
ILL Edna Lucia Cunha Lima, Guilherme Cunha Lima
pharmaceuticals

6

7

8

9

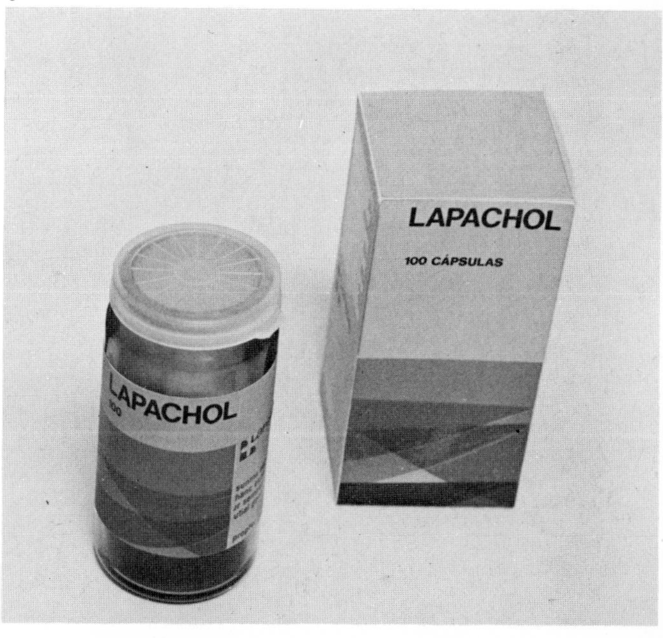

Screen advertising
Titles
Annonces de l'écran
Titres
Film und TV Werbung
Titel

1a Brazil
AD TV Globo
DIR (a, b, c,) Hans-J. Donner
(d, e, f, g) Rudi Böhm
DES (a, b, c, d, e, h) Hans-J. Donner
(f) Rudi Böhm, Hans-J. Donner, Sergio Liuzzi
ILL (f) Via Trenker

1a

1b

1c

1d

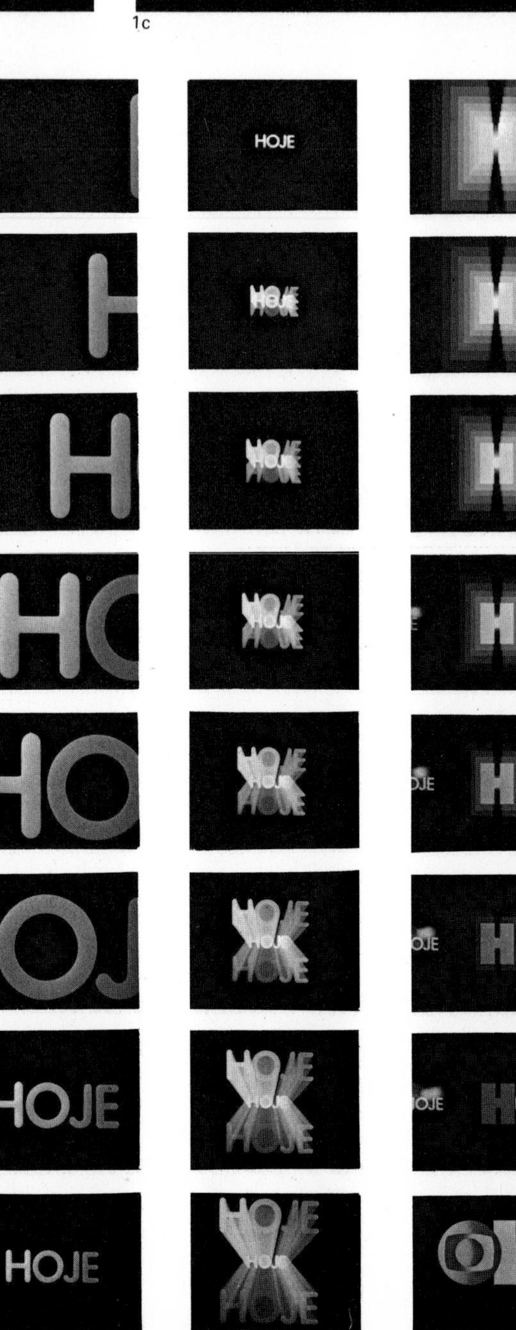

1e

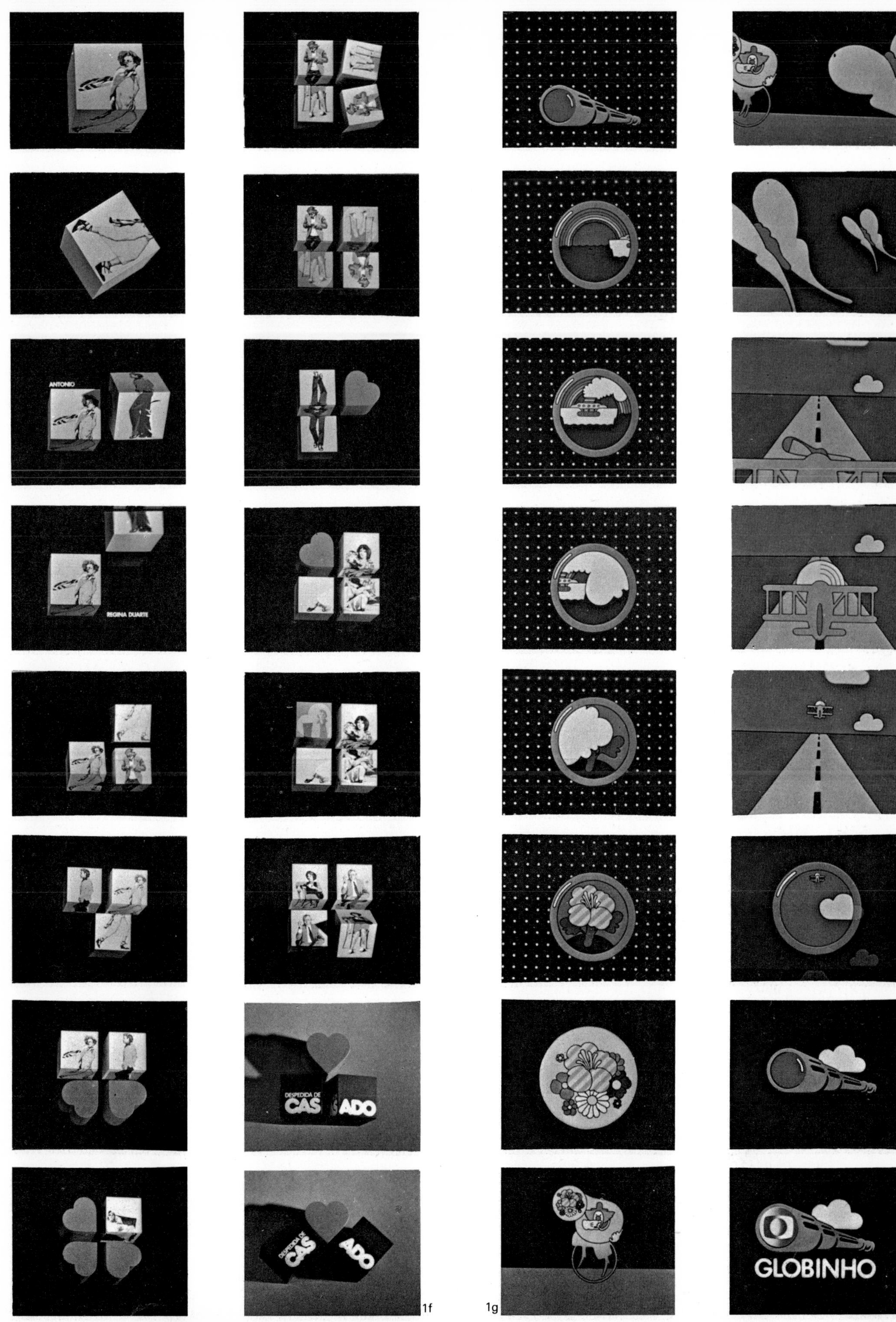
ANTONIO
REGINA DUARTE
DESPEDIDA DE
CAS
ADO
DESPEDIDA DE
CAS
ADO
GLOBINHO

1f

1g

Screen advertising
Titles
Annonces de l'écran
Titres
Film und TV Werbung
Titel

1a-c Holland
AD (a) Nationale-Nederlanden
(b) Dutch Dairy Corporation
(c) House Painters' Trade Corporation
AG NPO Nationale Publiciteits Onderneming BV
DIR (a) Bob Blechman
(b) Huib Ebbinge
(c) Erik de Vries
TV DIR (a, b) Toon Broeksma
(c) Max Velthuijs
ILL (a, b) Bob Blechman
(c) Max Velthuijs

COPY (a) Joop Cranendonk, Ben Rowold
(b, c) Joop Cranendonk
a) insurance, assurance, Versicherung
(b) butter, beurre
(c) premium for indoor painting in winter

2 Great Britin
AD C.O.I. Department of Energy
AG Young & Rubicam Ltd
DIR Richard Dearing
ANIMATORS Richard Williams Studios
COPY Clive Atkins
'save it' energy commercial

3 India
AD Oberoi-Sheraton
AG Ogilvy Benson & Mather Private Ltd
DIR B. Merwan
DES Anil Dangi
ILL Sydney D'Souza
TV screen titles

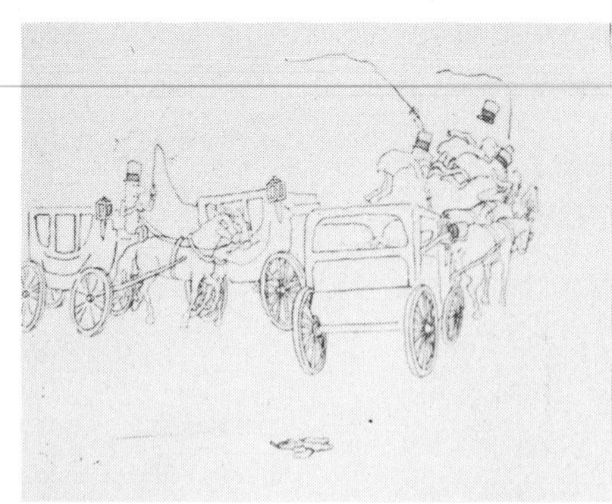

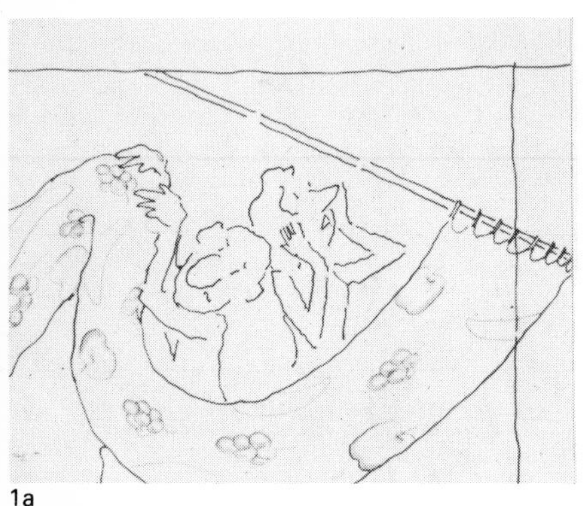

1a

1b

1c

4 Hong Kong
AD Hong Kong Land
AG Clic Studios Ltd
Chi Fu Fa Yuen — new town

2

3

4

Screen advertising
Titles
Annonces de l'écran
Titres
Film und TV Werbung
Titel

1a-c Great Britain
AD (a) General Accident, Fire, Life Assurance Corp
(b) H.P. Bulmer Ltd
(c) Scottish & Newcastle Breweries Ltd
AG Leo Burnett Ltd
DIR (a) Chris Baker
(b) Stuart Cooper
(c) Doug Buntrock
PRODUCER (a, c) Eric Straw
(b) Stuart Cooper
PRODUCTION COMPANY (a) Illustra Films
(b, c) Spots Film Services
COPY (a) Martin Walsh
(c) Barry Fox
(a) motoring policy
(b) cider, cidre, Apfelwein
(c) whisky

2a-b Great Britain
AD (a) Gallaher Ltd
(b) Amjo Productions
AG Richard Williams Animation Ltd
DIR (a) Peter Harold
(b) Tony White
DES (a) Dick Purdum
(b) Tony White, Roy Naisbitt
COPY (a) Alan Tilby, Peter Harold
(a) tobacco, (b) film

1a

1b

1c

NIEMEYER
SAMSON
HALFZ
SHAG

ALFZWARE SHA

ALFZWARE SH

2a

2b

in THE
STRIKES AGAIN

Screen advertising
Titles
Annonces de l'écran
Titres
Film und TV Werbung
Titel

1a-f Great Britain
AG (a) International Creative Group, B.P. Oil
(b) Dorland Advertising, Irish Cheddar Cheese
(c,e) Geers Gross Advertising
(d) Prad Amsterdam, Seven-Up
(f) Troost Dusseldorf Bus and Tram Transport
PRODUCTION Wyatt Cattaneo Productions
DIR/DES (a,f) Chris Randall
(b) Ron Wyatt
(c,e) Tony Cattaneo
(d) Alison de Vere

(a) oil
(b) cheese, fromage, Käse
(c) tea, tée, The
(d) cosmetics
(e) butter, beurre
(f) transport

2a-c Great Britain
AD (a) Allcome Hamburg
(c) The Genesis Project
AG Halas & Batchelor Animation
DIR (a) Dietrich Lowe
(b) John Halas
(c) Elphin Lloyd-Jones
DES (a) John Halas
(c) Dino Kotopoulis
(a) insurance
(b) story — Skyrider
(c) film of 'Noah's Ark'

1a

1b

2a

2b

2c

3 Germany
AD Opel
AG McCann, Frankfurt
DIR Claus-Joachim Koch
DES Robert Abel, Mitchell Brisker
motor cars

1c

1d

1e

1f

3

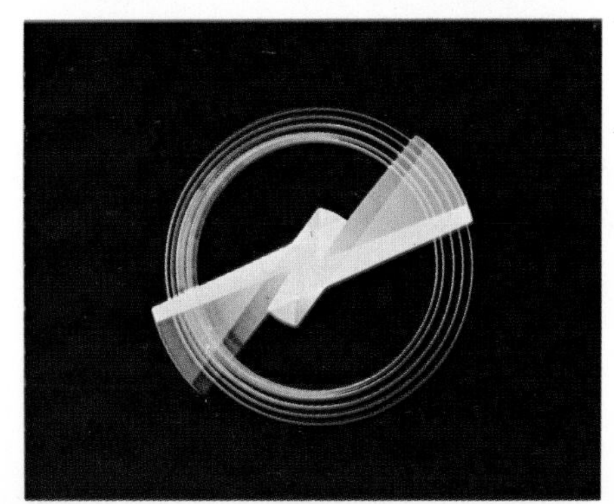

Screen advertising
Titles
Annonces de l'écran
Titres
Film und TV Werbung
Titel

1a-d Italy
AD RAI Radiotelevisione Italiana
AG (a,b,c) Ruffolo
(d) Studio de Santis
DIR/DES (a,b,c) Sergio Ruffolo
(d) Alfredo de Santis
a,c) cultural TV programme
(b) agricultural TV programme
(d) educational TV programme

2a-c Finland
AD/AG The Finnish Broadcasting Co
DIR/DES and ANIMATION Tapio Savio
ILL (c) Aarre Aalto
COPY Marita Linqwist
(a) title of TV programme
(b,c) animations

1a

1b

1c

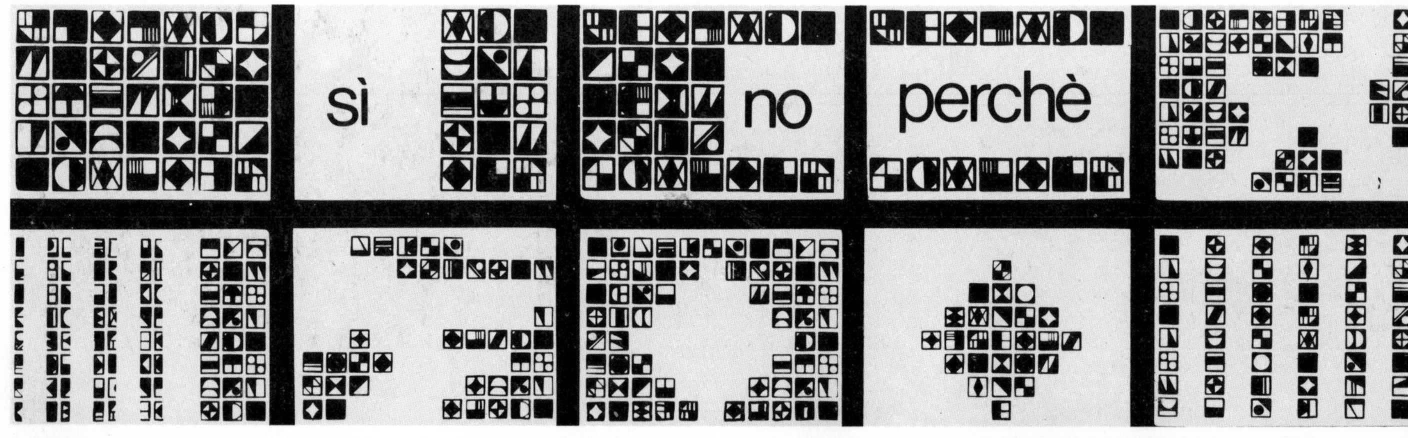

a

a

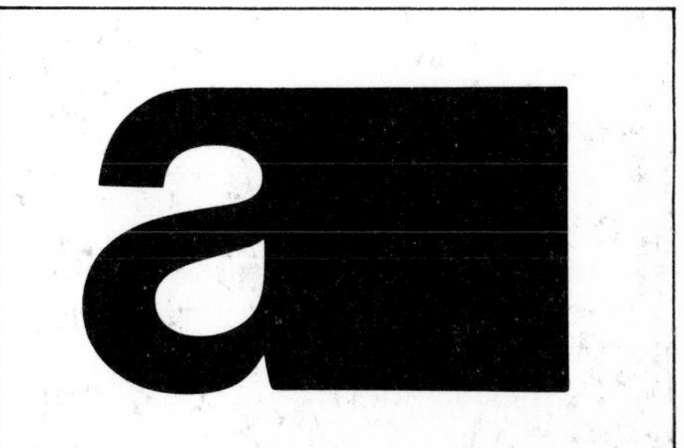
a

a
a cura di

a
a cura di
Sandro Lai
Angelo Sferrazza

a

1

2a

2b

HUNDEN
SOM INTE
FANNS

2c

HUNDEN
SOM INTE
FANNS

Screen advertising
Titles
Annonces de l'écran
Titres
Film und TV Werbung
Titel

1a-d Great Britain
AD BBC
DES (a) Dick Bailey
(b) Liz Friedman
(c) Anne Smith
(d) Pauline Talbot
PRODUCER (a) Stewart Hardy
(c) Chris Jelley
(a) drama,
(b) quiz programme
(c) further education
(d) children's programme

2a-g Great Britain
AD Granada TV
AG Granada TV Graphics Dept
DIR/DES (a) J. G. Adshead
(b) Jim Quick
(c,d) Ben Davies
(e,f,g) Keith Aldred
(a,e) film
(b,c,d) weather slide promotions
(g) children's programme
(f) video

3a-b Bulgaria
AD Bulgarian Television
DES Nikola Petrov Nikolov
cinema on TV

1a

1b

1c

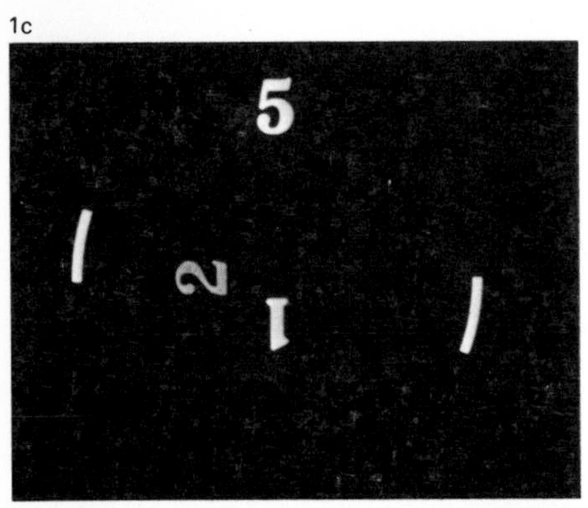

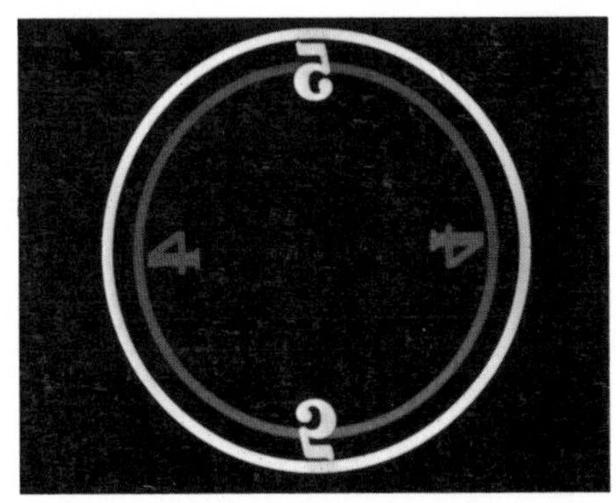

1d

2a

2b

2c

2d

2e

2f

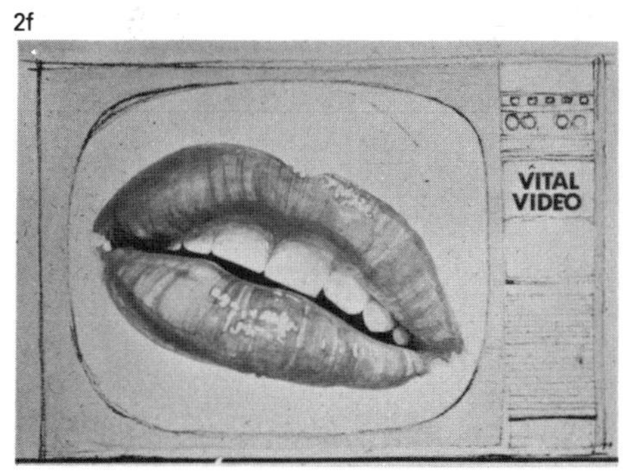

2g

3a

3b

Screen advertising
Titles
Annonces de l'écran
Titres
Film und TV Werbung
Titel

1 Great Britain
AD BBC TV
DIR Stefan Pstrowski
ANIMATION B. M. Animation
light entertainment

2a-b Great Britain
AD Granada TV
AG Granada TV Graphic Design Dept
DIR/DES (a) John Leech
(b) Phil Buckley
(a) comedy series
(b) pop programme

3 Brazil
AD TV Globo
DIR Rudi Böhm
DES Via Trenka
TV show

4 Great Britain
AD BBC TV
DES John Speirs, Howard Moses
ILL Howard Moses
current affairs programme

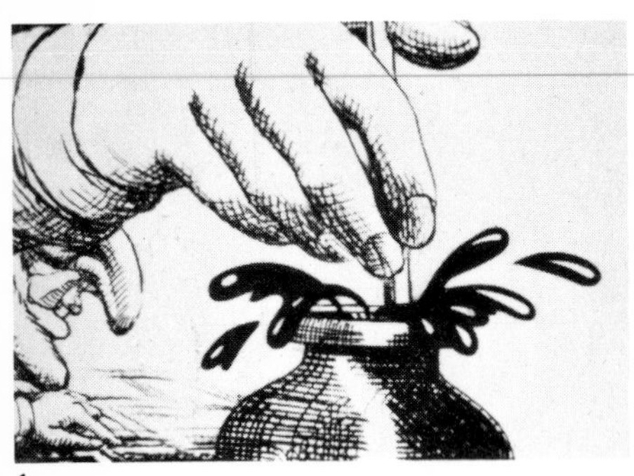

1

2a

2b

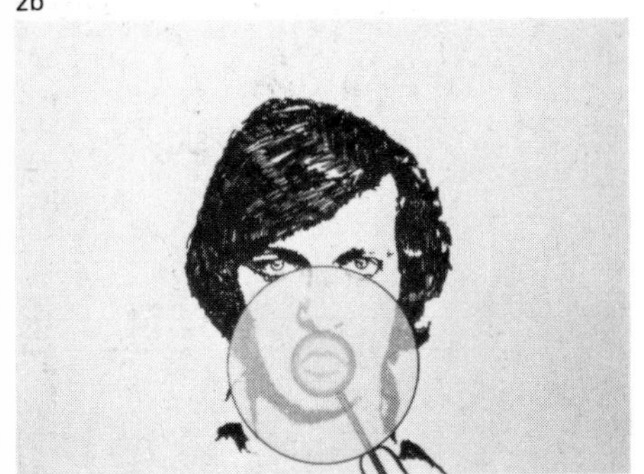

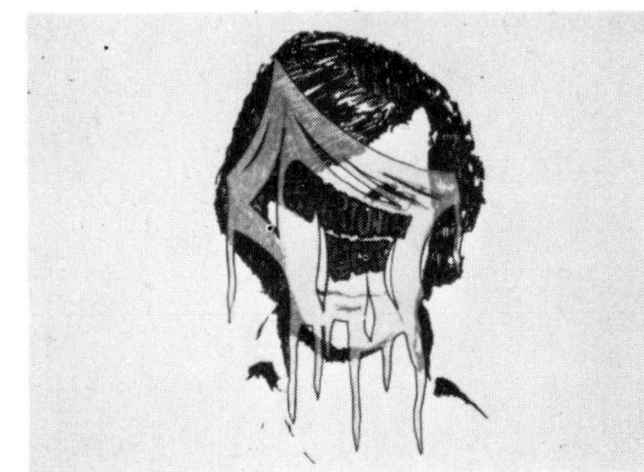

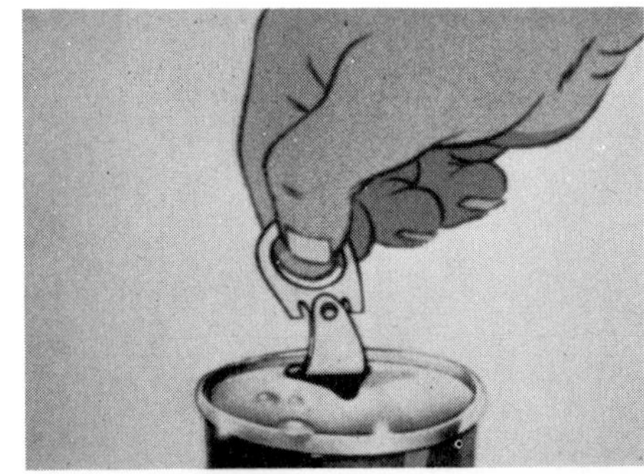

Marshall McLuhan
über Pop-Kultur

Marshall McLuhan über die
Identitätssuche der Jugend

Marshall McLuhan
über Kunst und
Kommunikation

Marshall McLuhan
über den
Generationskonflikt

3

4

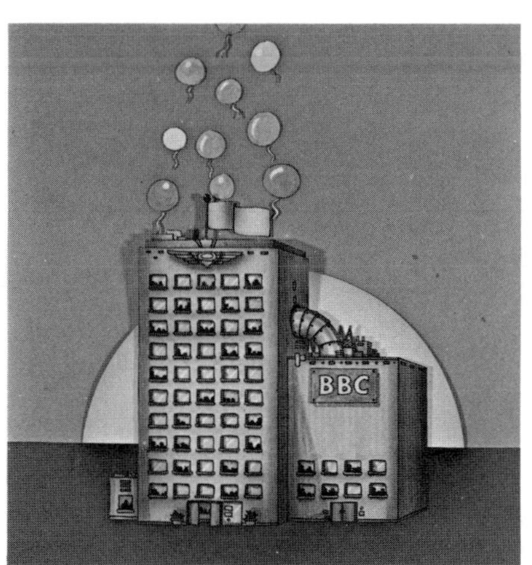
BBC

Direct Mail
Brochures
Broschüren

1a-d United States
AD/AG Container Corporation of America
DIR/DES Bill Bonnell

1a

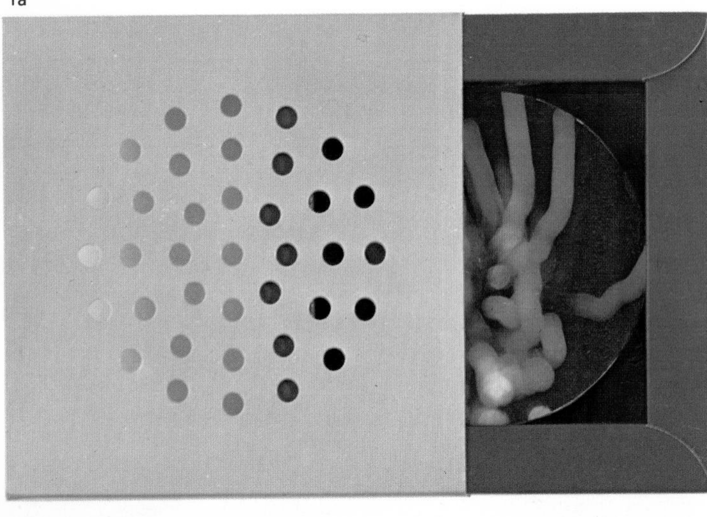

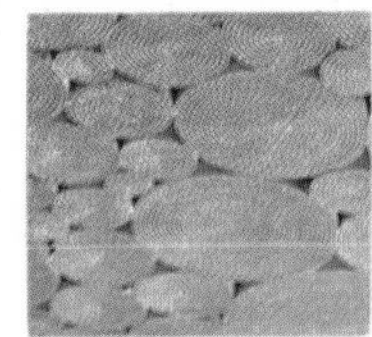

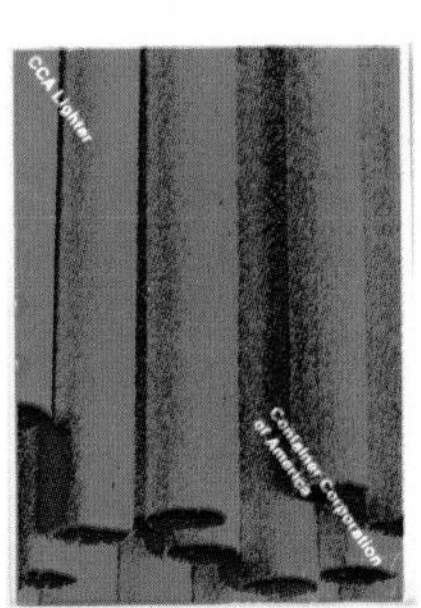

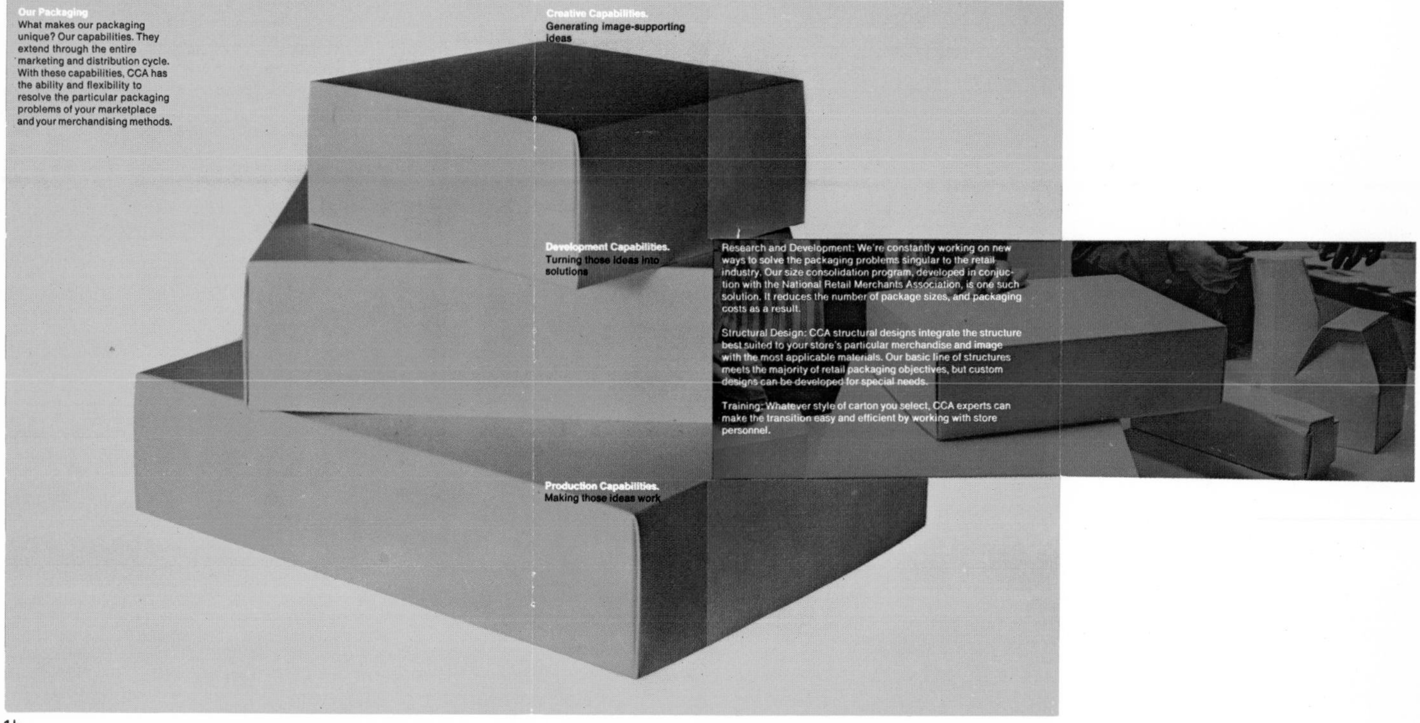
Our Packaging
What makes our packaging unique? Our capabilities. They extend through the entire marketing and distribution cycle. With these capabilities, CCA has the ability and flexibility to resolve the particular packaging problems of your marketplace and your merchandising methods.
Creative Capabilities.
Generating image-supporting ideas
Development Capabilities.
Turning those ideas into solutions
Research and Development: We're constantly working on new ways to solve the packaging problems singular to the retail industry. Our size consolidation program, developed in conjuc-tion with the National Retail Merchants Association, is one such solution. It reduces the number of package sizes, and packaging costs as a result.
Structural Design: CCA structural designs integrate the structure best suited to your store's particular merchandise and image with the most applicable materials. Our basic line of structures meets the majority of retail packaging objectives, but custom designs can be developed for special needs.
Training: Whatever style of carton you select, CCA experts can make the transition easy and efficient by working with store personnel.
Production Capabilities.
Making those ideas work

1b

1c

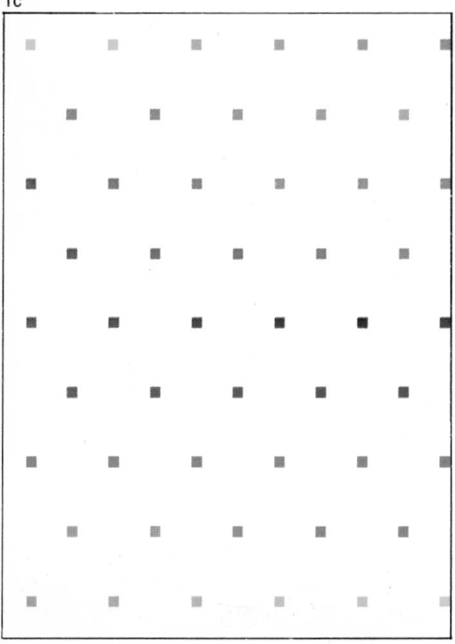

1d

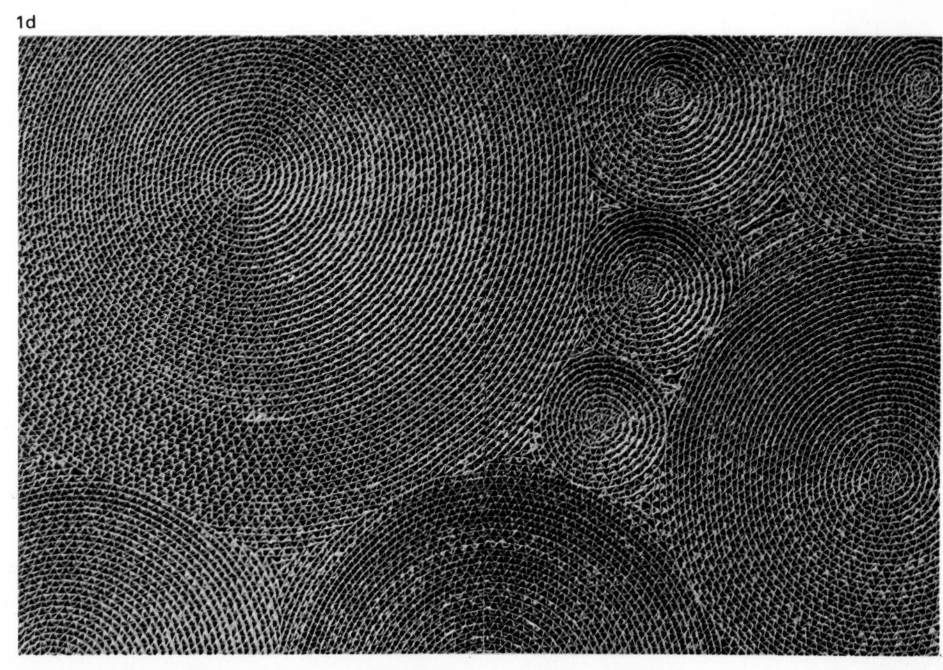

Direct Mail
Brochures
Broschüren

1 United States
AD Brickel Associates Inc
AG Peter Bradford & Associates
DIR Peter Bradford
DES Peter Bradford, Jonette Jackobson
ILL Michael Pateman
furniture, meuble, Möbel

2 United States
AD Hiebert
AG John Follis and Associates
DIR John Follis
DES T. Wayne Hunt
ILL Fritz Taggert
furniture, meuble, Möbel

3a-b Germany
AD Atrium Hotel Sepp Voglar
AG Udo Zisowsky
DIR/DES Zisowsky + Oehring
ILL Günter Bleyl
(a) wine list, Weinkarte
(b) menu, Speisekarte

4 South Africa
AD Karos Hotels
AG Jeremy Sampson Associates (Pty) Ltd
DIR/DES John Maskew
ILL Barry Sampson
menus, Speisekarte

5a-b United States
AD Netchair
AG Sam Smidt Associates
DIR/DES Sam Smidt
ILL Dennis Grey
furniture, meuble

6 United States
AD Copco Inc
AG Peter Bradford & Associates
DIR Peter Bradford, Joseph Rodd
DES Peter Bradford
ILL Michael Pateman
cookware, material pour la cuisine, Küchengeschirr

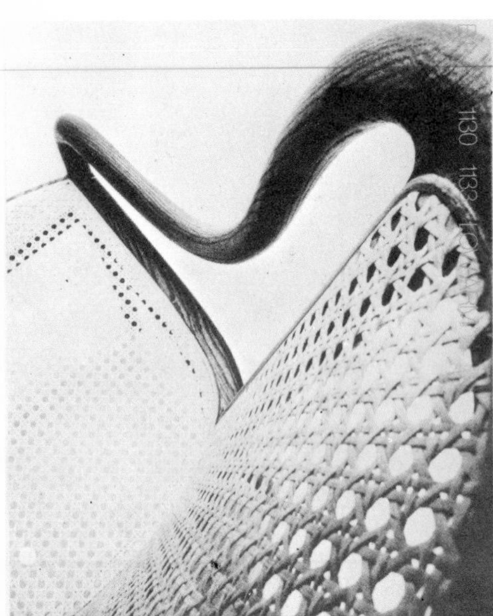

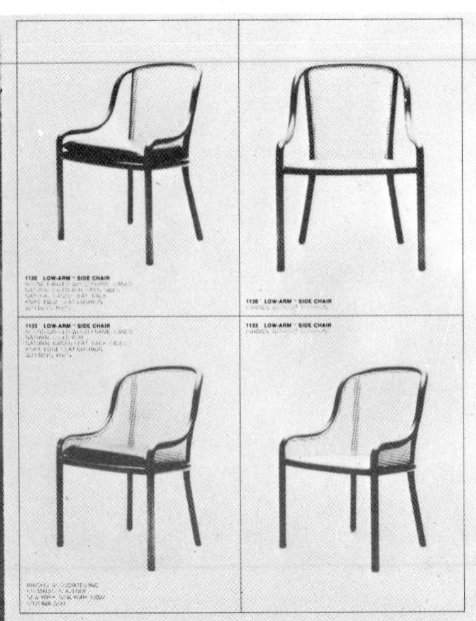

1

2

3a

3b

4

7a-b Great Britain
AD Telford Development Corporation
AG Minale, Tattersfield Provinciali Ltd
housing development project,
Baugesellschaft

5a

5b

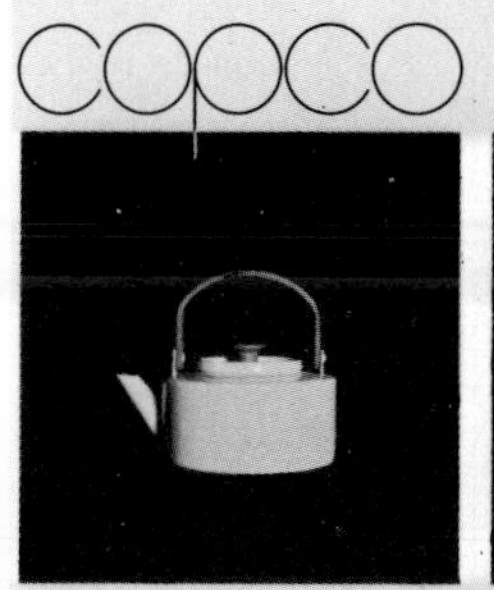

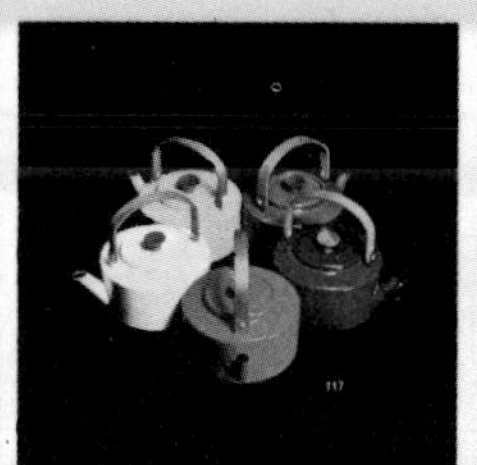

SINCE WE INTRODUCED OUR **TEA KETTLE** IT HAS BECOME THE CLASSIC IN THE FIELD MADE OF PORCELAINIZED ENAMEL ON STEEL. IT'S A GREAT PERFORMER AS WELL AS A GREAT LOOKER. AN AWARD WINNING DESIGN BY MICHAEL LAX. YOU CAN GET THE CLASSIC IN OUR FIVE COPCO COLORS.

THE PERFECT KITCHEN IS A **COPCO KITCHEN.** BEAUTIFULLY DESIGNED USABLE UTENSILS. COPCO WORKS AS HARD AS YOU DO TO CREATE PERFECT DISHES AND A BEAUTIFUL TABLE. CHOOSE THE COPCO COLOR THAT BEST MATCHES YOUR DECOR: TOMATO RED, CHOCOLATE BROWN, BLUE, WHITE OR YELLOW.

COPCO DESIGNS ITS PIECES TO GIVE YOU THE BEST IN LOOKS, PERFORMANCE, AND THEY'RE ALL EASY TO CLEAN. IT'S NOT JUST COOKWARE, IT'S COPCO.

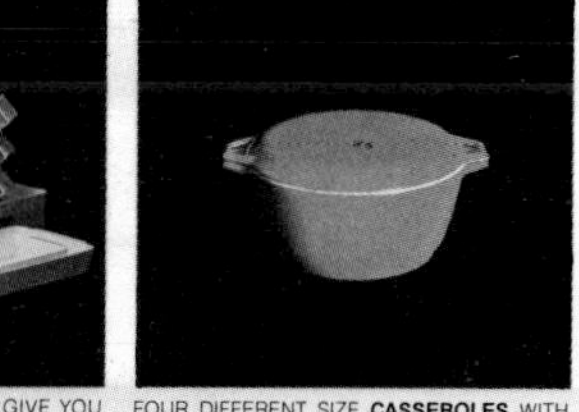

FOUR DIFFERENT SIZE **CASSEROLES** WITH MATCHING COVERS ASSURE YOU THE PERFECT SIZE FOR THE PERFECT MEAL. LIKE ALL OUR CAST IRON COOKWARE, EACH PIECE IS CREATED FROM RAW CAST IRON TO PORCELAINIZED PERFECTION TO INSURE PERFECT HEAT DISTRIBUTION.

EACH PIECE OF COPCO IS TWICE COATED WITH ENAMEL FOR EASY CLEANING. DESIGNED BY COUNT SIGVARD BERNADOTTE.

6

7a

7b

Direct Mail
Brochures
Broschüren

1a France
AD 3 Suisses
AG Mafia (Maïmé Arnodin, Fayolle, International, Associés)
fashion, modes

1b-c France
AD Absorba
AG Mafia (Maïmé Arnodin, Fayolle, International, Associés)
childrens fashion, Kinderbekleidung

2 Great Britain
AD Funcore Ltd
AG Ad Graphics Ltd
DIR Ken Brown
DES Brian Davis
COPY (translator) Marion Lum
rocking horses, chevaux à bascule, Schaukelpferde

3a-d Australia
AD Vega Press Pty Ltd
AG Cato Hibberd Hawksby Design Pty Ltd
ILL Penelope Cato, Ray Condon
COPY David Webster
printing house

4 France
AD Air France
AG Garamond
DIR R. Mangiavacca
DES Jacques Nathan-Garamond
airline

5 Great Britain
AD The Grosvenor House Antiques Fair
DIR/DES Ronald Clark
ILL Derrick Witty
antiques

1a

1b

1c

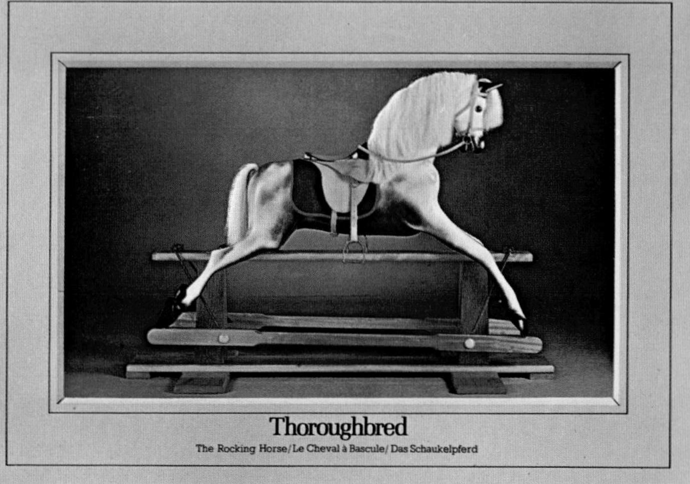

2

3

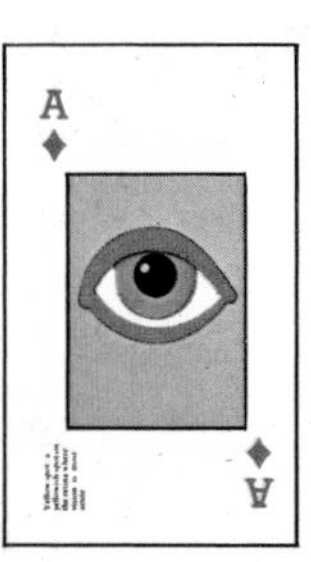

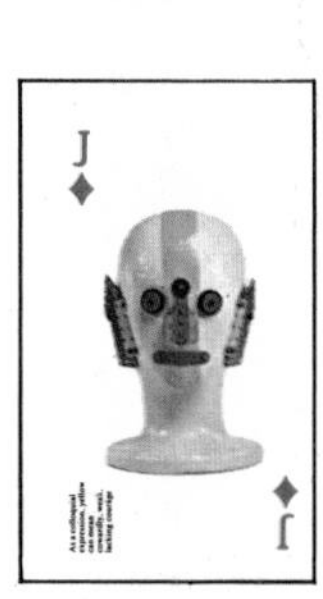

4

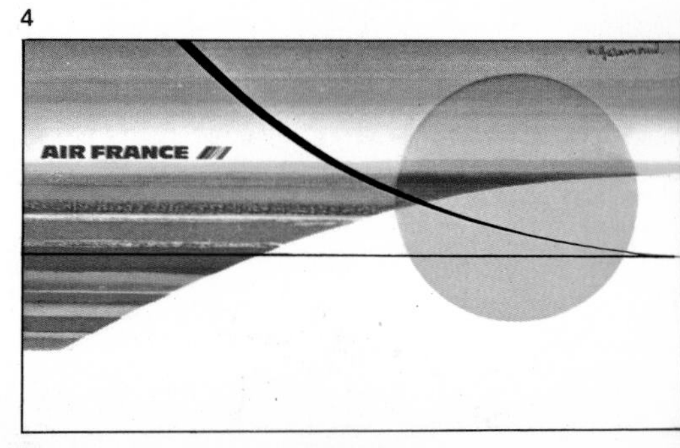

6 Great Britain
AD The General Trading Company
AG National Advertising Corporation
DIR/DES K. Friedeberger
ILL Roger Tuff
COPY Elva Carey
antiques

7a-c Great Britain
AD Volvo Concessionaries Ltd
AG Trickett & Webb Ltd
DIR Lynn Trickett, Brian Webb
DES (a) Lynn Trickett, Brian Webb, Andrew Thomas
(b,c) Lynn Trickett, Brian Webb, Colin Sands
COPY (a) Neil Mattingley
cars, autos

7d Great Britain
AD Spillers Foods
AG Trickett & Webb Ltd
DIR Lynn Trickett, Brian Webb
DES Lynn Trickett, Brian Webb, Andrew Thomas
cookery book, livre de cuisine, Kochbuch

5

THE LONG SHORT STORY OF THE VOLVO 343

It's safe to say that few of us even held a driving licence when the concept behind the 343 first saw the light of day. For it was in 1926 that the Volvo founding fathers decided that quality would take precedence when designing their cars. And this principle is as closely adhered to in the design concept of the new Volvo 343 as in previous generations of Volvo cars.

The 343 project team knew one important element in achieving this enviable and traditional standard of quality would be that of safety. And, of course, it was to be expected that reliability and handling would also take priority. But when the team were asked to equal the spaciousness and comfort of larger models with the economy of a smaller car, it seemed almost too difficult a target to reach. Yet as this story unfolds, it is clear that the team reached their six-point objective: comfort, spaciousness, reliability, handling, economy and safety.

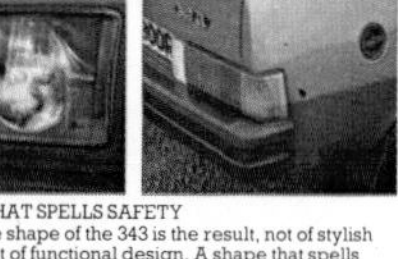

THE SHAPE THAT SPELLS SAFETY
The distinctive shape of the 343 is the result, not of stylish inspiration, but of functional design. A shape that spells safety with every curve from sturdy front bumper to the compact arrangement of warning lights at the rear end. And this shape will look as exciting tomorrow as it does today precisely because it is a product of logic. Just look at the facts. The aerodynamic design has excellent stability, good side-wind resistance and enough window space to give exceptional all-round visibility to driver and passengers alike.

UNDERNEATH THE SKIN, THE FAMOUS SAFETY CAGE
Volvo's safety cage design with reinforced doors and roof is constructed so that on impact the cage absorbs crash energy before it reaches the occupants. Inside the cage are other Volvo safety features: collapsible steering system, integral head restraints, energy absorbing dashboard, laminated windscreen.

A SHORT STORY OUTSIDE, A LONG STORY INSIDE
But safety was not the only target. The team also had to design a spacious interior with a compact exterior. As the director of car production put it: 'the occupants of a 343 should feel they are in a far larger car'. Careful planning arrived at a solution giving a good driving position in a roomy interior with unusually large windows. The result, from the driver's point of view, is that he has both the outlook as well as the driving space of a far larger car.

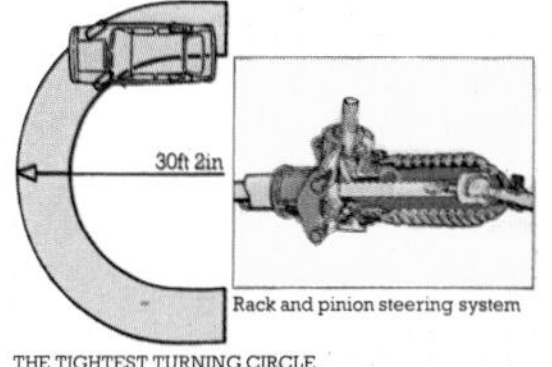

Rack and pinion steering system

THE TIGHTEST TURNING CIRCLE
Yet the exterior length of the 343 is only 13ft 7in. That's about the same (or even shorter) than cars of the same engine size. One of the main advantages resulting from this shorter car length is a tight turning circle of 30ft 2in. And as the Volvo rack and pinion steering makes light work of manoeuvring, parking is made that much easier. An important point in rush hour traffic conditions when kerbside space is so limited.

BALANCE OF POWER
The 343 has a 4 cylinder, 70 hp, 1397 cc engine up front and a transaxle housing an integral transmission near the rear axle. This balance of power distributes the weight and adds greatly to the roadholding and stability of the 343, however greasy the surface.

ROOM FOR COMFORT
The 343's generous interior space has most of the comforts of a far larger car. There are fully reclining front seats with integral head restraints and, in the back, lots of leg-stretching room. The wide doors too, are easy to open and use. (Except of course, when the children's safety locks are on.)

A CONTROLLED ENVIRONMENT
Clearly titled, precisely placed, the 343 instrument panel and controls make driving simple. Illuminated letters indicating the transmission lever position is one indication of this care for detail. A line of indicators and warning lamps on the instrument panel feed information on everything from whether the seat belts (front and rear) are clicked into position to whether the rear warning fog lamps are working. And, the driver also controls a heating and ventilation system which keep the car interior at an exact temperature. Just another sophisticated big-car comfort.

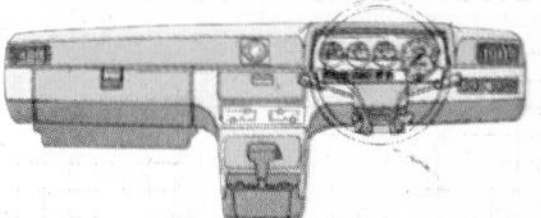

Warning lamps

THE ECONOMY OF THE 343
A low, total weight, just under one ton, and the aerodynamic shape are two facts that contribute to keeping costs down. In addition to fuel economy, there are Volvo touches such as wide bumpers, rust protection, ease of service and quality of materials.

END OF THE STORY?
A large tailgate gives access to a spacious boot and, if you wish to increase the luggage capacity, the rear bench seat folds down.
It would also be true to say there is no end to the story of the Volvo 343. Indeed, if this model lives up to every other Volvo story, you'll find most of the 343s on the road this year still going strong in sixteen years. It's a matter of facts.

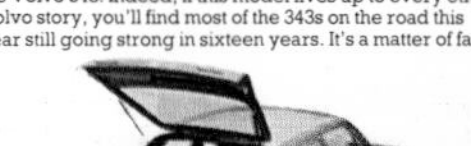

THE VOLVO 343 STORY.
IT'S A MATTER OF FACTS.

7a

6

Choose presents brilliantly from here. You cannot do better than order now by post for everyone unless of course you come yourself as soon as you can and have the pick not just of these but of a whole shop sparkling with ideas.

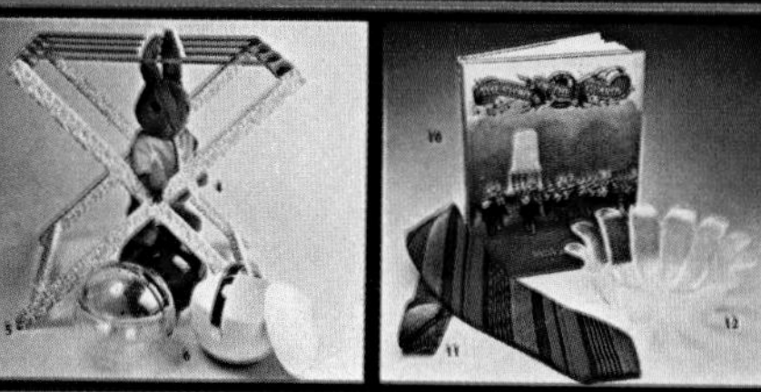

7b

7c

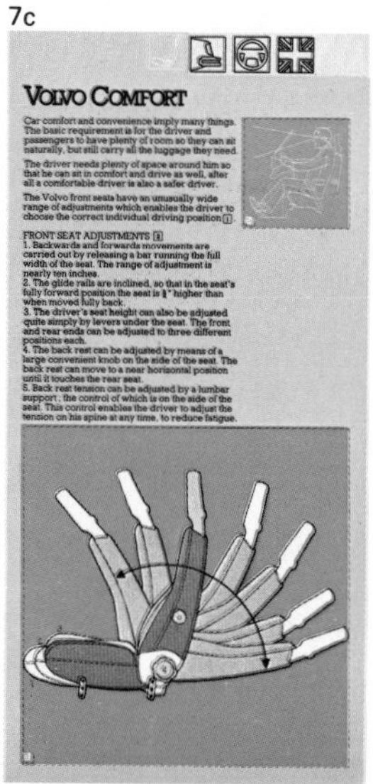

VOLVO COMFORT

Car comfort and convenience imply many things. The basic requirement is for the driver and passengers to have plenty of room so they can sit naturally, but still carry all the luggage they need.

The driver needs plenty of space around him so that he can sit in comfort and drive as well, after all a comfortable driver is also a safer driver.

The Volvo front seats have an unusually wide range of adjustments which enables the driver to choose the correct individual driving position [1].

FRONT SEAT ADJUSTMENTS [2]
1. Backwards and forwards movements are carried out by releasing a bar running the full width of the seat. The range of adjustment is nearly ten inches.
2. The glide rails are inclined, so that in the seat's fully forward position the seat is ¾" higher than when moved fully back.
3. The driver's seat height can also be adjusted quite simply by levers under the seat. The front and rear ends can be adjusted to three different positions each.
4. The back rest can be adjusted by means of a large convenient knob on the side of the seat. The back rest can move to a near horizontal position until it touches the rear seat.
5. Back rest tension can be adjusted by a lumbar support; the control of which is on the side of the seat. This control enables the driver to adjust the tension on his spine at any time, to reduce fatigue.

7d

Direct Mail
Brochures
Broschüren

1a-b Great Britain
AD Hygiena
AG Conran Associates
DIR/DES Stafford Cliff
COPY Terence Conran, Alexandra Towle
kitchen furniture, ameublement de cuisine, Küchen Möbel

2a-b Holland
AD Cannon Amsterdam NV
AG Will van Sambeek Design Associates
DIR Will Van Sambeek
DES Shigeru Watano
ILL Joost Guntenaar
photocopying machine

3 Japan
AD Toyota Motor Sales Co Ltd
AG Nippon Design Center
DIR Kenzo Nakagawa
DES Hiro Nobuyama
ILL Hiro Nobuyama, Hiroshi Yoshida
refrigerator

4a-b United States
AD Jeff Leedy
AG Gauger Sparks Silva
DIR/DES David Gauger
ILL Jeff Leedy
illustrator's work

5 United States
AD American Express Co
AG Creative Services American Express Co
DIR Martin Leeds
DES Roy Van Eick
presentation booklet for 25-year employees

6 United States
AD/AG AIGA
exhibition

1a

Stuart Britain
saw great changes in eating habits when she reaped the benefits of the discoveries in the New World. New types of beans, the pimento, pumpkins, banana, sugar, treacle and chocolate were all introduced to an astonished Europe. (The potato, however, first presented by Raleigh to Queen Elizabeth I, and repeatedly brought to the notice of seventeenth century agriculturists, languished until Parmentier made it popular a century later.)

When Charles II was restored to the throne in 1660, he and his entourage brought fresh life-style ideas from France, where the Sun King's chefs ensured that the Grand Siecle was also gastronomically remarkable. In this they were helped by a great number of new utensils, some of them tin-plated by a newly invented process.

With the age of enlightenment under Charles II, the sciences began to flourish. Many of the experiments conducted under the auspices of the newly founded Royal Society concerned the kitchen. 'Papin's digester', a forerunner of the pressure-cooker presented in 1680, was considered too dangerous for ordinary households. Smokeless fuel, also, became a subject for study, as did various heating machines – as well they might after the Great Fire of London in 1666 made people more safety-conscious.

The Industrial Revolution
This was heralded by further improvements: mechanical weights and clockwork spit-jacks relieved servants of this infernal task.

The open fires, still merrily burning in spite of the inventors, became enclosed in grates, which were to develop into ranges. Meat could now also be baked in Dutch ovens – metal sentry box-like constructions which faced the fire – but Georgian kitchens did not yet differ to any important extent from their forerunners.

The fact that coffee and tea, at first suspiciously regarded and accused of causing every ailment under the sun, gained popularity (in time replacing ale for breakfast) did not affect the kitchen, making these beverages was a drawing-room occupation. This change in taste, meant, however, that pewter tankards and glasses were now joined by cups. The first of these were of Chinese porcelain, but in the course of the century, the English potteries started to meet the ever-growing need for cups, plates, saucers, dishes and platters besides, so that more storage space was needed in kitchen and/or dining room.

As the Industrial Revolution gathered momentum, more innovations followed, the first enamel saucepan was made in 1805. A canning process was invented in 1810, but, unfortunately, the iron cans weighed over 1lb when empty, and purchasers were optimistically instructed to 'cut round the top with a chisel ...' It was not until the thinner steel cans, with a rim round the top, came into general use (in the 1860s) that the can-opener was invented. Refrigeration of foodstuffs was introduced in 1834, but was not developed until 'later', large households still relied on their 'icehouses' – caves in which great slabs of ice kept food in the coolest possible conditions.

10

1b

2a

2b

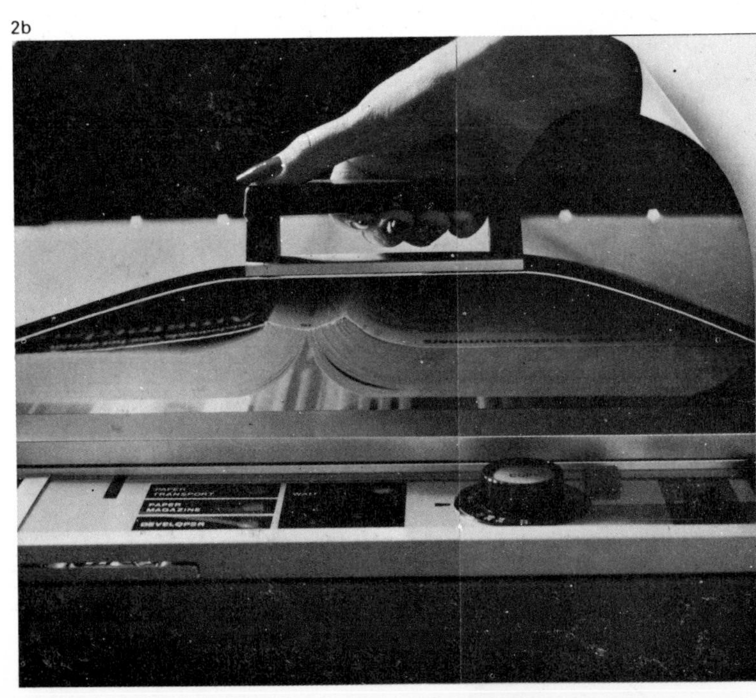

United States
D The Beckett Paper Company
ES Susan Jackson Keig
L James L. Ballard
aper, papier

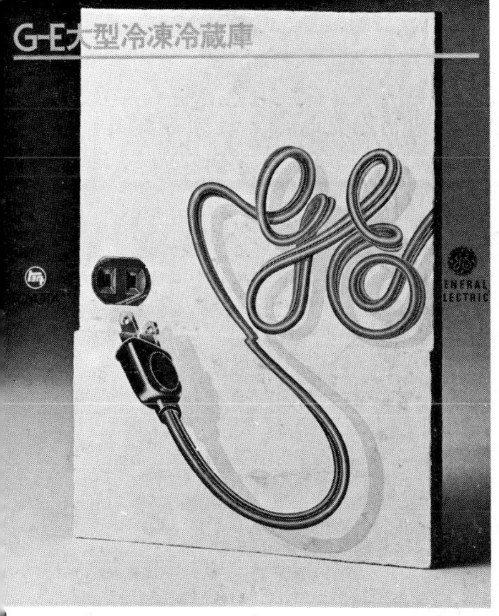

209 North Street, Sausalito, California 94965 (415) 332-9100 or 332-9596. 209 North Street, Sausalito, California 94965 (415) 332-9100 or 332-9596. 209 North Street, Sausalito, California 94965 (415) 332-9100 or 332-9596. 209 North Street, Sausalito, California 94965 (415) 332-9100 or 332-9596. 209 North Street, Sausalito, California 94965 (415) 332-9100 or 332-9596. 209 North Street, Sausalito, California 94965 (415) 332-9100 or 332-9596. 209 North Street, Sausalito, California 94965 (415) 332-9100 or 332-9596. 209 North Street, Sausalito, California 94965 (415) 332-9100 or 332-9596. 209 North Street, Sausalito, California 94965 (415) 332-9100 or 332-9596. 209 North Street, Sausalito, California 94965 (415) 332-9100 or 332-9596. 209 North Street, Sausalito, California 94965 (415) 332-9100 or 332-9596. 209 North Street, Sausalito, California 94965 (415) 332-9100 or 332-9596. 209 North Street, Sausalito, California 94965 (415) 332-9100 or 332-9596. 209 North Street, Sausalito, California 94965 (415) 332-9100 or 332-9596. 209 North Street, Sausalito, California 94965 (415) 332-9100 or 332-9596. 209 North Street, Sausalito, California 94965 (415) 332-9100 or 332-9596. 209 North Street, Sausalito, California 94965 (415) 332-9100 or 332-9596. 209 North Street, Sausalito, California 94965 (415) 332-9100 or 332-9596. 209 North Street, Sausalito, California 94965 (415) 332-9100 or 332-9596. 209 North Street, Sausalito, California 94965 (415) 332-9100 or 332-9596. 209 North Street, Sausalito, California 94965 (415) 332-9100 Design: Gauger Sparks Silva 441-0303

Jeff Leedy

163 LB. 32X69 IN. 10 SHEETS

4a

4b

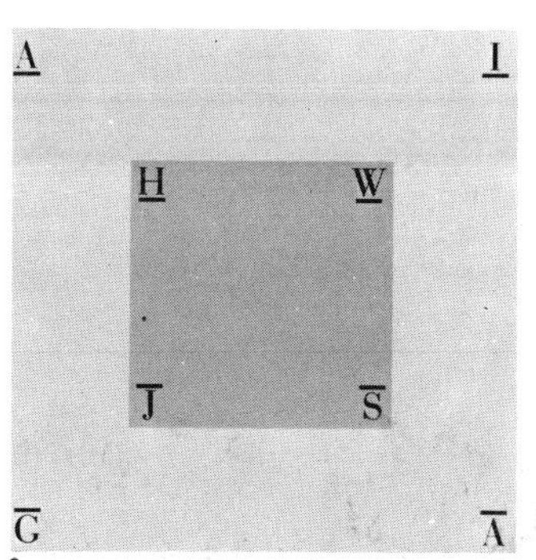

6

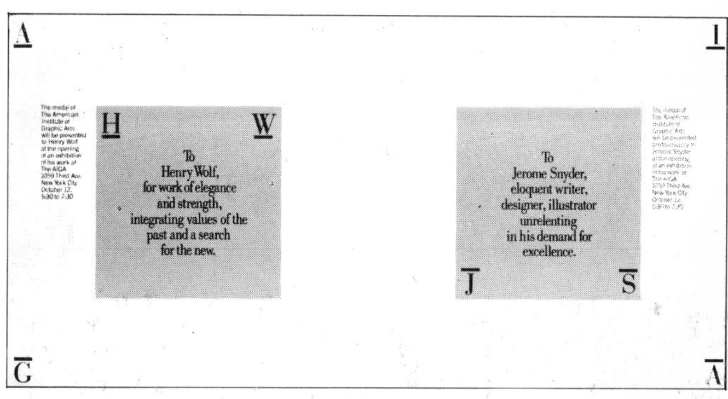

Of all the enterprises the Shakers engaged in, the sale of garden seed was one of the best known and most profitable. Highly decorative labels on wood shipping boxes (above) reflected the styles of the era and were used to merchandise seeds to the world's people.

Special equipment was designed for the extensive seed business, such as compartmented drawers for storage (above), display racks for the seed bags, and Shaker-designed machinery for printing and filling the bags (right). Journal records note that in the winter of 1860 at Pleasant Hill the East Family alone prepared 81,400 envelopes or bags, of garden seed. There was a yearly increase in the business until the Civil War, when sales and production fell off as Southern markets collapsed.

14

Seed boxes had a list of contents, as above, which was often used by customers as an order blank. A box from South Union (top right) is typical of the thousands of boxes made by the Shakers in Kentucky. The lid, when opened, served as a display or broadside. The confidence the Shakers had in their product was expressed by the statement on the label: "We give more and better seeds for the money than any other company." Hinges and fasteners of the box were made of wire.

The enterprising South Union Shakers issued a 32-page Farm Annual catalog in 1885 (right) which described not only seeds and slips, but also brooms, preserves, livestock and poultry, pigs, turkeys, ducks and eggs.

15

Direct Mail
Brochures
Broschüren

1a-b Germany
AD Fried, Krupp GmbH
AG SSM Werbeagentur
DIR/DES Harald Schlüter
COPY Jürgen Mehl
hard metal

2 Great Britain
AD ICI — plastics division
AG Kynoch Graphic Design
DIR/DES Len Harvey
ILL A. Hedderwick
plastics

3 Germany
AD Format Zeitschrift
AG Verlag Dieter Gitzel
DIR Dieter Gitzel
DES Manfred Glemser
verbal and visual communications magazine

4 United States
AD Ford Foundation
AG Peter Bradford & Associates
DIR/DES Peter Bradford
research on effects of television on children

5 United States
AD/AG Scholastic
DIR Skip Sorvino
DES Stefanie Green
ILL James Barkley
magazine

6 Italy
AD Civilta' delle Macchine
AG Ruffolo
DIR/DES Sergio Ruffolo
magazine

1a

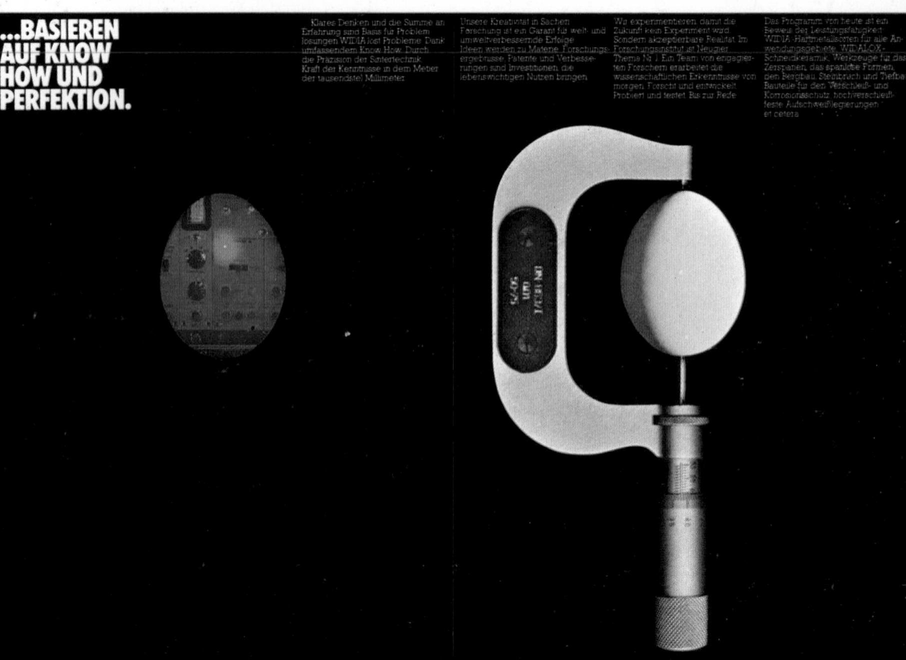

1b

2

ICI Plastics Today 55

Zeitschrift für verbale und visuelle Kommunikation 12. Jg. Heft 5 Sept. 76 P 20638 F

63 ›Format›

photokina 76
Neuheiten
Kodak Instant Produkte
Bilderschauen
Kodak Kulturprogramm

7a Great Britain
AD Scottish Tourist Board
AG Forth Studios Ltd
DIR Andrew Hunter
ILL Douglas Cottance and others
tourism — winter festival

7b-c Great Britain
AD National Trust for Scotland
AG Forth Studios Ltd
DIR John Martin
DES Malcolm Park
ILL Tom Scott
guide book

8 France
AD Le Livre de Paris
AG Primart
DIR/DES Ulrich Meyer
book society prospectus

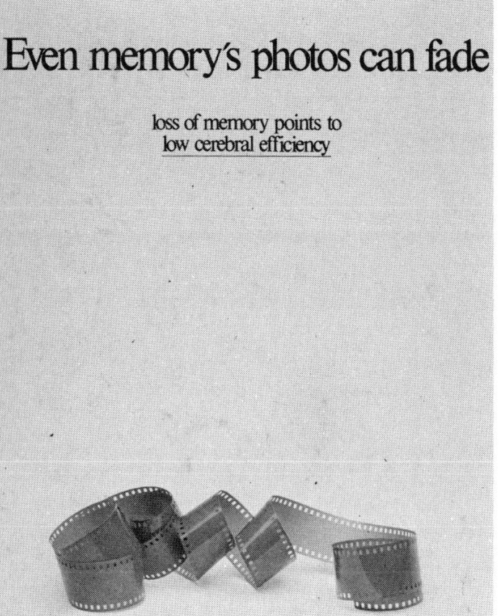

4

5

6

7a

7b

7c

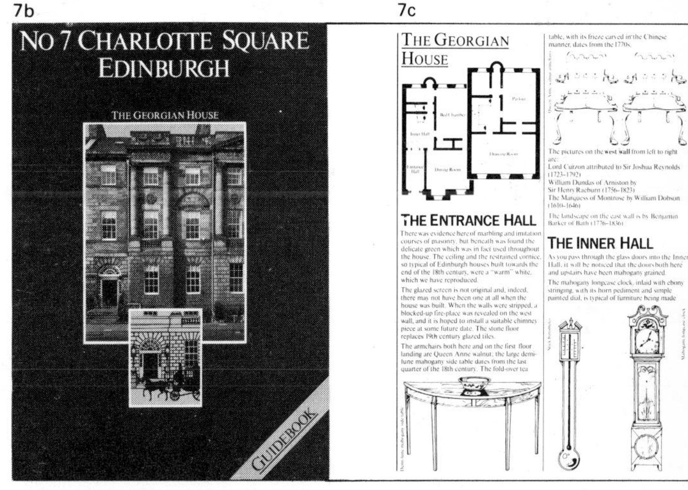

8

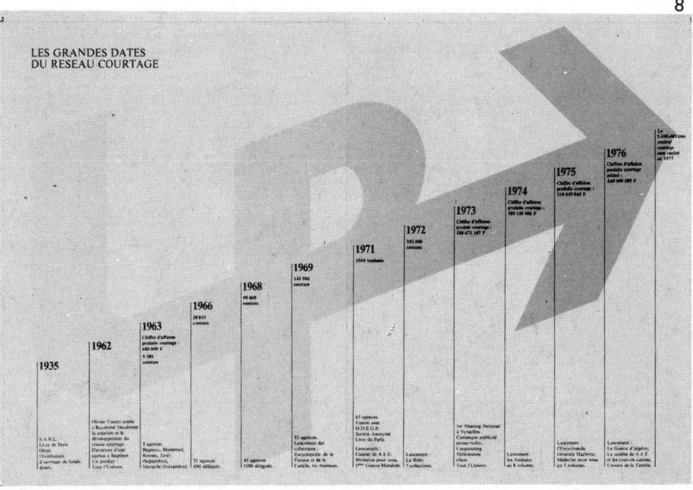

Direct Mail
Brochures
Broschüren

1a-b Great Britain
AD Nedo
AG Lock/Pettersen Ltd
DIR/DES Glenn Tutssel
ILL Warwickshire Illustrators

2a-b United States
AD/DES Henry Wolf
self-promotion

3 United States
AD Detroit Fee Press
AG Free Press Promotion Dept
DIR H. Szerlag
DES Roger Hicks
COPY K. Field
food section in Free Press

4 Great Britain
AD Scottish Agricultural Industries
AG Kynoch Graphic Design
DIR/DES Clive Allsop
ILL A. Reid
seeds, graines, Samen

5 United States
AD College Press Review
AG Art Dept Colorado State University
DIR/DES John J. Sorbie
college press review

6 United States
AD The Municipal Art Society
AG Peter Bradford & Associates
DIR Peter Bradford
DES Peter Bradford, Wendy Byrne
ILL Stan Stark, Jonette Jakobson
magazine-newsletter on urban problems
and programmes for New York City

7 United States
AD The Weavers Guild
AG Lipson-Jacob Associates
DIR Stan Brod
DES Ruth Brod
craft show for fibers

1a

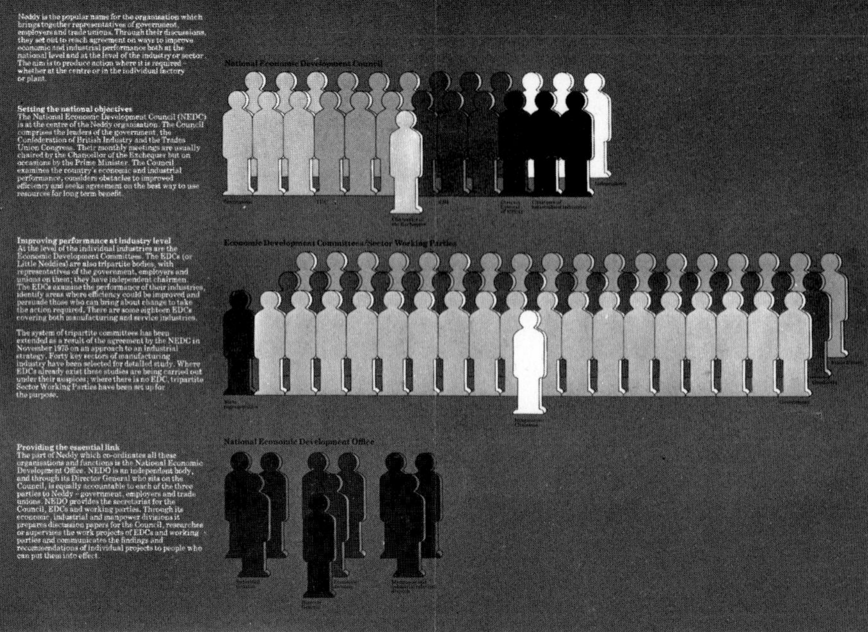

1b

2a

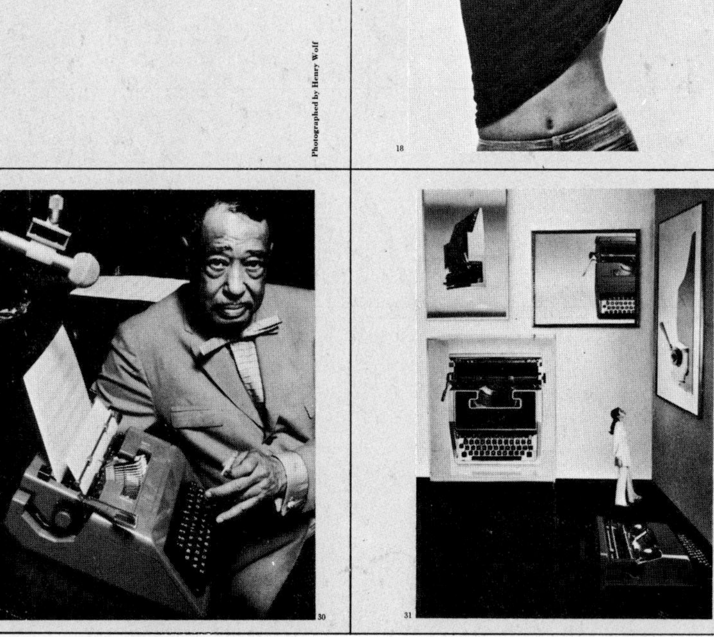

2b

3

8 Austria
AD Funder Aktiengesellschaft
AG Graphikstudio Hauch
DIR/DES Walter J. Hauch
timber, Spanplattew

9 Great Britain
AD/AG Unit Five Design Ltd
DIR/DES John Gibbs
ILL Jonathan Bayer
self-promotion

4

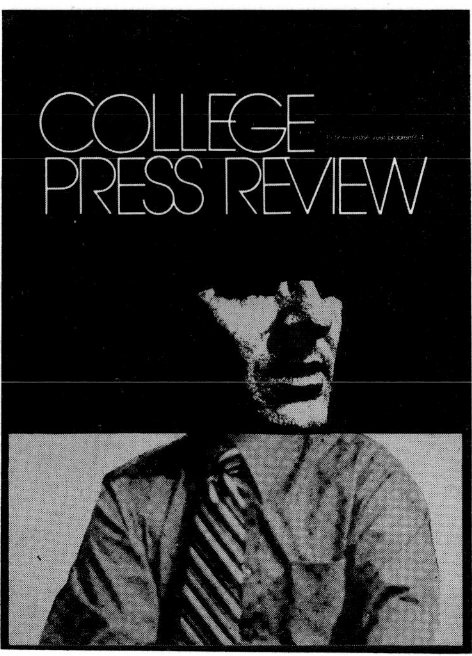

5

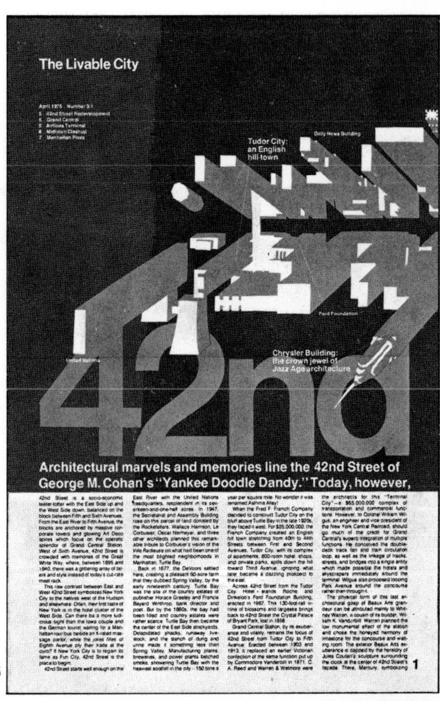

6

7

8

9a

9b

9c

Direct Mail Brochures Broschüren

1a-b Canada
AD Air Canada
AG Guillon/Designers Inc
DIR/DES Frédéric Metz
ILL Susan Pritchard
airline

2 United States
AD Honeywell Inc
DIR/DES Cyril John Schlosser
neighborhood involvement booklet

3 United States
AD NBC Sports
AG NBC Advertising Sales and Promotion
DIR/DES Nicholas M. Stano
COPY Hal Altermann
1976 baseball book

4 United States
AD San Francisco Symphony Orchestra
AG Charles Fuhrman & Edith Allgood Design
DIR/DES Charles Fuhrman
youth concerts

5 Denmark
AD Forlaget Audio A/S
AG SB Grafisk Design
DIR/DES Soren Balle
ILL John Fowlie

6 Spain
AD Campaña
DES Fernando Medina
magazine

7 Spain
AD/AG Carlos Rolando & Asociados
self-promotion

1a

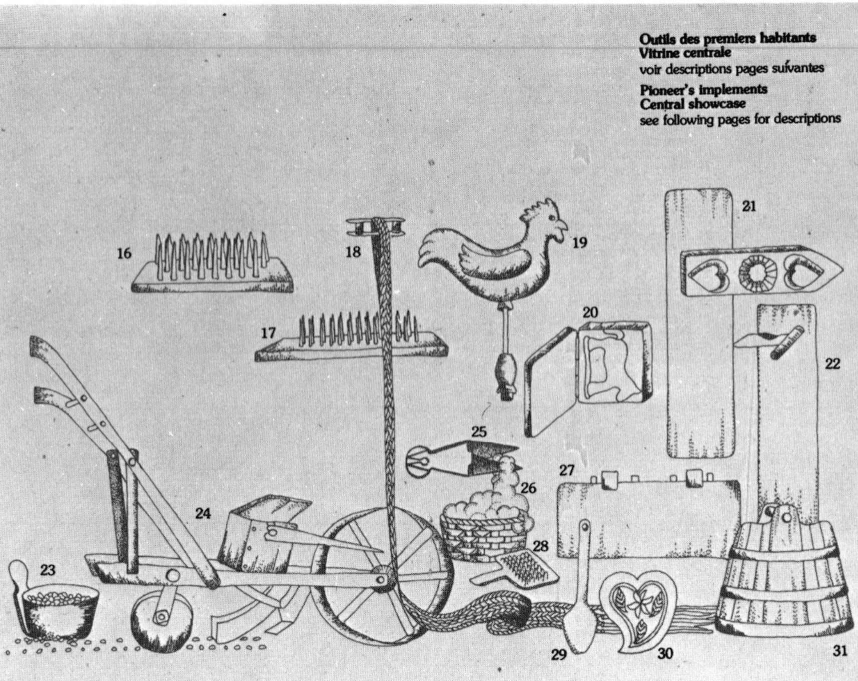

1b

2

3

8 Germany
AD Brauerei Schloss Wächtersbach
DES Wilhelm Malkemus
beer congress, Bierkongress

9 United States
AD National Fire Protection Association
AG Robert P. Gersin Associates Inc
DIR Louis Nelson
DES Barbara Daley, Jack Morgan, Ronald Wong
fire safety techniques, précautions contre l'incendie

4

5

6

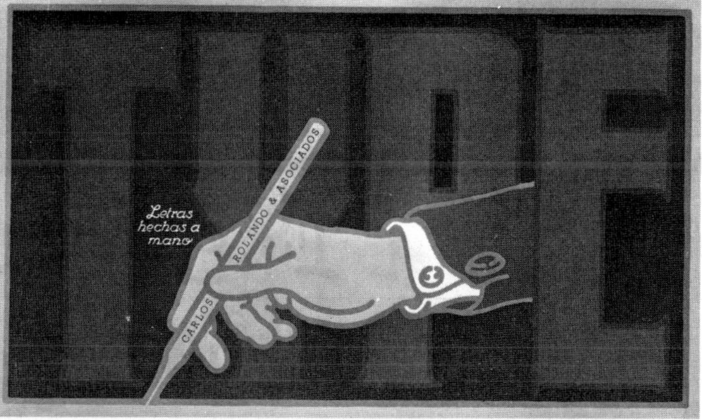

7

8

9

Direct Mail
Brochures
Broschüren

1a-b Yugoslavia
AD Theatre itd
DES Zeljko Borcić
ILL Zeljko Stojanovic
COPY Nenad Puhovski
theatre

2a-c Germany
AD Thalia Theater
DES Holger Matthies
theatre

3 Germany
AD Bayerischer Rundfunk München
DES Walter Tafelmaier
concerts

4 Germany
AD Fa Siebdruck Geier Ingolstadt
DES Walter Tafelmaier
screen printing, Siebdruck

5 Turkey
AD State Opera and Ballet
AG San Grafik
DIR/DES Mengü Ertel
magazine

6 Germany
AD Graphic-Edition 'q'
DES Wieland Schütz

7a-b Germany
AD (a) Landesarbeitsamt Berlin
(b) Senator für Gesundheit und Umweltschutz
AG Atelier Noth & Hauer
DES Noth, Hauer, Sodemann
ILL (a) Klappert
(a) career information,
(b) health information

8a-b Germany
AD Berliner Absatz-Organisation
AG Atelier Noth & Hauer
DES Noth, Hauer, Sodemann
ILL Klappert
brochure

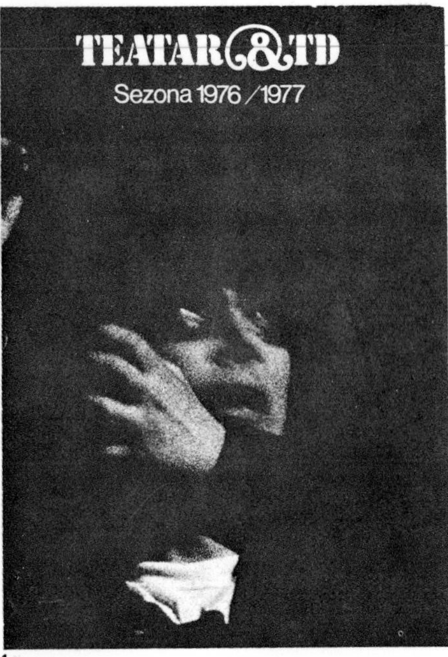

1a

TEATAR&TD

PROŠLOST & SADAŠNJOST

TEATAR &TD adaptiran je kao teatarski prostor 1962. godine, a do 1966. djeluje pod nazivom KOMORNA POZORNICA STUDENTSKOG CENTRA. U tom razdoblju "Komorna pozornica" prikazuje niz predstava, od kojih su neke radjene u njenoj organizaciji, dok su druge realizirane gostovanjima.

10.1.1966., predstavom "Balkon" Jeana Geneta u režiji Tomislava Durbešića, započinje rad Teatra &td. Promjenom imena, dolaskom upravitelja Vjerana Zuppe, likovnim uobličenjem teatarskih prostora Mihajla Arsovskog, a ponajviše novim organizacijskim rješenjima, Teatar &td započinje razdoblje jednog drugačijeg razmišljanja o teatru. Suština organizacijske izuzetnosti Teatra &td može se objasniti jednostavnom činjenicom da se ta organizacija stalno mijenjala u skladu s umjetničkim zadacima. Takav način teatarskog života učinio je Teatar &td privlačnim prvenstveno za mlade ljude i za sve one, bili oni "kazališni ljudi" ili ne, koji su željeli progovoriti na nov, nekonvencionalan i kritičan način.

Jedan od odlučujućih elemenata takvog okupljanja oko Teatra &td svakako je čvrsta repertoarna usmjerenost. Repertoar se godinama mijenjao, ali je uvijek zadržavao konstante jasnog opredjeljenja SUVREMENOG POVIJESNOG TEATRA, teatra izrazite kritičke orijentacije. Takvo opredjeljenje donijelo je Teatru &td i niz priznanja i nagrada - Nagradu grada Zagreba, Sterijinu nagradu, niz nagrada na domaćim i stranim teatarskim festivalima, kao i pozive na gostovanja u našoj zemlji, SSSR-u, Italiji, Francuskoj, Španjolskoj, Poljskoj, S.R. Njemačkoj, Venezueli, Meksiku, Panami, Guatemali i Costariki.

U okvirima takve repertoarne usmjerenosti sazdan je i repertoar za sezonu 1976/77. To se prije svega odnosi na predstave "1984" Orwella, "Proces" Kafke, "Nečastivi..." Brešana, te "Marat/Sade" Weissa, koje vremenski i tematski najbolje omedjuju problem sukoba individualne svijesti i mehanizma vlasti. Osim tog tematskog ciklusa tu su i druge predstave koje spremamo za ovu sezonu. Na kraju je potrebno spomenuti da od ove sezone Teatar &td započinje sa radom TEATARSKE RADIONICE, specifičnim načinom okupljanja pojedinih ekipa ili grupa koje će raditi svoje predstave i zatim ih prikazati i teatru i javnosti.

1b

2a

2b

2c

3

Bayerischer Rundfunk Konzerte des Münchner Rundfunkorchesters 1975/76

4

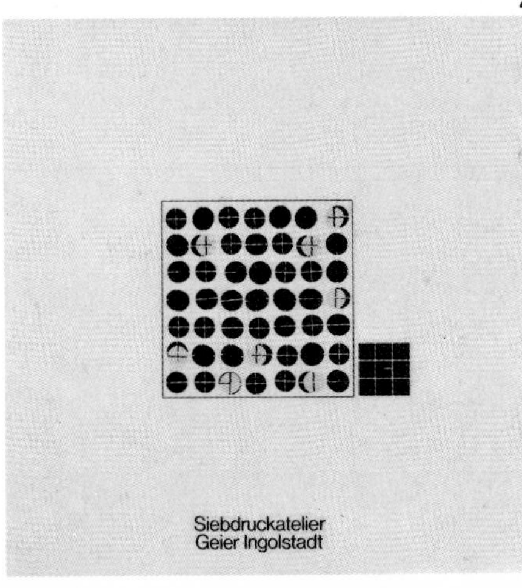

5

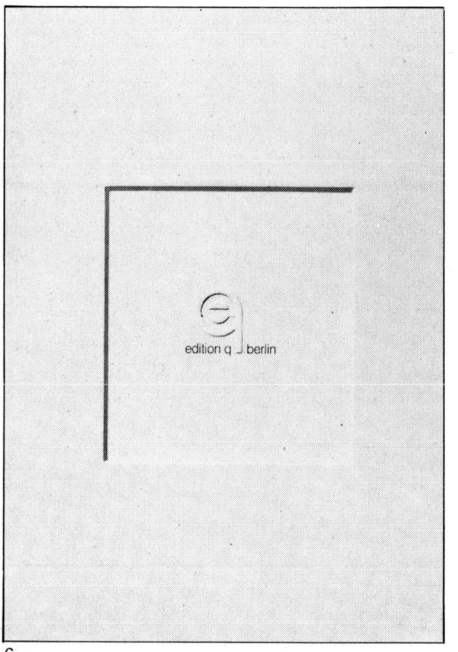

6

7a

7b

8a

Kommunikations-Mix à la Berlin

Dienstleistungen der Werbe- und Absatzwirtschaft

8b

Branchentätigkeit und Branchenerfahrung

Hersteller und Dienstleistungsunternehmen																			Handel												
Getränke	Bauwirtschaft, Immobilien	Bildung, Freizeit, Touristik	chem. Industrie, Energiewirtschaft	Haushalts- und Einrichtungsgegenstände	Körperpflegemittel	Kraftfahrzeuge und Zubehör	Maschinen, Apparate, Anlagen	Nahrungsmittel	Papier- und Druckindustrie	Pharmazeutika	Reinigungsmittel	Tabakwaren	Textilien und Bekleidung	Verkehrs- und Transportwesen	Versicherungen, Banken	Verlage	Behörden, Institutionen, Personalwerbung	Gastronomie	Elektrogeräte	Foto, Optik	Handelsketten, Einkaufszentren	Kauf- und Warenhäuser	Kraftfahrzeuge und Zubehör	Lebensmittelfachhandel	Möbel	Radio, Fernsehen, Phono	Schuhe, Lederwaren	sonstige Haushaltsgeräte und -waren	Uhren, Schmuck	Textilien, Bekleidung, Wäsche	Teppiche, Gardinen, Fußböden
●	●	●			●		●	●		●					●		●		●		●	●			●	●		●		●	
		●													●	●	●	●				●				●					
●	●						●		●							●	●	●													●
									●							●	●								●	●			●		●
	●	●	●				●		●	●					●	●	●			●	●			●							
		●							●					●		●	●														
	●	●	●				●						●	●																●	
●	●	●	●		●	●	●	●	●				●	●	●	●	●	●	●	●	●		●	●	●		●		●	●	

39

Direct Mail
Brochures
Broschüren

1a-b Germany
AD Zanders Feinpapier GmbH
DIR Wolfgang Heunwinkel
DES Klaus Winterhager
paper, papier

2 Canada
AD Abitibi Provincial Paper Co
AG Burns, Cooper, Donoahue, Fleming & Co Ltd
DIR Robert Burns
DES Jim Donoahue
ILL Heather Cooper, (photo) Leigh Warren
COPY Jim Hynes
paper, papier

3a-b United States
AD Champion Papers
DIR/DES (a) Roger Cook, Don Shanosky
(b) Miho
ILL Art Kane
COPY (b) David Brown
paper, papier

4a-b Norway
AD (a) Den Norske Bokklubben
(b) Norpapp Industri
DES Hansdørgen Toming

1a

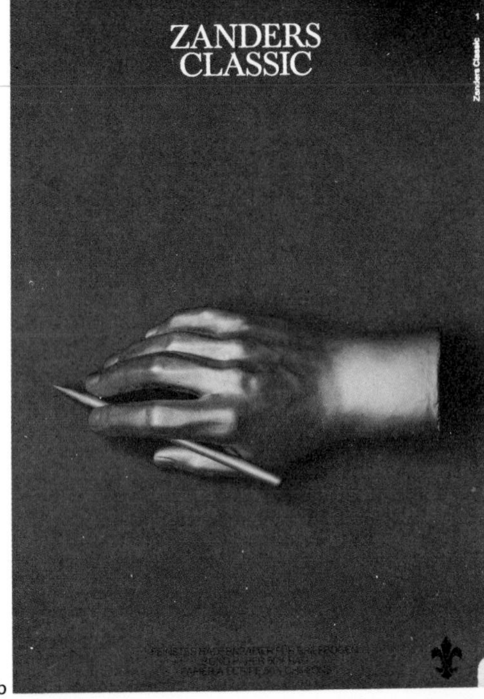

1b

2

ABITIBI PROVINCIAL PAPER PRESENTS THE DEFINITIVE RANGE OF COATED PAPERS. THE COATED CLASSICS. NUMBER ONE IN THE SERIES.

JENSON GLOSS

3a

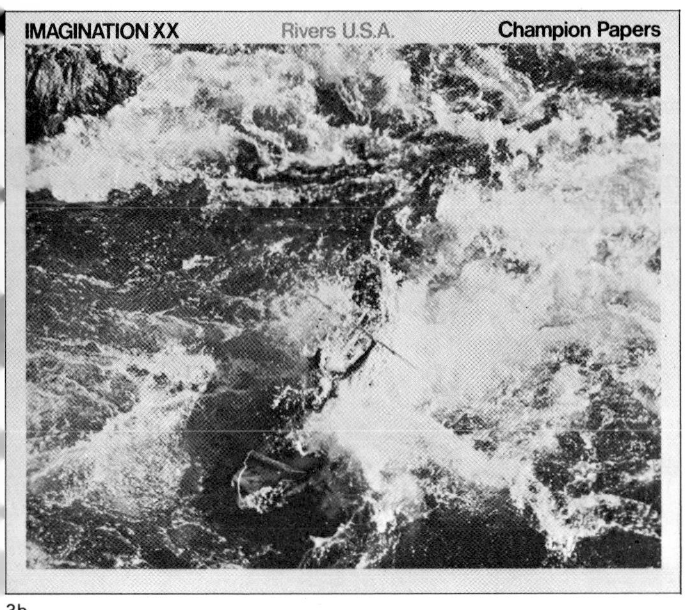
IMAGINATION XX
Rivers U.S.A.
Champion Papers

3b

4a

Bokklubben
Stjernereiser 76/77
høst
vinter

4b

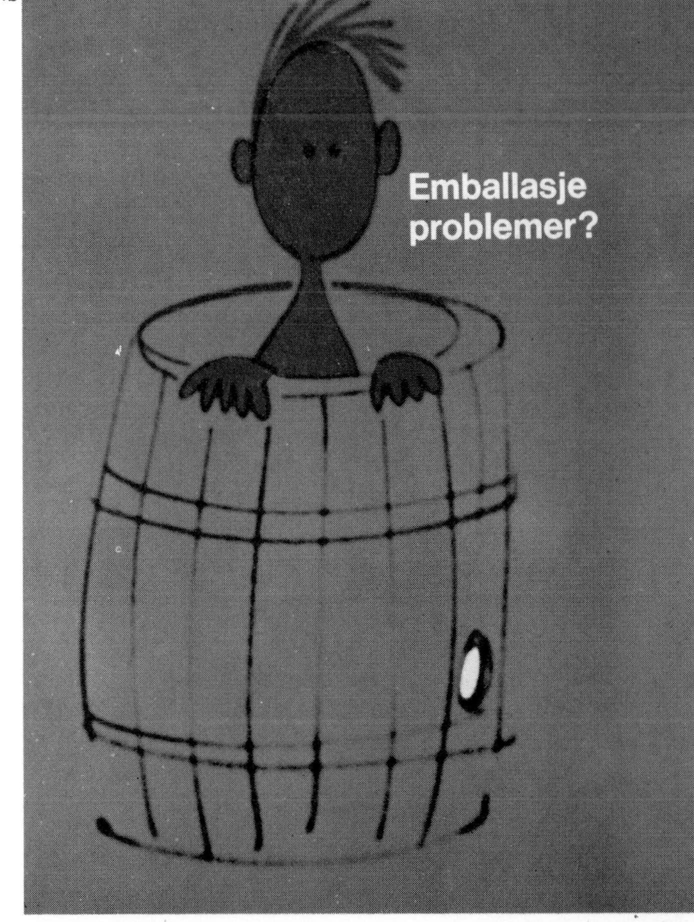
Emballasje
problemer?

Direct Mail
Brochures
Broschüren

1a-c Great Britain
AD (a) Alcan
(b) Aluminium Extruders Association
(c) Alcan Booth Systems
AG John Nash & Friends
DIR John Nash
DES (a) Malcolm Smith
(b,c) John Nash
ILL (b,c) Peter Higgins
(c) K. Randall, V. Brand
COPY (a,b) Ian McIness
(c) Hutton and Rostron
(a) foil packaging
(b) the extrusion process
(c) window and door assemblies

2 Canada
AD Hoffmann-La Roche Ltd
AG Design Collaborative
DIR Rolf Harder, Monique Simond
DES Rolf Harder
brochure on dangers of infectious diseases

3a-b Canada
AD/AG Gordon Hill Advertising Ltd
DIR/DES Billy Sharma
ILL David Jenkinson
COPY Russ Showell, Denyse Maheux
self promotion

4 Great Britain
AD Truc International (USA)
AG Peter Windett Associates
DIR/DES Peter Windett
ILL Roger Frederick
toilet articles

5 Israel
AD Gordon Gallery
DES Varda Raz
ILL Reuven Milon
exhibition

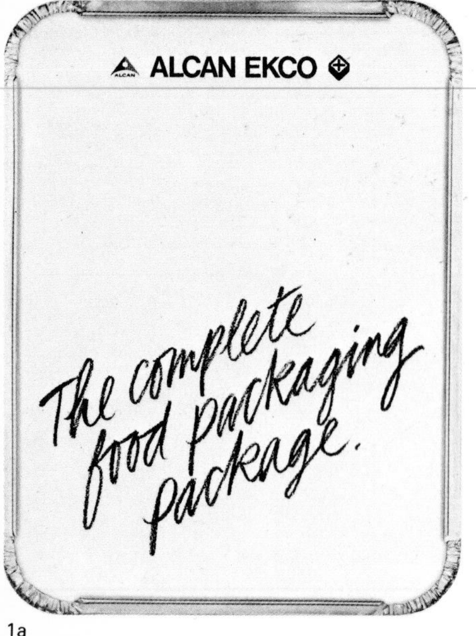

1a

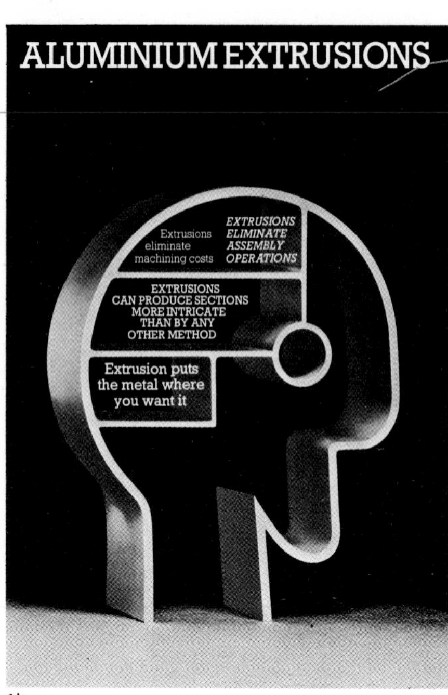

1b

1c

2

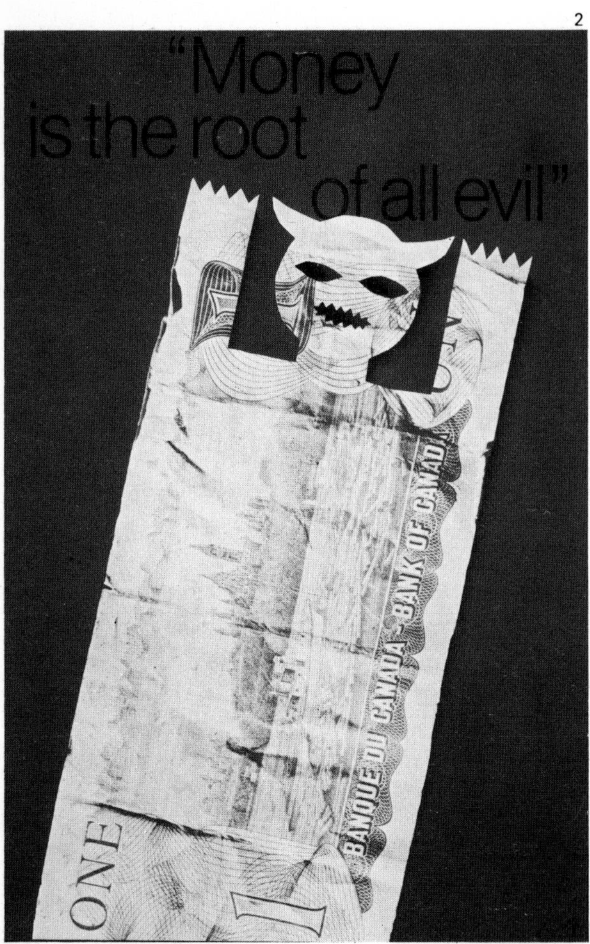

3a

3b

6 Italy
AD Muzak
AG Studio Vitale
DIR Ettore Vitale
book jackets

7a-c Canada
AD/AG Burns & Cooper Ltd
DIR Robert Burns
DES (a) Robert Burns
(b,c) Ann Ames
ILL Heather Cooper
COPY David Parry
self promotion

4a

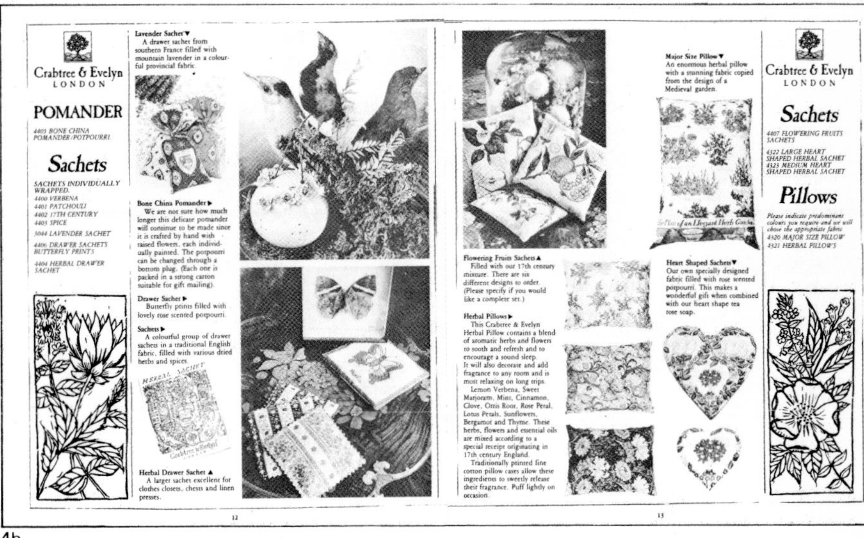

Crabtree & Evelyn
LONDON

POMANDER

4405 BONE CHINA POMANDER/POTPOURRI

Sachets

SACHETS INDIVIDUALLY WRAPPED.
4400 VERBENA
4401 PATCHOULI
4402 17TH CENTURY
4403 SPICE
5044 LAVENDER SACHET
4406 DRAWER SACHETS BUTTERFLY PRINTS
4404 HERBAL DRAWER SACHET

Lavender Sachet ▼
A drawer sachet from southern France filled with mountain lavender in a colourful provincial fabric.

Bone China Pomander ▶
We are not sure how much longer this delicate pomander will continue to be made since it is crafted by hand with raised flowers, each individually painted. The potpourri can be changed through a bottom plug. (Each one is packed in a strong carton suitable for gift mailing).

Drawer Sachet ▶
Butterfly prints filled with lovely rose scented potpourri.

Sachets ▶
A colourful group of drawer sachets in a traditional English fabric, filled with various dried herbs and spices.

Herbal Drawer Sachet ▲
A larger sachet excellent for clothes closets, chests and linen presses.

12

Flowering Fruits Sachets ▲
Filled with our 17th century mixture. There are six different designs to order. (Please specify if you would like a complete set.)

Herbal Pillows ▶
This Crabtree & Evelyn Herbal Pillow contains a blend of aromatic herbs and flowers to sooth and refresh and to encourage a sound sleep.
It will also decorate and add fragrance to any room and is most relaxing on long trips.
Lemon Verbena, Sweet Marjoram, Mint, Cinnamon, Clove, Orris Root, Rose Petal, Lotus Petals, Sunflowers, Bergamot and Thyme. These herbs, flowers and essential oils are mixed according to a special receipt originating in 17th century England.
Traditionally printed fine cotton pillow cases allow these ingredients to sweetly release their fragrance. Puff lightly on occasion.

Major Size Pillow ▼
An enormous herbal pillow with a stunning fabric copied from the design of a Medieval garden.

Heart Shaped Sachets ▼
Our own specially designed fabric filled with rose scented potpourri. This makes a wonderful gift when combined with our heart shape tea rose soap.

Crabtree & Evelyn
LONDON

Sachets

4407 FLOWERING FRUITS SACHETS
4322 LARGE HEART SHAPED HERBAL SACHET
4323 MEDIUM HEART SHAPED HERBAL SACHET

Pillows

Please indicate predominant colours you require and we will chose the appropriate fabric
4320 MAJOR SIZE PILLOW
4321 HERBAL PILLOWS

13

4b

5

6

7a

7b

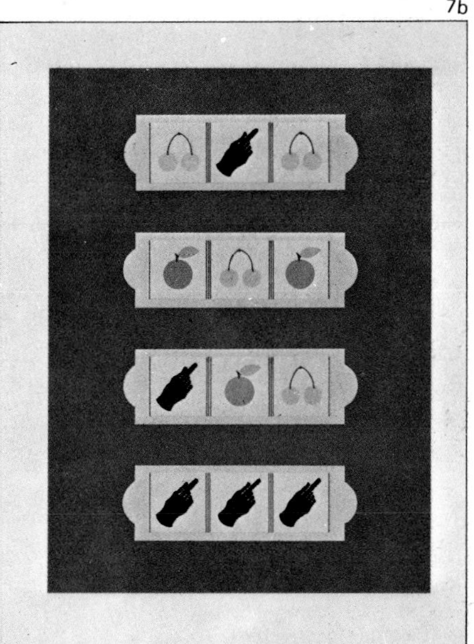

7c

Direct Mail
Brochures
Broschüren

1 Great Britain
AD Honeywell Europe SA
AG Gavin Healey Design
DIR/DES Gavin Healey
ILL Paul Dolden
COPY A. J. Sparks

2 Great Britain
AD Filtrona Cigarette Components Ltd
AG Don Burston & Assoc
DIR Don Burston
DES Pete King
ILL Geoffrey Sturdy photography
COPY Chris Boddy
tip cutting machine

3 Great Britain
AD Spunalloys Ltd
DES Peter Bragg
bronze tubes and bars, tubes et barres de bronze

4 Great Britain
AD Davall Ltd
AG Peter Proto Associates
DIR Peter Proto
DES Peter Proto, Jon Bodsworth
electronic equipment for aviation industry

5 Germany
AD Hans Schmidlin AG
AG Atelier Zeugin

6 United States
AD Ciba Geigy Corporation
AR Art Services
DIR/DES Markus Low
dyes, teintures, Färbemittel

7 India
AD Voltas Ltd
AG Studio Ogilvy Benson & Mather Private Ltd
DIR/DES M. Swaminathan

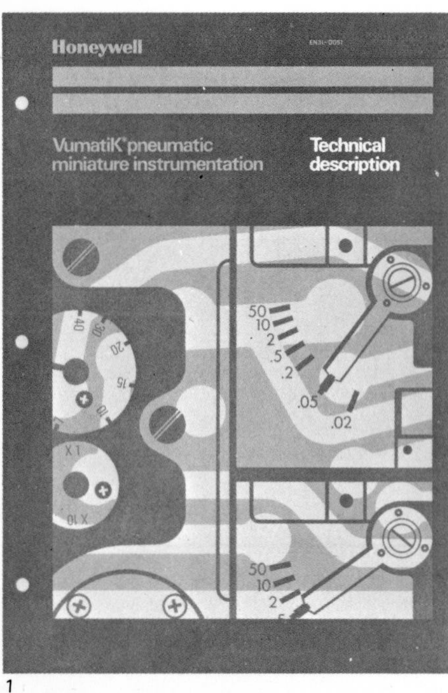

1

2

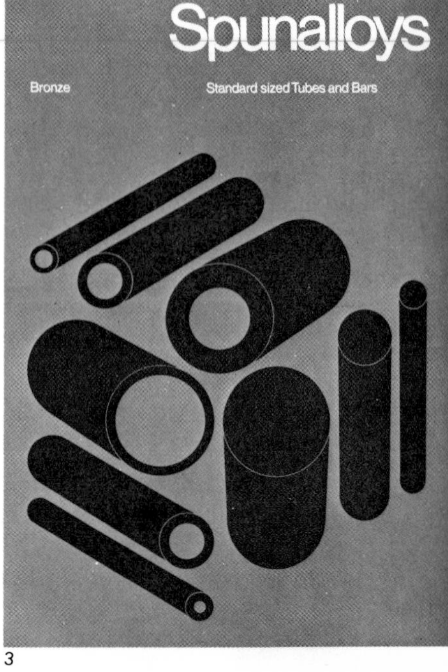

3

4

5

8 Great Britain
AD Alcan Booth Extrusions Ltd
AG Michael Werner Ltd
DIR/DES Michael Werner
COPY Russel Broman
extruded aluminium for furniture

9 Australia
AD McPherson's Ltd
AG E. G. Holt & Associates Pty Ltd
DIR Kevin Lees
DES Jonathan Milne
ILL Ian McKenzie
COPY Peter W. Tritsch, M. Lewis
corporate identity

10 United States
AD National Ass. of Convenience Stores
AG Pepsi Cola Studios
DIR/DES Bruce James Duhan
convention

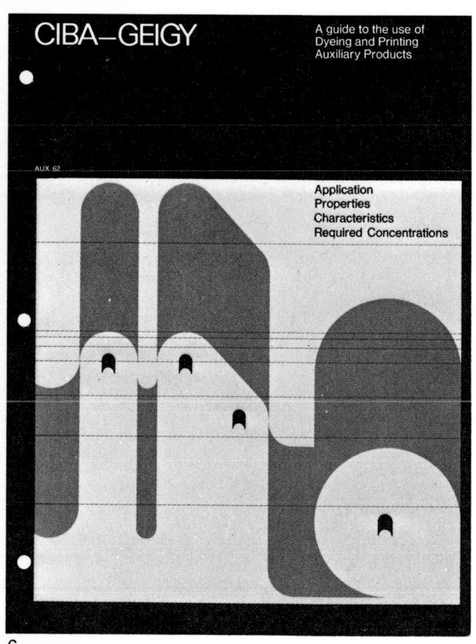

6

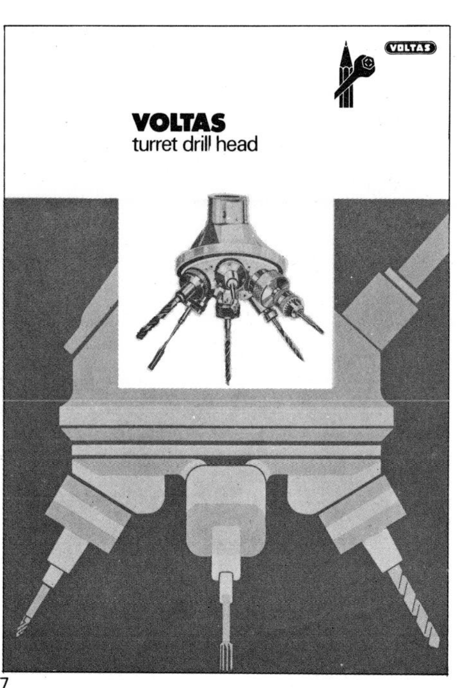

7

8

9

10

Direct Mail
Brochures
Broschüren

1a-b Mexico
AD Estado de Mexico y Instituto Nacional de Bellas Artes
AG Laboratorio de Diseno y Mercadotecnia — Carton y Papel de Mexico SA
DIR/DES Arie J. Geurts
COPY Bertha Taracena
exhibitions

2 Great Britain
AD Central Office of Information
AG Design and Reproduction Department COI

3a-b Australia
AD Comeng Engineering
AG Graphic Concept
DIR/DES Maurice Schlesinger
stainless steel railway carriages, wagons en acier inoxydable

4 Great Britain
AD The Museum of London
DES David Stuart
ILL John Gorham
museum guidebook

5 France
AD Publicem
ILL Jean Claverie

6 Brazil
AD Banco de Desenvolvimento do Parana
DES Oswaldo Mirando (Miran)
bank

7 Portugal
AD Sociedade Nacional de Belas Artes
DIR Jose Candido
visual education course

1a

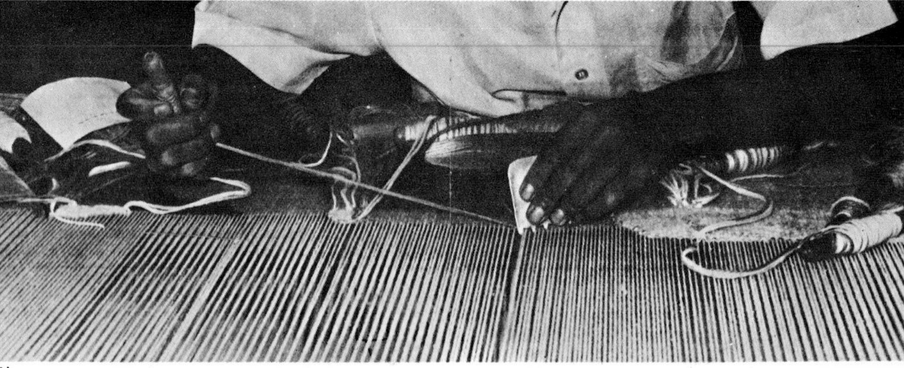

1b

2

3a

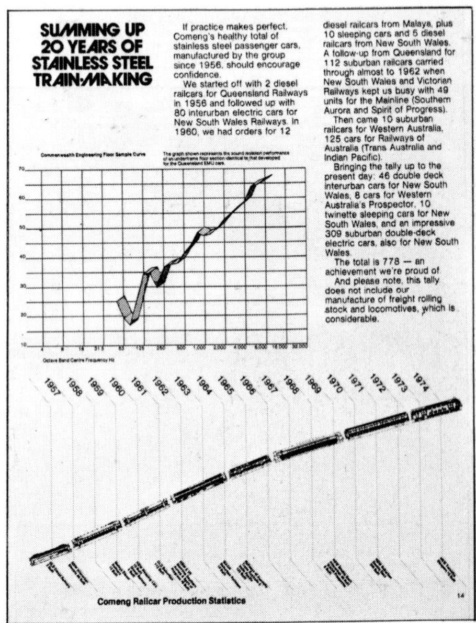

3b

4

5

6

8 United States
AD Johnson & Johnson
AG George Tscherny, Inc
DIR/DES George Tscherny
ILL Gary Gladstone
COPY R. Robert Kniffin
corporate annual report

9 Switzerland
AD Swissair
AG GGK Basel
DIR/DES Gerd Hiepler

10a-c Great Britain
AD (a) Hartley Reece
(b) MacIntyre
(c) Reuters
AG Pentagram
DIR Mervyn Kurlansky
DES Mervyn Kurlansky, Lora Starling
ILL (b) John Stone, Bill Warhurst
(c) Wolf Spoerl
(a) pens, porte-plumes
(b) home for mentally handicapped, asile d'aliénés
(c) commemorative booklet

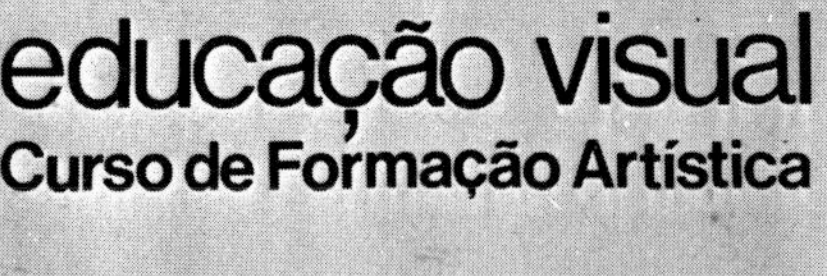

7

8

9

10a

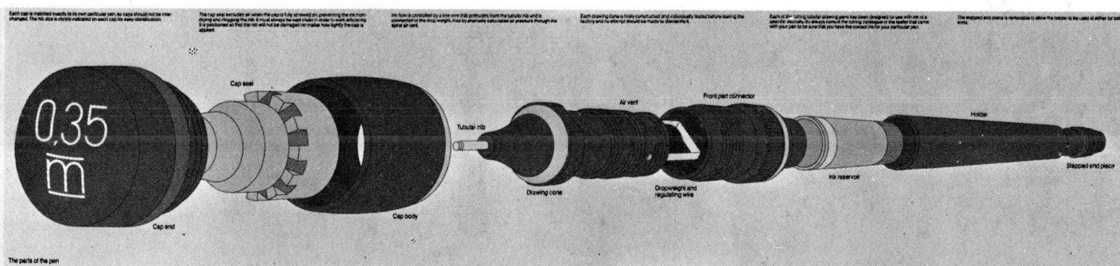

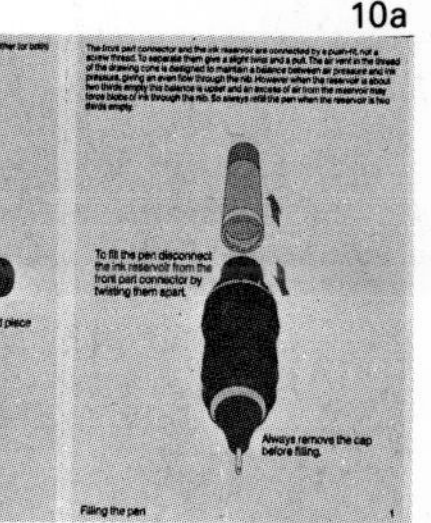

10b

Paul Julius Reuter: **21 July 1816** Born Israel Beer Josaphat in Kassel, Hesse, Germany, son of Samuel Levi, a Rabbi. **1844** Josaphat becomes a Christian and takes name of Paul Julius Reuter. **25 October 1845** Marries Ida Maria Magnus. **1848** Works as translator in Paris for Charles Havas, founder of the Havas news agency, later to become Agence France-Presse. **1849** Edits own news sheet in Paris for few months, moves to Aachen and starts news service using mail trains and telegraph. **1850** Flies stock market prices from Brussels to Aachen by pigeon. **1851** Moves to London. **14 October 1851** Rents two rooms on first floor of No 1 Royal Exchange Buildings, London. **13 November 1851** Dover-Calais cable opens. Reuter supplies Paris and London with stock prices from the other capital. **8 October 1858** Starts news service to London newspapers. **20 February 1865** Reuter's Telegram Company incorporated. **14 April 1865** Abraham Lincoln assassinated – Reuter two days ahead with story in Europe. **March 1866** Office opened in Bombay. **September 1866** Lays cable from Lowestoft, England, to Norderney, in the East Frisians, off the north coast of Germany. **31 January 1870** Triumvirate agreement signed with Havas news agency of France and Wolff of Germany. **February 1870** Sells Norderney cable to British Government. **7 September 1871** Awarded barony of Saxe-Coburg-Gotha. Now known as Baron Julius de Reuter. **1871** Offices opened in Singapore and Shanghai. **February 1872** Representative first visits Tokyo. **25 July 1872** Shah of Persia grants Reuter wide-reaching concession to develop Persian economic resources. **1874** Europe to Brazil cable completed; opens joint office with Havas in Rio de Janeiro. **May 1878** Retires as Managing Director of Reuter's Telegram Company; succeeded by son, Herbert. **30 January 1889** Founds the Imperial Bank of Persia which was later to become the British Bank of the Middle East, and gives up the economic resources concession. **25 February 1899** Dies aged 83 in Nice, France; buried in West Norwood cemetry, London, beside the grave of children, Albert Julius and Lucy Alice.

10c

**Direct Mail
Brochures
Broschüren**

1 Germany
AD Roth-Händle
AG Olaf Leu Design Ffm
DIR/DES Olaf Leu, Fritz Hofrichter

2 Mexico
AD Desc, Sociedad de Fomento Industrial s.a. de c.v.
AG Laboratorio de Diseno y Mercadotecnia — Carton y Papel de Mexico SA
DIR/DES Arie J. Geurts
ILL Ruben Padova, Axel B. Garcia
COPY I. Raymundo Leal Marquez, Guillermo Sottil
annual report

3 United States
AD Cavitron Corporation
AG Barnett/Goslin/Barnett
DIR Cuncan Hunt, Harriet Kriegel
DES David Barnett, Charles Goslin
ILL Harry Wilks
COPY Harriet Kriegel
annual report

4 South Africa
AD Empisal (South Africa) Ltd
AG Jeremy Sampson Associates (Pty) Ltd
DIR/DES John Maskew
annual report

5 Australia
AD Australian National University
AG ANU Graphic Design
DIR/DES Adrian Young
university courses

6 Iran
AD Iranians' Bank
AG Publiciteam
DES Melanie Kaveh, Jila Mansourpour
annual report

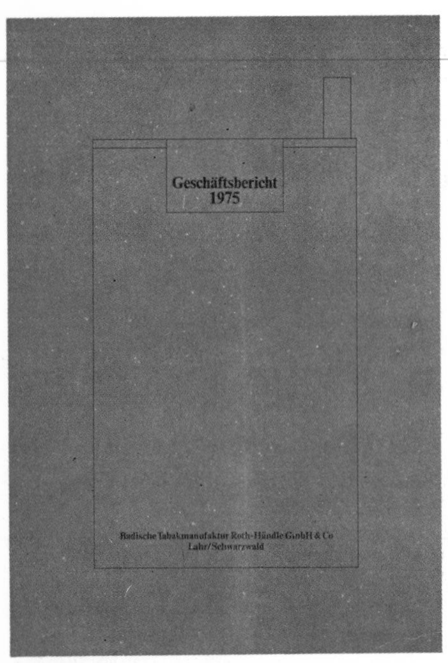

1

2

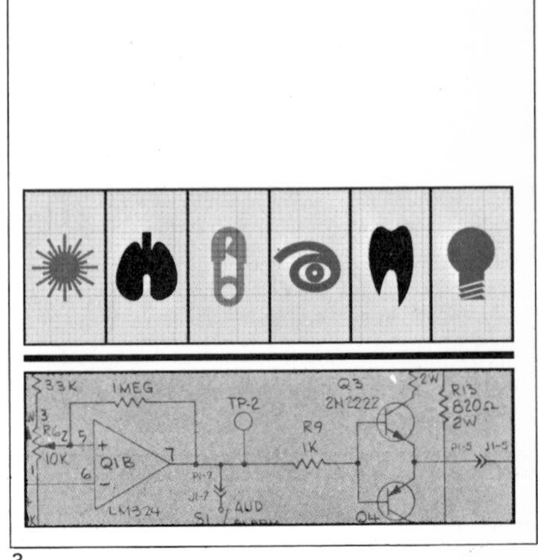

3

4

5

7 Hong Kong
AD Textile Alliance Ltd
AG Graphic Communication Ltd
DIR/DES Henry Steiner
ILL John Nye
textiles

8 United States
AD Standard Brands Paint Company
AG Weller Institute for the Cure of Design
DIR/DES Don Weller/Chicako Matsubayashi
ILL Don Weller
PHOTO Stan Caplan
COPY Sheldon Weinstein
annual report

9a-b Germany
AD Zweites Deutsches Fernsehen
DES Christof Gassner
TV programme brochure

10a-b Hong Kong
AD The Hong Kong & Changhai Banking Corporation
AG Graphic Communication Ltd
DIR/DES Henry Steiner
ILL Norman Macdonald
(a) annual report
(b) group magazine

6

7

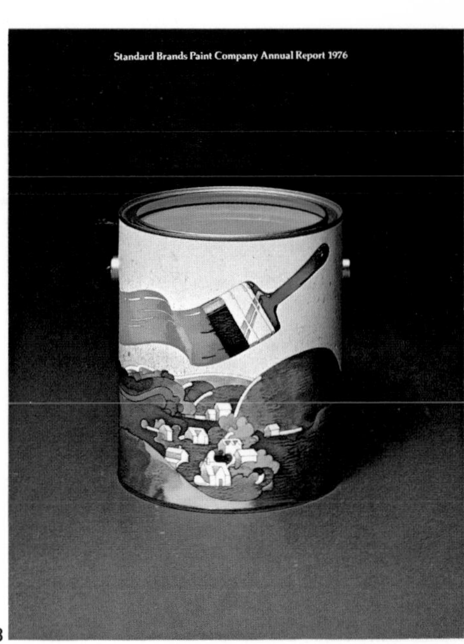

8

9a

9b

10a

10b

Direct Mail
Brochures
Broschüren

1 Mexico
AD Laboratorios Endo de Mexico Sa
AG Young & Rubicam
DIR Justo Somonte
DES John Nahmias
ILL Pedro Meyer
COPY Luis Salinas
antibiotic

2 Spain
AD Laboratorios Rocador
AG Pharma/Consult SA
DIR Vicente Olmos
DES Javier Noguera
ILL Javier Noguera, Joan Enric
pharmaceutical

3 Germany
AD Chemiewerk Homburg Frankfurt/M
AG Werbeagentur Peter Selinka
DES Atelier Oskar Weiss
ILL Friedmann Hett

4 United States
AD/AG Smith Kline & French Laboratories
DIR J. Robert Parker
DES Bruno-Mease
ILL Len Cohen
COPY Dick Kennerley
pharmaceuticals

5 Canada
AD Hoffmann — La Roche Ltd
AG Design Collaborative
DIR/DES Rolf Harder
booklets on sleep, livrets au sujet du sommeil

6 Spain
AD Laboratories ISDIN
AG Pharma/Consult SA
DIR Vicente Olmos
DES Javier Noguera
ILL Javier Noguera, Joan Enric
pharmaceuticals

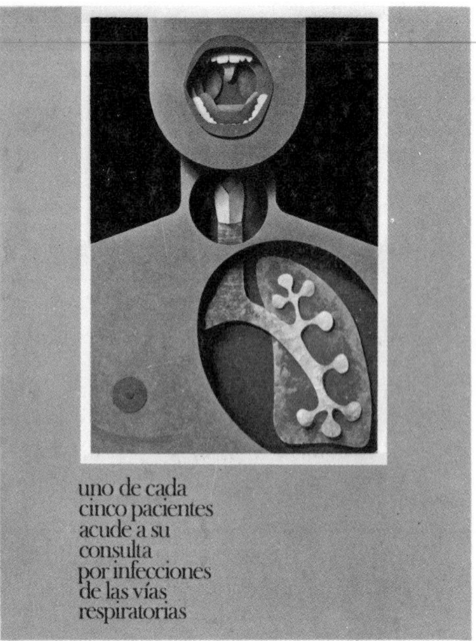

1

2

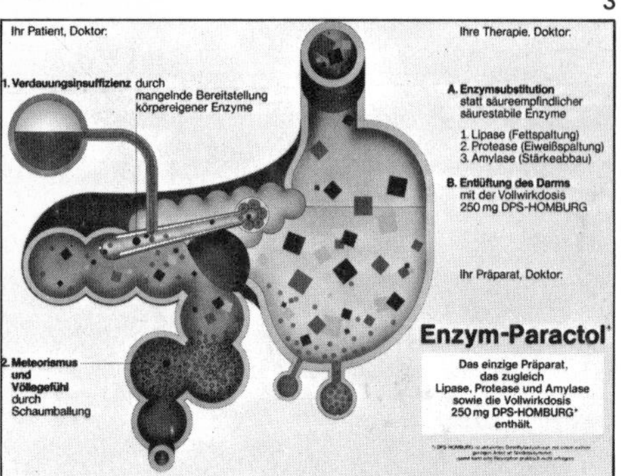

3

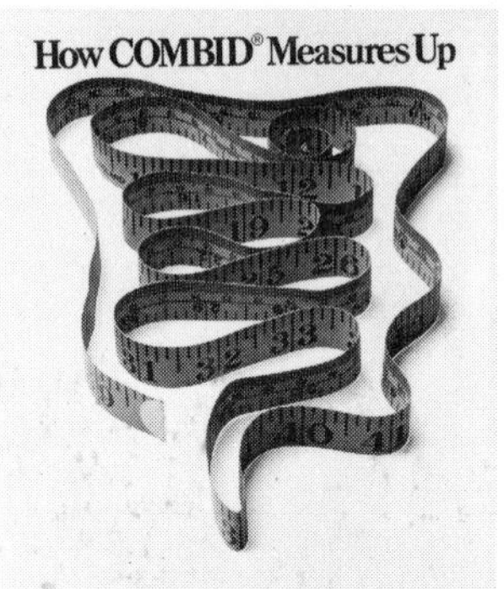

4

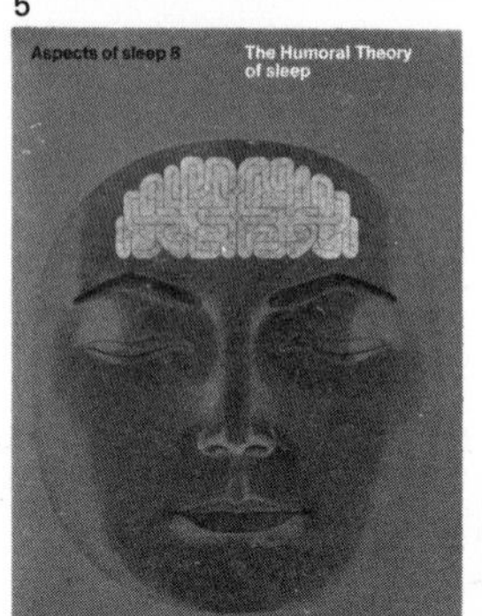

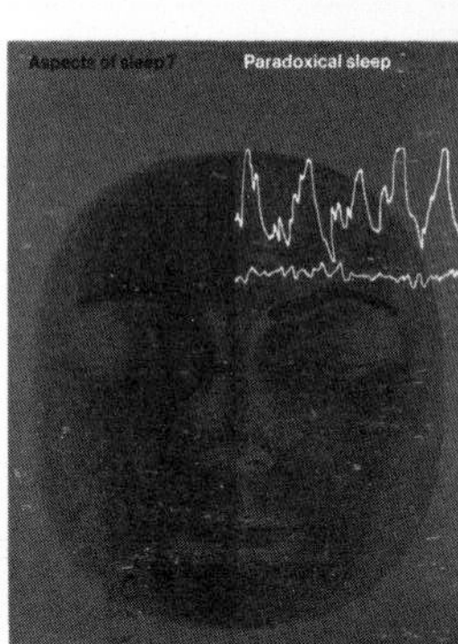

5

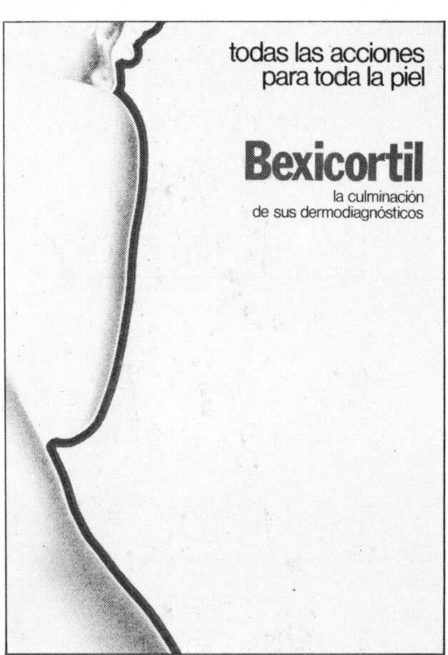

6

7

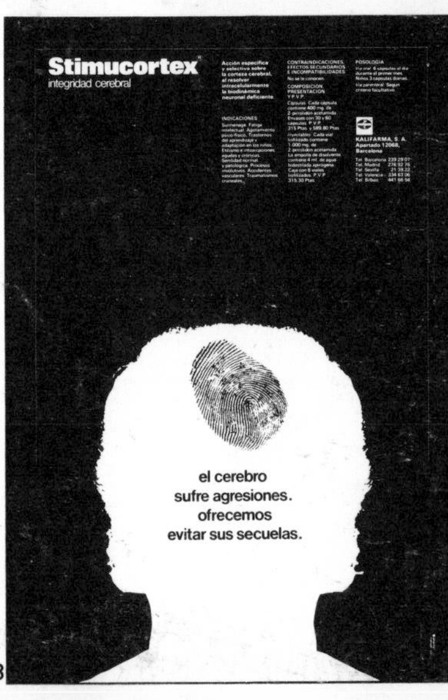

8

7 Switzerland
AD Solco Basel AG
AG Institute Dr. Friesewinkel AG
DES Maya Stange ASG
ILL Christian Vogt
pharmaceuticals

8 Spain
AD Kalifarma SA
AG Pharma/Consult SA
DIR/DES Vicente Olmos
ILL Vicente Olmos, Joan Enric
pharmaceutical

9 Italy
AD Merck, Sharp & Dohme Italia SpA
DES Rinaldo Cutini
medical journal

10 Argentina
AD Bagó Laboratory
DES Estudio Cánovas
COPY Jose Bienvenite
booklet on brain diseases, livret au sujet des maladies de la cervelle

11 Spain
AD Sandoz SAE
AG Ribas/Creus
pharmaceuticals

12a-b United States
AD/AG Smith Kline & French Laboratories
DIR Alan J. Klawans
DES Jonson Hinrichs Pedersen
ILL Robert Weaver
COPY Len Aulenbach
psychiatrist's reference guide

9

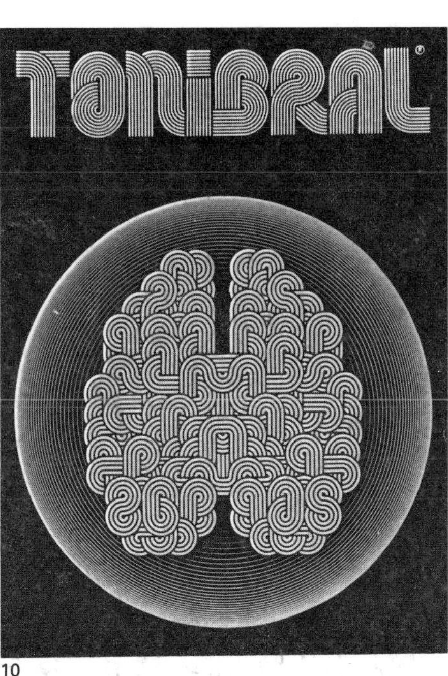

10

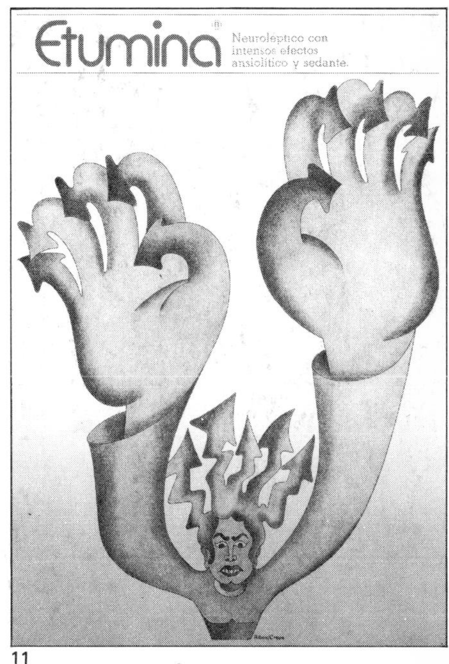

11

12a

12b

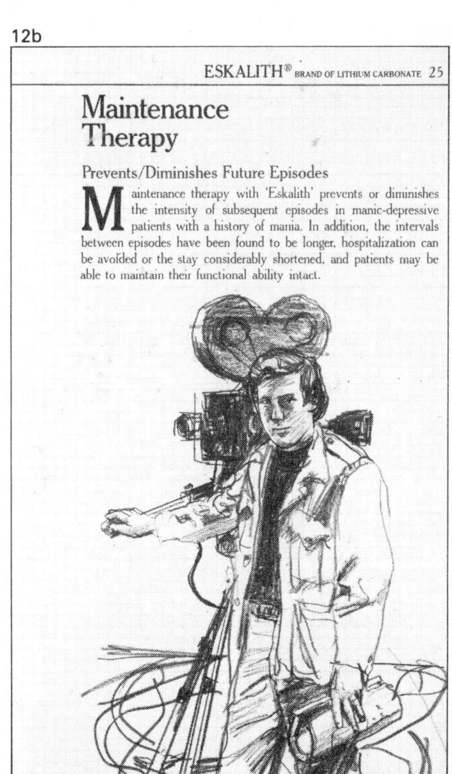

Direct Mail
Brochures
Broschüren

1 Belgium
AD Esso — Division Presse et Information
AG Partner
DIR Patrick Queva
ILL Josse Goffin

2a-b United States
AD Exxon Corporation
DIR Harry O. Diamond
ILL (a) Nordbok
(b) Fred Otnes
'The Lamp' housemagazine

3 Great Britain
AD HMSO/National Portrait Gallery
AG HMSO Graphic Design
DES Christabel Hardacre
ILL Angelo Hornack, David Williams (calligrapher)
COPY Hugh Clayton

4 Great Britain
AD Prime Computer (UK) Ltd
AG Bloy Eldridge
DES Robert Custance

5 France
AD Ailleurs
DIR Paul Henri Moisan
DES Michel Granger

6 Denmark
AD F. L. Smidth & Co AS
AG Poul Lund Hansen/Reklame
DIR Poul Anker
ILL Ellegaard
COPY Poul Lund Hansen
engineering

Contacts avec les dealers.

Pour la vente de ses carburants, notre société fait appel à un réseau de stations-service exploité par des commerçants indépendants, opérant soit sous la forme d'une exploitation familiale, soit sous une forme juridique de société commerciale. L'intégration verticale qui caractérise l'industrie pétrolière ne trouve pas d'application au niveau de la distribution de nos carburants où, au contraire, nous nous trouvons en présence d'un grand nombre de petites et moyennes entreprises liées à notre société pour la revente de ses produits par un contrat de durée déterminée.

Compte tenu des fonctions importantes que les Petites et Moyennes Entreprises (PME) remplissent dans notre système économique de marché, nous croyons que notre rôle ne se confine pas à la seule fourniture de carburants aux conditions régissant nos relations contractuelles avec nos revendeurs. Nous sommes persuadés qu'il nous appartient de promouvoir le rôle des PME dans la distribution et de contribuer à leur développement économique en les faisant bénéficier de techniques de vente, de connaissances comptables, de moyens de promotion et de possibilités de training dont nous disposons.

Aussi nous nous réjouissons de voir que, malgré les tendances actuelles d'intégration et de concentration, les PME parviennent à se maintenir grâce au rôle spécifique qu'elles jouent dans la distribution des carburants. De par leur structure et en fonction du dynamisme du chef d'entreprise, les PME ont des avantages certains par rapport aux grandes sociétés et, notamment, dans le domaine du service personnalisé à rendre à la clientèle, ainsi que par une flexibilité plus grande à des conditions de marché en évolution constante. Des heures d'ouverture adaptées aux besoins du trafic automobile, un contact personnel avec le client et une gamme étendue de services pour l'entretien de véhicules sont les atouts majeurs entre les mains des revendeurs indépendants.

En outre, des échelons hiérarchiques limités et l'absence de procédures encombrantes permettent aux PME, qui sont en contact permanent et direct avec le marché, de prendre rapidement des décisions d'investissement afin de profiter pleinement de l'avantage d'être parmi les premiers à introduire, par exemple, dans sa zone d'achalandage un point de vente en self-service ou une pompe automatique avec lecteur de billets de banque.

Reconnaître le rôle important joué par les PME entraine également une approche nouvelle des relations entre société pétrolière et revendeurs.

Nous sommes par conséquent convaincus que des relations harmonieuses et constructives entre ces PME et nous-mêmes ne peuvent être élaborées et — a fortiori — ne peuvent être maintenues uniquement sur base des clauses d'un contrat signé entre les deux parties.

Des relations durables ne sont possibles que pour autant que chaque partie y trouve un avantage et que chacun ait l'occasion de faire valoir ses intérêts et son point de vue. Le besoin s'est donc fait sentir de structurer davantage nos relations avec nos revendeurs selon les deux lignes de force suivantes : en premier lieu, la contribution qu'en tant que société pétrolière intégrée, nous pouvons apporter à l'organisation et au développement des PME qui assurent la vente de nos produits. Ensuite, la participation de notre réseau à l'élaboration de nos stratégies de vente.

En effet, le succès d'un réseau de stations-service ne dépend pas seulement d'un nombre relativement grand de points de vente, situés stratégiquement, vendant des produits de qualité avec une identification propre aux couleurs de la marque.

Le succès d'un réseau et, par conséquent, de la société qui vend ses produits par l'intermédiaire d'un tel réseau, réside bien plus dans le dynamisme et l'esprit commercial du revendeur qui, en tant que chef de son entreprise, peut agir comme véritable « entrepreneur » dans le sens du terme rendu célèbre par Peter F. Drucker.

A titre d'illustration, rappelons que traditionnellement toutes les sociétés pétrolières se sont évertuées à obtenir la collaboration de leurs revendeurs, afin d'inciter ces derniers à faire bénéficier le client automobiliste des principes de service propres à chaque société. Le résultat de ces campagnes n'a hélas pas toujours été en ligne avec les efforts qui y avaient été consacrés.

Sans délaisser les moyens traditionnels mis en œuvre tels que trainings, campagnes promotionnelles, conseils réguliers des représentants, matériel point de vente, nous croyons par contre que la collaboration du revendeur ne peut être obtenue que grâce à une communication franche et ouverte où chaque partie a l'occasion d'exprimer librement son point de vue, afin que, dans un esprit de compréhension mutuelle, une ligne de conduite commune puisse être mise au point.

A cet effet, nous avons graduellement mis sur pied une série de moyens de communication par lesquels notre société entend jouer plus efficacement son rôle non seulement de revendeur de produits pétroliers, mais également et surtout de partenaire commercial d'un ensemble de moyennes et petites entreprises.

A titre d'exemple, citons le fonctionnement des comités de contact avec nos revendeurs. Ces comités ont été créés il y a maintenant trois ans et ont pour but de promouvoir une meilleure communication entre notre réseau et la société, d'informer nos clients des derniers développements dans les différents domaines qui touchent de près à leurs activités et, enfin, de leur donner un canal supplémentaire par lequel ils peuvent nous faire connaître leurs vues sur les stratégies de vente que nous développons ou sur l'évolution du marché telle qu'ils la ressentent eux-mêmes.

Il existe deux comités régionaux et un comité national composé chacun de douze membres. Tous les revendeurs, tant hommes que femmes, sont éligibles et le choix est fait par un vote par correspondance auquel l'ensemble des revendeurs est appelé à participer.

Les membres du comité national sont élus par les membres des comités régionaux au sein de ceux-ci.

En dehors des réunions statutairement prévues, une réunion peut être convoquée à tout moment à la demande de 7 membres. Un compte-rendu de chaque réunion est communiqué à l'ensemble du réseau, afin que chacun soit au courant de la suite réservée aux points soulevés, soit par leurs collègues, soit par notre société.

Plusieurs réalisations importantes et des changements notables à notre politique de vente figurent à l'actif de ces comités de contact. Nous voudrions d'ailleurs ici mettre en lumière le travail personnel que chacun des délégués mène pour préparer la discussion de chaque point et pour défendre au mieux une position représentative de la majorité de ceux qui l'ont élu.

Néanmoins, malgré les résultats déjà atteints, notre souci est d'obtenir un apport d'un plus grand nombre de revendeurs, afin de mieux appréhender les problèmes de tout notre réseau. Ce souci est d'ailleurs partagé par les délégués qui voudraient ainsi être en mesure de mieux représenter les idées et les remarques de tous leurs électeurs.

Nous aurions pu continuer cet aperçu des moyens mis en œuvre par notre société pour améliorer le contact avec ses clients-revendeurs. Nous espérons cependant avoir pu illustrer de cette façon comment une société intégrée peut contribuer au développement d'un grand nombre de petites et moyennes entreprises et combien un dialogue bien compris entre ces dernières et notre société peut être bénéfique pour les deux parties.

En guise de conclusion, nous voudrions souligner que tout dialogue positif dont question ci-dessus et que tout essor des PME — que nous estimons nécessaires ne sera vraiment réalisable que pour autant que celui qui se trouve à la tête de son entreprise fasse preuve de créativité, de sens commercial et d'une flexibilité suffisante pour adapter continuellement son entreprise aux besoins changeants du marché.

R.C. VAN DEN BERGH,

Directeur des Ventes aux Automobilistes.

1

2a

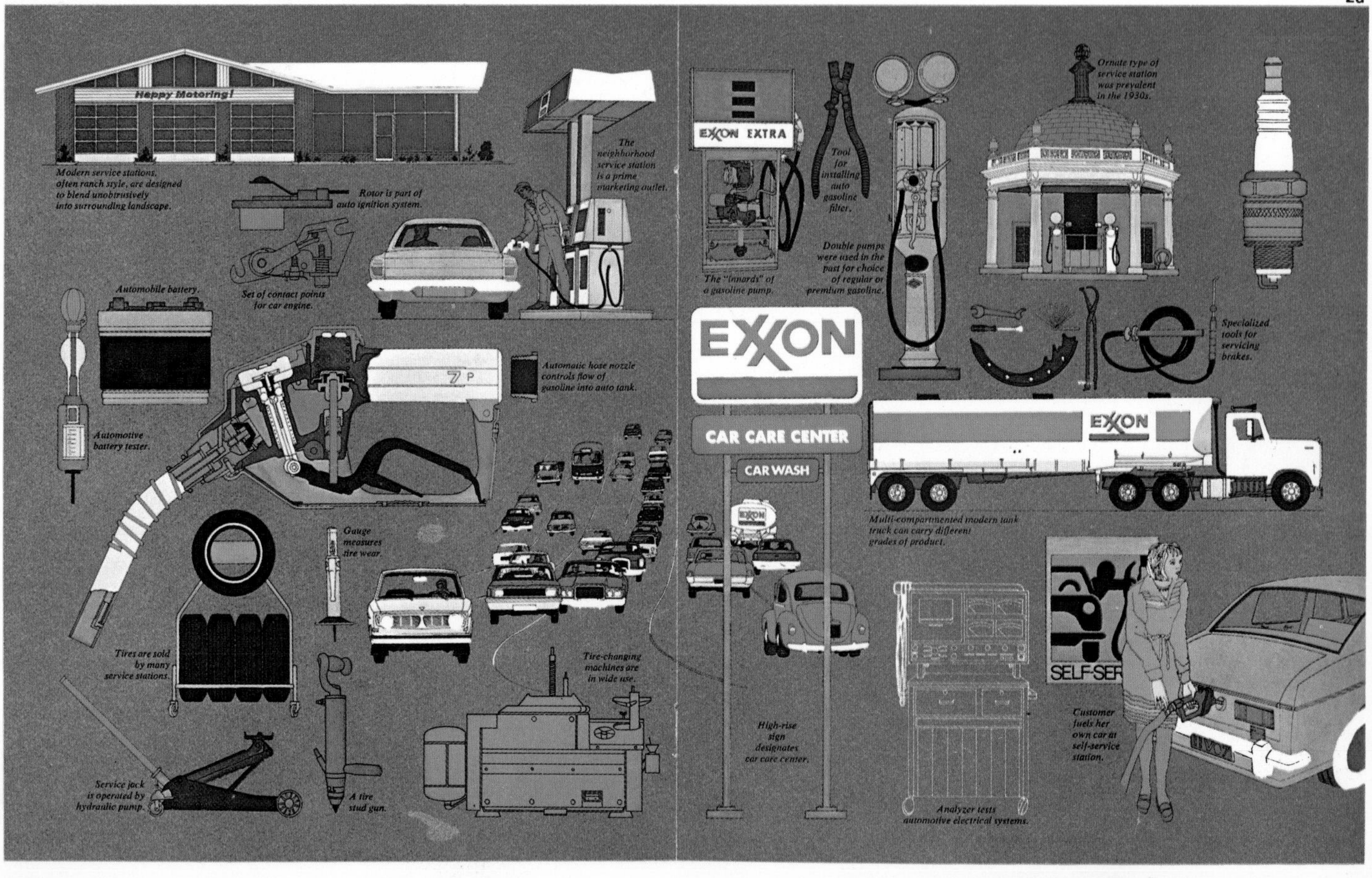

Happy Motoring!

Modern service stations, often ranch style, are designed to blend unobtrusively into surrounding landscape.

Rotor is part of auto ignition system.

The neighborhood service station is a prime marketing outlet.

Automobile battery.

Set of contact points for car engine.

Automatic hose nozzle controls flow of gasoline into auto tank.

Automotive battery tester.

Gauge measures tire wear.

Tires are sold by many service stations.

Tire-changing machines are in wide use.

Service jack is operated by hydraulic pump.

A tire stud gun.

EXXON EXTRA

The "innards" of a gasoline pump.

Tool for installing auto gasoline filter.

Double pumps were used in the past for choice of regular or premium gasoline.

Ornate type of service station was prevalent in the 1930s.

EXXON

CAR CARE CENTER

CAR WASH

Specialized tools for servicing brakes.

EXXON

Multi-compartmented modern tank truck can carry different grades of product.

High-rise sign designates car care center.

Analyzer tests automotive electrical systems.

SELF-SER

Customer fuels her own car at self-service station.

Royal Faces
900 YEARS OF BRITISH MONARCHY

3

The Prime File

4

5

2b

The Lamp

6

FLS
32283
101
FLS

Greetings cards
Calendars
Cartes de voeux
Calendriers
Glückwunschkarten
Kalender

1 Australia
AD/AG Cato Hibberd Hawksby Design Pty
ILL Ray Condon
COPY David Webster
self promotion

2 Holland
AD Drukkerij Westerbaaw/Westerhuis
AG Weda/D & A
DES Theo de Witte
calendar

3 Germany
AD/AG Mohn Gordon Studios
ILL Pepi Merisio

4 Brazil
AD Esso Brasileira de Petroleo
AG Maccann Erickson Publicidade
DIR Carlos Martins
ILL Jose Franceschi
COPY Herminio Naddeo
calendar

5 Great Britain
AD Habitat
AG Conran Associates
DES Stafford Cliff
ILL Graham Percy
COPY Austair Best
calendar

6 Australia
AD McPherson's Ltd
AG E. G. Holt & Associates Pty Ltd
DIR/DES Kevin Lees
ILL Jonathan Milne
COPY A. B. Paterson

7 United States
AD That Stat Place
AG Bob Coonts Design
DIR Bob Coonts
DES John Sorbie
calendar

Signal Flags These have been designed to meet the normal signalling requirements of Merchant vessels. They conform to the International Code of Signals, which has been printed in seven languages. Each letter of the alphabet is represented by a single flag, which when hoisted can read as the letter it represents, or may convey particular information according to the Code. The meaning of the signal changes, depending upon the number of flags hoisted. A message may consist of up to five flags. Single-flag signals relate to the 26 specific meanings listed. Two-flag signals relate to distress, navigational warnings, and the handling of ships and aircraft. Three-flag signals relate to Points of Compass, Relative Bearings, Standard Time, and the Model Verb Section and General Vocabulary Section of the Code. Four-flag signals relate to geographical signals or the signal letters of ships. Five-flag signals relate to signal letters of aircraft. A complete set of signal flags consists of 26 alphabetical flags, 10 numeral pendants, 3 substitutes, and an answering flag.
Cato Hibberd Pty Ltd 46 Nicholson Street South Yarra Victoria 3141 Telephone 26 1337
Printcells Pty Ltd 1 Parslow Street Clifton Hill Victoria 3068 Telephone 489 9377

1

2

3

4

1977

MAIO

D	S	T	Q	Q	S	S
1	2	3	4	5	6	7
8	9	10	11	12	13	14
15	16	17	18	19	20	21
22	23	24	25	26	27	28
29	30	31				

JUNHO

D	S	T	Q	Q	S	S
			1	2	3	4
5	6	7	8	9	10	11
12	13	14	15	16	17	18
19	20	21	22	23	24	25
26	27	28	29	30		

Esso
Esso Brasileira de Petróleo

5

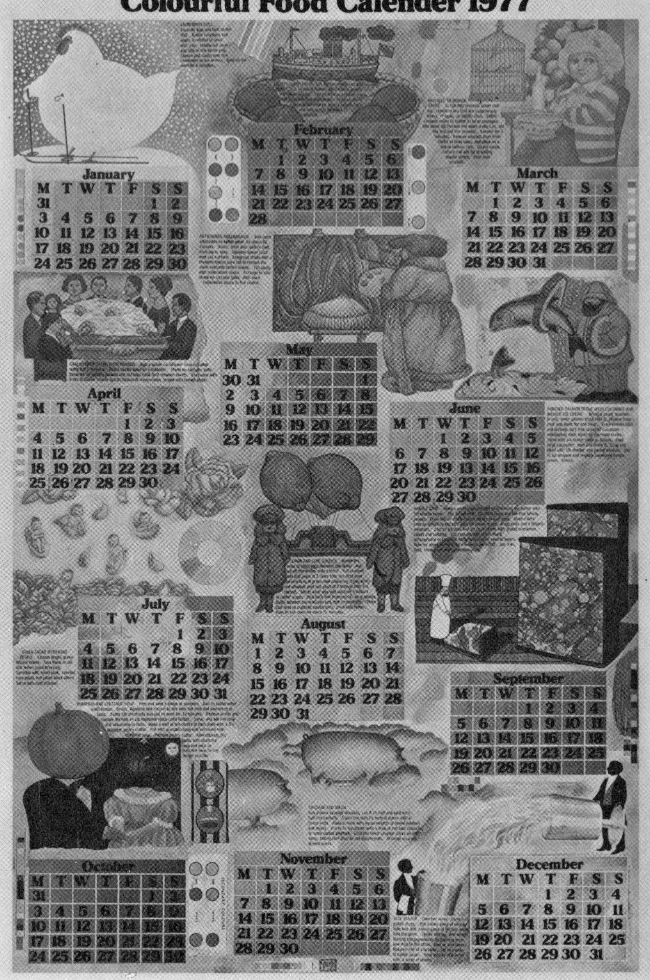

8 Germany
AD Opel
AG McCann, Frankfurt
DIR Claus-Joachim Koch
DES Peter Englehard, C.-J. Koch
ILL Peter Forster
calendar

9 Israel
AD Makhteshim-Agam
DES Mordechai Kellner
calendar for farm chemicals

6

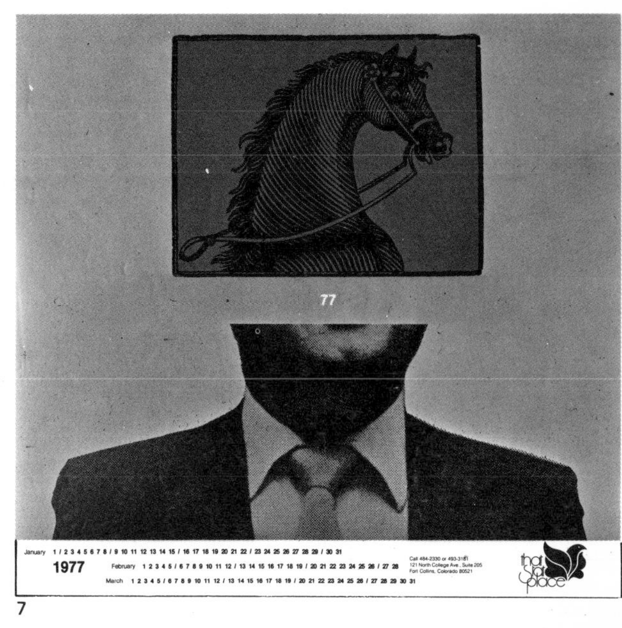

7

8

9

Greetings cards
Calendars
Cartes de voeux
Calendriers
Glückwunschkarten
Kalender

1a-b Great Britain
AD GAF
AG Design Group Chris Meiklejohn
DIR Laurence Fairfax Jones
DES David Bull
ILL Sarah Moon (photography)
calendar

2a-b Germany
AD Zanders Feinpapier GmbH
AG Werbeabteilung Zanders
DIR/DES Wolfgang Heuwinkel
ILL Wim Cox

3 Greece
AD Citibank
AG K&K Univas Advertising Centre
DIR Frederick Carabott
DES Agni Katzourakis
COPY Pelia Kambanellis
calendar

4 Holland
AD Drukkerij van Wijland b.v.
DES Dick de Moei
ILL Ed van der Elsken
COPY Bas Roodnat

5a-b Germany
AD BASF Farben + Fasern AG
DIR H. G. Mietzner
DES Prof. Kurt Weidemann
ILL Lajos Keresztes
printing inks, encres d'imprimerie, Druckfarben

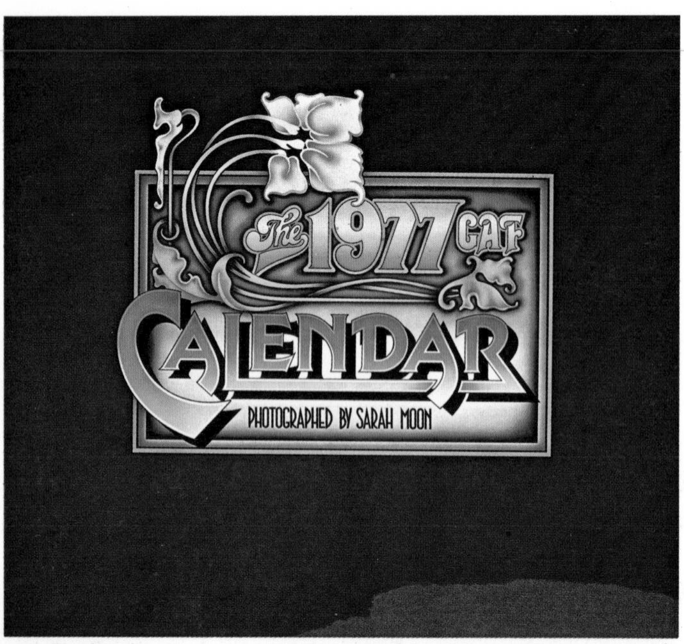

1a

1b

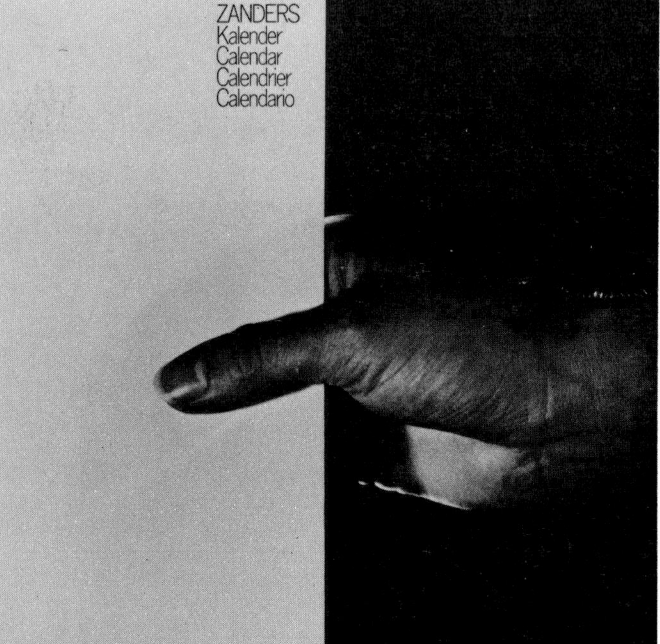

2a

2b

Citibank
1977

3

JANUARI 1 2 3 4 5 6 7 8 9 10
11 12 13 14 15 16 17 18 19 20 21 22 23 24 25 26 27 28 29 30 31
ED VAN DER ELSKEN
DRUKKERIJ VAN WIJLAND BV, CALISKAMP 7, LAREN NH, TEL. 02153-82534

4

5a

5
K+E
30
19
1 8 15 22 29

5b

10
K+E
2 9 16 23 30

Greetings cards
Calendars
Cartes de voeux
Calendriers
Glückwunschkarten
Kalender

1 Hungary
AD Hungarian Philatelic Bureau
DES Pál Varga (stamp designer)

2 United States
AD/AG Barnett/Goslin/Barnett
DIR David Barnett, Charles Goslin
DES David Barnett
COPY Charles Goslin, David Barnett
calendar

3 Spain
AD Picancel — Ferrer SA
DES Francesc Guitart
ILL Toni Catany
calendar

4 United States
AD/DES Bob Coonts
Christmas card, carte de Noel,

5 Great Britain
AD Face Photosetting
AG Pentagram
DIR/DES John McConnell
calendar

6 Israel
AD Hasneh Insurance Co Ltd
AG United Graphics
DES Haim Bar
calendar

7 Germany
AD Wilhelm Kumm Verlag
DES Paulus Schlageter
calendar

8 Holland
AD Drukkerij Reclame
AG. Loridan Studios
printer's calendar

9a-b United States
AD Colonial Penn Group Inc
George Tscherny Inc
DIR/DES George Tscherny
calendar

2

3

8

JANUARY
MONDAY
10
5

הסנה
6

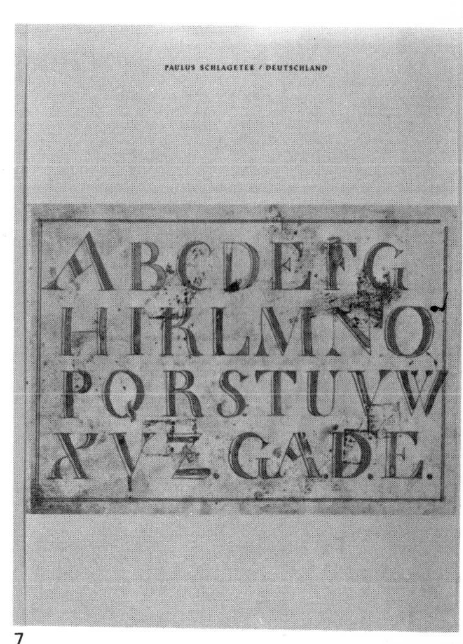
PAULUS SCHLAGETER / DEUTSCHLAND
ABCDEFG
HIKLMNO
PQRSTUVW
XYZ.GADE.
7

bob, carmen, brent & brian coonts
PEACE
1977
4

9a

OPEN
ANTIQUES
9b

Greetings cards
Calendars
Cartes de voeux
Calendriers
Glückwunschkarten
Kalender

1 Italy
AD F. Begliomini — Typographer
DIR Rinaldo Cutini
DES Stefano Babic
calendar

2 Germany
AD Eberhard Bauer
DES Ursula Weckherlin
ILL Ernst Raas

3 Germany
AD BASF Aktiengesellschaft
AG Studio Gerhard Gerger
DES Gerhard Berger
ILL Roland Fürst
calendar

4 Belgium
AD/AG De Schutter SA
DES Rob Buytaert
calendar

5 Germany
AD Internationales Katholisches Missionswerk
DIR Herbert Wenn
ILL students from the school of weaving, Mariannhill, South Africa

6 Australia
AD Vega Press Pty Ltd
AG Cato Hibberd Hawksby Design Pty Ltd
ILL John Pollard
printing house promotion

1

2

3

MAY
MAI
MAI
77
BASF

4

7 Great Britain
AD Roland Offset
DIR/DES Olaf Leu Design
ILL David Goddard

8 Germany
AD Valkswagenwerk AG
AG Alpha 9 Phototeam
DIR J. Albrecht Cropp
ILL J. Albrecht Cropp
cars, autos

9 Great Britain
AD 'Shell World' magazine
DIR Ray Gautier
DES/ILL Richard Tilley
calendar

5

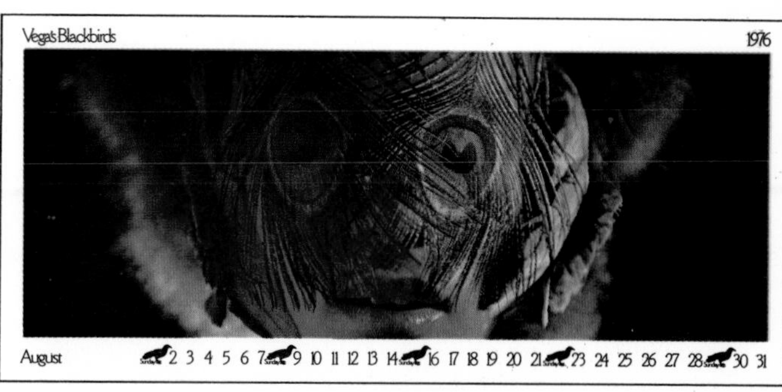

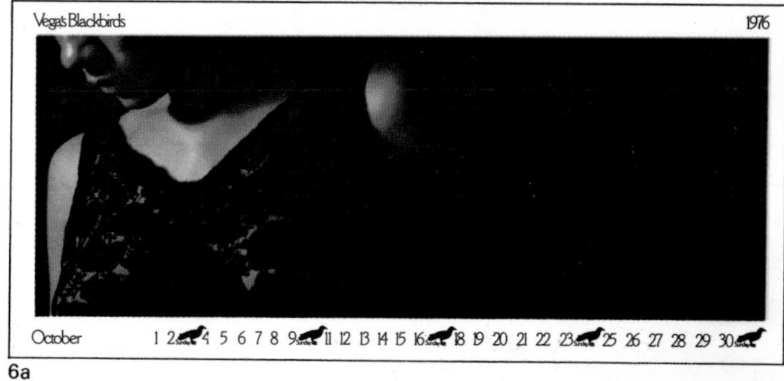

6a

7

8

9

Greetings cards
Calendars
Cartes de voeux
Calendriers
Glückwunschkarten
Kalender

1 Great Britain
AD Mervyn J. Franklyn
ILL Lyn Gray
Christmas card, carte de Noël, Weihnachtskarte

2 Belgium
AD/DES Charles Rohonyi
Christmas card

3 Spain
AD ECTA 3
DIR/DES Albert Isern i Castro
ILL Jordi Isern

4 Spain
AD/DES Bartolome Liarte
Christmas card

5 Great Britain
AD/AG Your Company by Design Ltd
DIR/DES Derrick Holmes
Christmas card

6 Spain
AD John Gomez Hall
DES Ribas, Creus
Christmas cards

7 Great Britain
AD/AG Negus & Negus
ILL Dominic Negus
COPY Maurice Herson
Christmas card

8 Great Britain
AD/AG Guilding Design Partnership
DIR Alan Livingston
DES Robin Stanford
Christmas party, fête de Noël

1

3

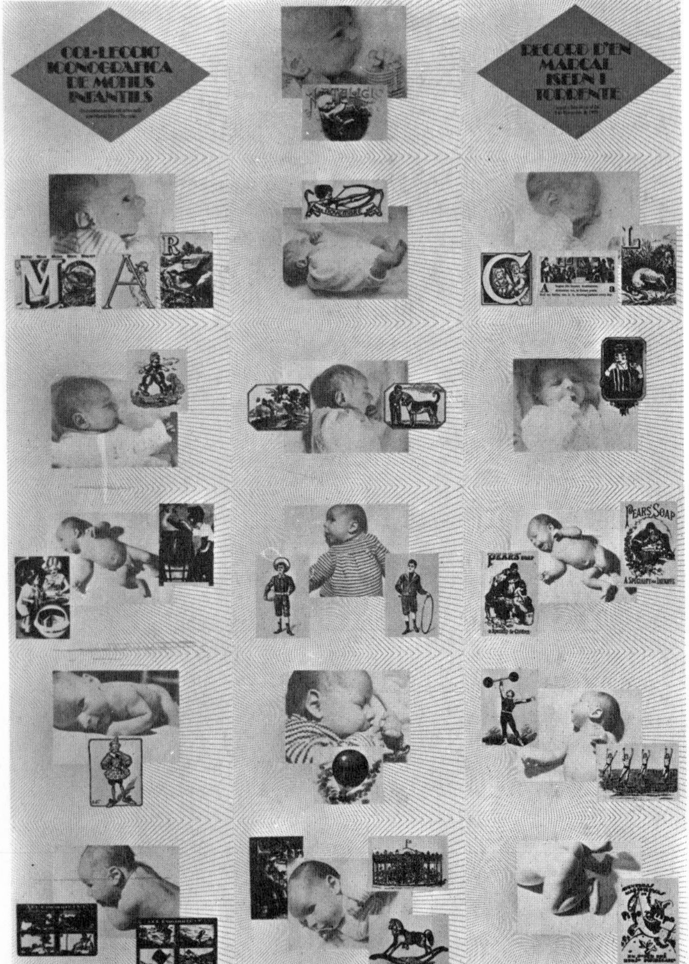

4

5

6

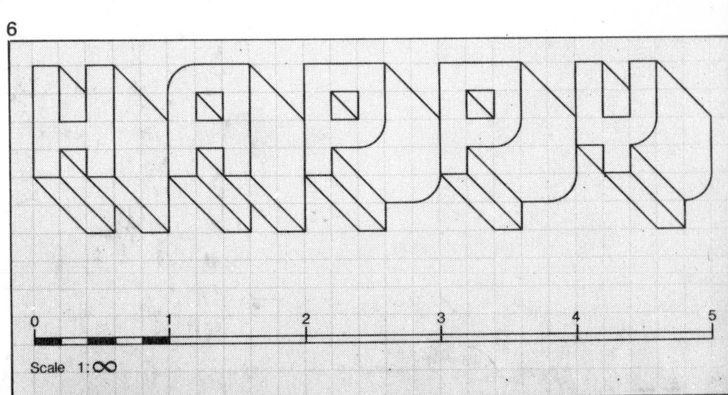

9a-b United States
AD Margaret Martin Eakin
AG Recto Verso Bookworks
DIR/DES Don Albert
COPY Wallace Stevens
Christmas gifts, cadeaux de Noël, Weihnachtsgeschenke

10 Great Britain
AD Castle Chappel & Partners Ltd
G The Pack Design Company
DIR Keith Chappell
DES John Castle
Christmas gift, cadeau de Noël, Weihnachtsgeschenk

11 Great Britain
AD/AG Rod Springett Associates
DES Rod Springett
hristmas greetings book, livre pour le Noël, Weihnachtsbuch

2

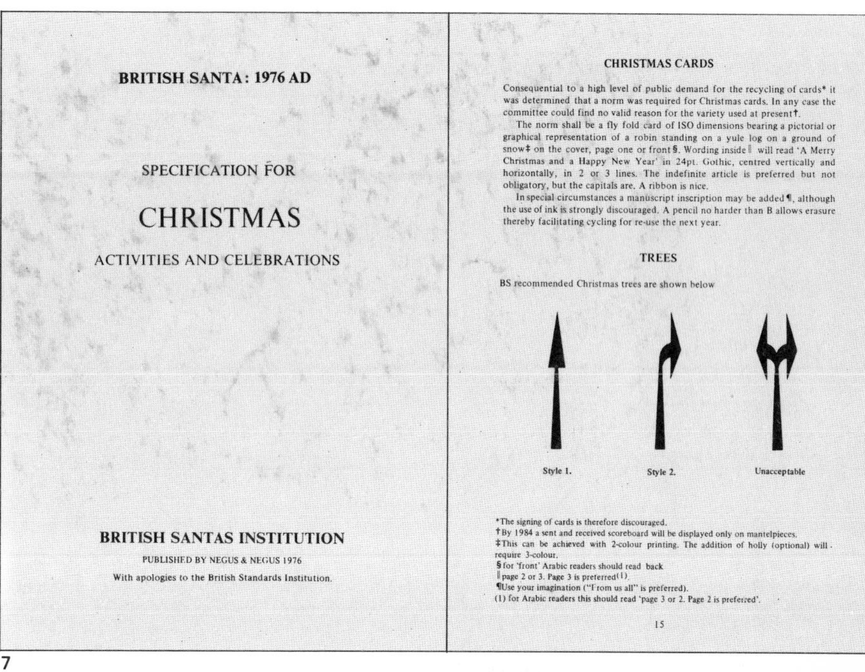

BRITISH SANTA: 1976 AD

SPECIFICATION FOR

CHRISTMAS

ACTIVITIES AND CELEBRATIONS

BRITISH SANTAS INSTITUTION

PUBLISHED BY NEGUS & NEGUS 1976

With apologies to the British Standards Institution.

CHRISTMAS CARDS

Consequential to a high level of public demand for the recycling of cards* it was determined that a norm was required for Christmas cards. In any case the committee could find no valid reason for the variety used at present†.

The norm shall be a fly fold card of ISO dimensions bearing a pictorial or graphical representation of a robin standing on a yule log on a ground of snow‡ on the cover, page one or front§. Wording inside‖ will read 'A Merry Christmas and a Happy New Year' in 24pt. Gothic, centred vertically and horizontally, in 2 or 3 lines. The indefinite article is preferred but not obligatory, but the capitals are. A ribbon is nice.

In special circumstances a manuscript inscription may be added¶, although the use of ink is strongly discouraged. A pencil no harder than B allows erasure thereby facilitating cycling for re-use the next year.

TREES

BS recommended Christmas trees are shown below

Style 1. Style 2. Unacceptable

*The signing of cards is therefore discouraged.
†By 1984 a sent and received scoreboard will be displayed only on mantelpieces.
‡This can be achieved with 2-colour printing. The addition of holly (optional) will require 3-colour.
§for 'front' Arabic readers should read back
‖page 2 or 3. Page 3 is preferred(1).
¶Use your imagination ("From us all" is preferred).
(1) for Arabic readers this should read 'page 3 or 2. Page 2 is preferred'.

15

7

8

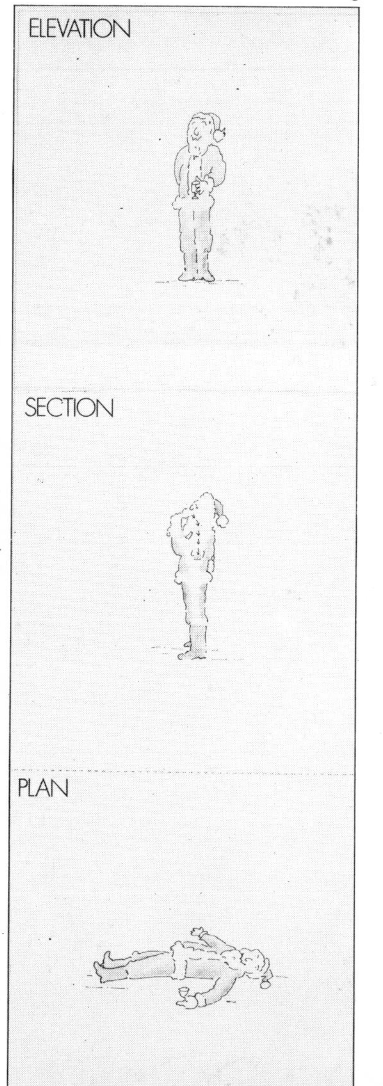

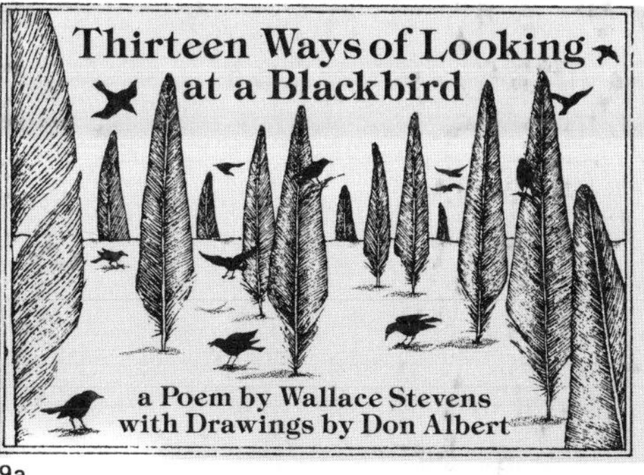

9a

9b

10

11

Greetings cards
Calendars
Cartes de voeux
Calendriers
Glückwunschkarten
Kalender

1 Great Britain
AD Habitat
AG Conran Associates
DES Stafford Cliff
ILL Susan Collier, Sarah Campbell
COPY Caroline Conran
cook's diary

2 Holland
AD/AG I.D. Unit
DES Robert & Jeanne Schaap
New Year card

3a-c Great Britain
AD Graphic Design Studies School of Creative Arts and Design, Leeds Polytechnic
DIR/DES Jonathan de Morgan
calendar

4 Great Britain
AD/AG Trickett & Webb Ltd
DIR/DES Lynn Trickett, Brian Webb
Christmas card

5 Holland
AD Transvemy/Hoogeveen
DIR/DES Ton Hoogendoorn
New Year card

6a-c South Africa
AD/AG Grapplegroup CJA
DIR/DES Richard Ward
COPY Richard Ward, Jill Clucas, Roy Clucas
Christmas card

1

2

3a

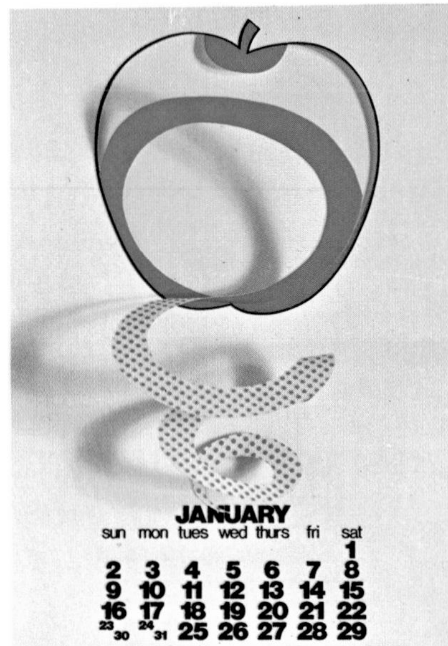

3b

4

5

6a

6b

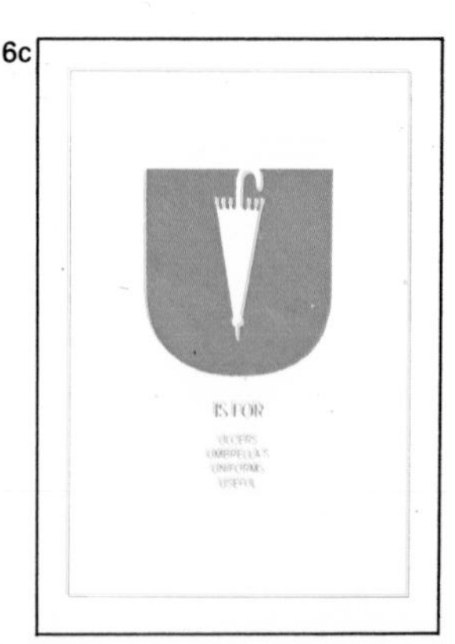

6c

3c